Ein Yaakov

Berachot | ברכות

Chapter 1 | Chapter 1

Berachot: FROM what time on may we read the Sh'm'a of the evening "From the time the priests enter to eat their Terumah until the end of the first watch, said R. Eliezer. But the other sages say "Until midnight," and Rabban Gamaliel says "Until the appearance of the morning star." It happened that the sons of Rabban Gamaliel came [very late at night] from a banquet and told Rabban Gamaliel that they had not yet read the Sh'm'a, whereupon he said to them: "If the morning star has not yet appeared you must read it."

(Gemara) Let us see: when do the priests enter to eat the Terumah? Is it not when the stars appear? Let then the Mishnah say: "From the time the stars appear!" In using this expression, he lets us hear something by the way; namely, that with the appearing of the stars, the priests are allowed to eat their Terumah, because the forgiveness-offering [which will be brought on the morrow] is not a hindrance, as we have been taught; "And when the sun hath set, he shall be clean. (Lev. 22, 7.) i. e., the waiting for the setting

ברכות: מאימתי קורין את שמע בערבית. משעה שהכהנים נכנסים לאכול בתרומתן עד סוף האשמורה הראשונה דברי רבי אליעזר וחכמים אומרים עד חצות רבן גמליאל אומר עד שיעלה עמוד השחר. מעשה ובאו בניו מבית המשתה אמרו לו לא קרינו את שמע. אמר להם אם לא עלה עמוד השחר חייבין אתם לקרות.

גמ' מכדי כהנים אימת קא אכלי בתרומה משעת צאת הכוכבים ליתני משעת צאת הכוכבים מלתא אגב אורחיה קא משמע לן כהנים אימת קא אכלי בתרומה משעת צאת הכוכבים והא קמ"ל דכפרה לא מעכבא. כדתניא (ויקרא כב ז) ובא השמש וטהר ביאת שמשו מעכבתו מלאכול בתרומה ואין כפרתו מעכבתו מלאכול בתרומה. (ע"ב) א"ר יוסי בין השמשות

of the sun prevents him from eating the Terumah, but not his forgiveness-offering." (Ib. b) R. Jose said: "Twilight lasts as long as a twinkling; this one comes and that one goes, and it is impossible to determine its exact time."

(Fol. 3a) "Until the end of the first watch," said R. Eliezer. Let us see: with whom does R. Eliezer agree? If he hold that the night is divided into three watches, then let him say "until the end of the fourth hour"; and if he hold that the night is divided into four watches, then let him say "Until the end of the third hour?" He holds indeed that the night has three watches, but he intends to inform us that just as there exist watches in Heaven, so there exist watches here on the earth; as we are taught that R. Eliezer says: "Three watches has the night; and at the beginning of every watch the Holy One, praised be He! sits and roars like a lion, as it is said (Jer. 25, 30.) The Lord will roar from Heaven on high and from His holy dwelling shall He give forth His voice. Verily, He will roar over His habitation. And the divisions of the night are recognized by these signs: In the first watch the ass brays; in the second the dog barks; and in the third the baby nurses from its mother's breast and the wife converses with her husband." How does R. Eliezer arrive at these conclusions? Does he apply the signs to the beginning or to the end of each watch? If He applies his signs to the beginning of each watch, then it is unnecessary to have a sign for the first, as nightfall itself is a sufficient indication for it! If, however, he applies his signs to the end of each watch then the sign for the last is unnecessary, for the dawn is then sufficient! He applies his signs to the end of the first watch, the beginning of the last and the middle of the second. And if you please, you may say that he applies his signs to the end of each watch. In answer to your question as to the necessity of a sign for the last, I say: It is necessary for a man who sleeps in a dark place and does not know the time for reading the Sh'm'a: as soon as he hears the wife conversing with her husband, and the baby nursing from its mother's breast, he may begin to read the Sh'm'a. R. Isaac b. Samuel in the name of Rab said: "Three watches has the night and at the beginning of every watch the Holy One, praised be He! sits and roars like a lion and says 'Woe to the children that because of their sins I have destroyed my edifice, and burned my Temple, and exiled my children among the heathens.' "

We are taught that R. Jose says: "Once upon a time I was walking on a road and I entered one of the ruins of Jerusalem to pray. Elijah, blessed be his memory! came and watched me at the door until I finished my prayer. After I had finished, he said to me: 'Shalom, (peace, unto thee), my teacher,' to which I answered, 'Shalom, my teacher and my guide.' 'My son,' said he, 'why did you enter this ruin?' 'To pray,' I replied. You could have prayed on the road?' he said 'I was afraid lest I be interrupted by travelers.' 'You should then have prayed a short prayer.' From this conversation, I concluded three things: First: It is not safe to enter a ruin. Second: One is permitted to pray on the road, and third: A man on the road [having no place to pray] has the privilege of saying a short prayer. He then said to me: 'What voice did you hear in this ruin?' 'I heard,' I replied, 'a Bath-Kol (heavenly voice) which

משדי אמו ליקום וליקרי. אמר רב יצחק בר שמואל אמר רב ג׳ משמרות הוי הלילה ועל כל משמר ומשמר יושב הקב״ה ושואג כארי ואומר אוי לבנים שבעונותיהם החרבתי את ביתי ושרפתי את היכלי והגליתי את בני לבין העובדי כוכבים:

תניא א״ר יוסי פעם אחת הייתי מהלך בדרך ונכנסתי לחורבה אחת מחורבות ירושלים להתפלל ובא אליהו ז״ל ושמר לי על הפתח עד שסיימתי תפלתי לאחר שסיימתי תפלתי אמר לי שלום עליך רבי אמרתי לו שלום עליך רבי ומורי. אמר לי בני מפני מה נכנסת לחורבה זו אמרתי לו להתפלל אמר לי היה לך להתפלל בדרך אמרתי לו מתיירא הייתי שמא יפסיקוני עוברי דרכים. אמר לי היה לך להתפלל תפלה קצרה. באותה שעה למדתי ממנו ג׳ דברים למדתי שאין נכנסין לחורבה ולמדתי שמתפללין בדרך ולמדתי שהמתפלל בדרך מתפלל תפלה קצרה. אמר לי בני מה קול שמעת בחורבה זו

coos like a dove, saying, 'Woe to the children that because of their sins I have destroyed my edifice, burned my Temple, and exiled my children among the heathens.' 'My son,' said he again, '[I swear] by your life and the life of your head, that this occurs not only at that particular time, but thrice daily; furthermore, every time Israelites enter the Synagogues or places of learning and answer Let His great name be praised, the Holy One, praised be He! nods His head, and says, 'Happy is the king thus praised in his own house, but what availeth it a father who hath exiled his children among the heathens? Woe to the children who have been exiled from their father's table!' "

Our Rabbis have taught: For three reasons shall no person enter a ruin; because of suspicion (of an immoral intention); because the ruin may cave in; and on account of demons (dwelling in ruins).

(Ib. b) Our Rabbis have taught: "The night has four watches," so says Rabbi. R. Nathan says "Three." What is R. Nathan's reason? It is written (Judges 6, 19.) And Gidon, and the hundred men that were with him, came unto the edge of the camp in the beginning of the middle watch. And we are taught that Tichon (middle) cannot be used unless something precedes and something follows it. But Rabbi disputes this and says that "by the middle is meant one of the two middles." R. Nathan says: "Is it then written one of the middles? Behold! It is written the middle!" What is Rabbi's reason? R. Zerika in the name of R. Ami, who speaks in the name of R. Joshua ben Levi, said: "One passage says (Ps. 119. 62.) At midnight do I constantly rise to give

אמרתי לו שמעתי בת קול שמנהמת כיונה ואומרת אוי לבנים שבעונותיהם החרבתי ביתי ושרפתי את היכלי והגליתי את בני לבין העכו״ם. אמר לי בני חייך וחיי ראשך לא שעה זו בלבד אומרת כך אלא בכל יום ויום ג״פ אומרת כך. ולא זו בלבד אלא בשעה שישראל נכנסין לבתי כנסיות ולבתי מדרשות ועונין יהא שמיה הגדול מבורך הקב״ה מנענע ראשו ואומר אשרי המלך שמקלסין אותו בביתו כך. ומה לו לאב שהגלה את בניו לבין העכו״ם ואוי להם לבנים שגלו מעל שלחן אביהם:

ת״ר מפני שלשה דברים אין נכנסין לחורבה מפני חשד ומפני המפולת ומפני מזיקין:

(ע״ב) ת״ר ד׳ משמרות הוי הלילה דברי רבי. רבי נתן אומר שלשה מ״ט דר׳ נתן דכתיב (שופטים ו יט) ויבא גדעון ומאה איש אשר אתו בקצה המחנה ראש האשמורת התיכונה תנא אין תיכונה אלא שיש לפניה ולאחריה ורבי מאי תיכונה אחת מן התיכונה שבתיכונות ור׳ נתן מי כתיב תיכונה שבתיכונות תיכונה כתיב. מ״ט דרבי א״ר זריקא א״ר אמי אמר ריב״ל כתוב אחד אומר (תהלים קיט סב) חצות לילה אקום להודות לך על משפטי צדקך וכתוב אחד אומר (שם קיט קמח) קדמו

thanks unto Thee, etc., and another passage says (Ib. ib. 148.) My eyes are awake before the night watches. How is this possible? At midnight; because The night is divided into four watches, [midnight is therefore after two watches.]" But R. Nathan explains it by the statement of R. Joshua; as we are taught that R. Joshua says: "It is the custom of kings to rise on the third hour of the day. [i.e., six hours of the night and two hours of the day together make two night watches of four hours each]. R. Ashi said: "One watch and a half are also called watches (plural)."

Another thing said R. Zerika, in the name of R. Ami. who speaks in the name of R. Joshua b. Levi: "In the presence of the dead it is not proper to speak of anything except things concerning the dead." R. Abba b. Cahana said: "This refers only to affairs of the Torah, but worldly affairs do not matter." But some say that R. Abba b. Cahana said: "This refers to affairs of the Torah and even more positively to worldly affairs."

It is written (Ps. 119, 62.) At midnight do I constantly rise to give thanks unto Thee. Did David rise at midnight? Behold! He arose at the beginning of the night, for it is said, (Ib. ib. 147.) I came before thee in the twilight of night. And how do we know that the meaning of Neshef is the beginning of night? For it is written (Pr. 7, 9.) In the Neshef, in the evening of day. R. Oshiya said: "Thus [said David], 'I never passed half a night in sleep.'" R. Zerika said: "Until midnight he slumbered like a horse, thereafter he strengthened himself [fought sleep] like a lion." R. Ashi said: "Until midnight he was engaged in the study of the Torah; after that [he spent his time] in songs and praises."

עיני אשמורות הא כיצד ד' משמרות הוי הלילה ור' נתן סבר לה כר' יהושע דתנן ר' יהושע אומר עד שלש שעות שכן דרך מלכים לעמוד בשלש שעות שית דלילא ותרתי דיממא הוו לה שתי משמרות רב אשי אמר משמרה ופלגא נמי משמרות קרי להו:

וא״ר זריקא א״ר אמי אמר ריב״ל אין אומרין בפני המת אלא דבריו של מת א״ר אבא בר כהנא לא אמרן אלא בד״ת אבל מילי דעלמא לית לן בה ואיכא דאמרי א״ר אבא בר כהנא לא אמרן אלא אפי' בד״ת וכ״ש מילי דעלמא:

כתיב (תהלים קיט סב) חצות לילה אקום להודות לך וכי דוד בפלגא דליליא הוה קאי מאורתא הוה קאי דכתיב (שם קמז) קדמתי בנשף ואשוע. ומאי משמע דהאי נשף אורתא הוא דכתיב (משלי ז ט) בנשף בערב יום וגו' אמר רבי אושעיא דוד הכי קאמר מעולם לא עבר עלי חצות לילה בשינה רבי זירא אמר עד חצות לילה היה מתנמנם כסוס מכאן ואילך היה מתגבר כארי רב אשי אמר עד חצות לילה היה עוסק בדברי תורה מכאן ואילך בשירות ותשבחות.

And do you say Neshef means the beginning of night? Why do we find it used as the dawn of morning? For it is written (I. Sam. 30. 37.) And David smote them from the Neshef even unto the evening of the next day. Is it not meant from morning until evening? "Nay, from evening to evening." If so, then let it be written Me-haneshef Ad Haneshef or instead of Me-ha'ereb Ad Ha'ereb! [Why are the two words Neshef and Ereb, used for the same idea?] "But," says Raba, "Neshef means originally, 'The transition of anything' hence, night ends and day comes, the day ends and night comes." But how did David know the exact time at midnight? Behold! If Moses our teacher did not know it, for it is written (Ex. 11, 4.) Thus hath the Lord said, about midnight, etc. Why [does he come to say] about midnight? Should we say that he was told so by the Holy One, praised be He! Is there any possibility of God being in doubt? We must therefore explain it that Moses was told At midnight [as it really happened]; but Moses [on his own recognizance] said About midnight; consequently we infer that Moses was in doubt. And how did David know it? David had a sign [which indicated the exact time at midnight to him], for R. Chana b. Bizna said in the name of R. Simon the Pious that: a harp was hanging over David's bed and, as soon as midnight arrived, a northerly wind blew in upon the strings of the harp and caused it to play. Thereupon, David arose and studied the Torah until dawn. At dawn the sages of Israel visited David and said to him: "Our Lord, O King! Israel, thy people need a living!" "Go and support yourselves by dealing with one another," replied David. "But," said they, "a handful does not satisfy the lion nor can a pit be filled with its own

ונשף אורתא הוא נשף צפרא הוא דכתיב (ש״א ל לז) ויכם דוד מהנשף ועד הערב למחרתם מאי לאו מצפרא ועד ליליא לא מאורתא ועד אורתא. אי הכי לכתוב מהנשף ועד הנשף או מהערב ועד הערב. אלא אמר רבא תרי נשפי הוו נשף ליליא ואתא יממא נשף יממא ואתא ליליא. ודוד מי הוי ידע פלגא דליליא אימת השתא משה רבינו לא הוי ידע דכתיב (שמות יא ד) כה אמר ה׳ כחצות הלילה וגו׳. מאי כחצות אילימא דאמר ליה הקב״ה בחצות ומי איכא ספיקא קמי שמיא אלא דאמר לו למחר כחצות כי השתא ואתא איהו ואמר כחצות אלמא מספקא ליה ודוד הוה ידע (סנהדרין פרק א׳) דוד סימנא הוה ליה דאמר רב חנא בר ביזנא אמר ר״ש חסידא כנור היה תלוי למעלה ממטתו של דוד וכיון שהגיע חצות לילה בא רוח צפונית ונושבות בו ומנגן מאליו מיד היה עומד ועוסק בתורה עד שעלה עמוד השחר. וכיון שעלה עמוד השחר נכנסו חכמי ישראל אצלו ואומרים לו אדונינו המלך עמך ישראל צריכין פרנסה אמר להם לכו ויתפרנסו זה מזה אמרו לו אין הקומץ משביע את הארי ואין הבור מתמלא מחולייתו אמר להם לכו ופשטו ידיכם בגדוד מיד יועצים באחיתופל ונמלכין בסנהדרין ושואלין באורים ותומים. אמר רב יוסף מאי קרא דכתיב (דה״א כז לד) ואחרי אחיתופל

earth! [i. e., a community cannot live on its own resources]." Whereupon David said to them: "Go ye and stretch your hands out as a band [of warriors]. Immediately they held counsel with Achi'tophel and took advice from the Sanhedrin and inquired of the Urim and Tummim. R. Joseph said: "What is the passage [that refers to this]? It is written (I Chr.27, 34.) And after Achi'tophel (came) Joho'yada, the son. of Bena'yahu, and Ebya'thar, and the captain of the king's army was Joab, i.e., 'Achi'tophel' is the adviser; as it is said (II Sam. 16, 23.) And the council of Achi'tophel, which he counseled in those (Fol. 4a) days was as if a man had asked advice of the word of God: 'Jehoyada the son of Bena'yahu,' refers to the Sanhedrin; 'Ebyathar' refers to the Urim and Tummim; as the passage said (Ib. 20, 23.) And Bena'yahu, the son of Jeho'yada was over the Kareithi and Peleithi. But why are the Sanhedrin called 'Kareithi?' Because they cut their words clearly; and 'Peleithi?' Because their acts were wonderful [predestined]. And why was the name Urim given to the stones? Because they enlightened their words; 'Tummim?' Because they finished their words.' And after this, they applied to Joab, the king's captain." R. Isaac b. Ada said: "What biblical passage relates to this? [That the harp was hanging over David's bed.] Awake! my spirit, awake! my psaltry and harp; I will wake up the morning dawn! (Ps. 57, 9)." R. Zera said: "Moses, our teacher, knew very well [the exact time at midnight] and so did David; the harp was used not to tell him the time at midnight, but to awaken him from sleep. The reason for Moses' statement About midnight is that he feared lest the astrologers of Pharaoh might err in the time and would afterwards say that

יהוידע בן בניהו ואביתר ושר צבא למלך יואב אחיתופל זה יועץ וכן הוא אומר (ש״ב טז כג) ועצת אחיתופל אשר יעץ בימים ההם כאשר ישאל איש בדבר האלהים. יהוידע בן בניהו זה סנהדרין אביתר אלו אורים ותומים, וכן הוא אומר (שם כ כג) ובניהו בן יהוידע על הכרתי ועל הפלתי. ולמה נקרא שמם כרתי ופלתי. כרתי שכורתים דבריהם פלתי שמופלאים דבריהם. ואחר כך שר צבא למלך יואב. אמר רב יצחק בר אדא מאי קרא (תהלים נז ט) עורה כבודי עורה הנבל וכנור אעירה שחר. ר׳ זירא אמר משה רבינו מידע הוה ידע ודוד נמי הוה ידע וכיון דדוד הוה ידע כנור ל״ל לאתעוריה משנתיה. וכיון דמשה הוה ידע ל״ל למימר כחצות משה קסבר שמא יטעו אצטגניני פרעה ויאמרו משה בדאי הוה והיינו, דאמר מר למד לשונך לומר איני יודע שמא תתבדה ותאחז רב אשי אמר כפלגא אורתא דתליסר נגהי ארביסר הוה קאי וה״ק משה לישראל אמר הקב״ה למחר כחצות הלילה כי האידנא אני יוצא בתוך מצרים:

Moses lied; as the master has said, Use thy tongue to say, I do not know lest you be found mistaken and deceived!' " R. Ashi said: "The time when Moses spoke was midnight (between the thirteenth and the fourteenth day of Nisan) and thus he said to Pharaoh: 'The Holy One, praised be He! said, 'To-morrow, at this time, will I go out in the midst of Egypt.'"

[It is written] (Ps. 66, 1.) A prayer of David, preserve my soul, for I am pious. R. Levi and R. Isaac both explain this passage. One said: "Thus said David before the Holy One, praised be He! 'Sovereign of the universe, am I not pious? Whereas all the kings of the east and west sleep until the third hour of the day, I rise at midnight to praise Thee.'" And the other said: "Thus said David before the Holy One, praised be He! 'Sovereign of the universe, am I not pious, whereas all the kings of the east and west sit companies in their glory, my hands are soiled in blood, membraneous-bag and after-birth in order to decide questions pertaining to family life; and moreover, whatever I do, I first consult Mephi-bosheth my teacher, saving to him: Meplu-bosheth my teacher, have I properly convicted? Have I properly acquitted? Have I properly declared pure? Have I properly declared impure? And I do not feel degraded [asking this].'" R. Joshua, the son of Ide, said: "What is the Biblical passage [that refers to this]? It is written (Ps. 119, 46.) And I will speak of thy testimony before kings and will not be ashamed." We are taught that his name (David's teacher) was not Mephi-bosheth but Ish-bosheth. Why was he called Mephi-bosheth? Because he insulted David during Halachic discussions; therefore, [because David humbly accepted these

(תהלים סו א) לדוד שמרה נפשי כי חסיד אני רבי לוי ור' יצחק חד אמר כך אמר דוד לפני הקב"ה רבש"ע לא חסיד אני שכל מלכי מזרח ומערב ישנים עד ג' שעות ואני חצות לילה אקום להודות לך. ואידך כך אמר דוד לפני הקב"ה רבש"ע לא חסיד אני שכל מלכי מזרח ומערב יושבים אגודות אגודות בכבודם ואני ידי מלוכלכות בדם ובשפיר ובשליא כדי לטהר אשה לבעלה ולא עוד אלא שכל מה שאני עושה אני נמלך במפיבושת רבי ואומר לו מפיבושת רבי יפה דנתי יפה חייבתי יפה זכיתי יפה טהרתי יפה טמאתי ולא בושתי. אמר רב יהושע בריה דרב אידי מאי קרא (שם קיט מו) ואדברה בעדותיך נגד מלכים ולא אבוש. תנא לא מפיבושת שמו אלא איש בשת שמו ולמה נקרא שמו מפיבושת שהיה מבייש פני דוד בהלכה לפיכך זכה דוד ויצא ממנו כלאב. ואמר ר' יוחנן לא כלאב שמו אלא דניאל שמו ולמה נקרא שמו כלאב שהיה מכלים פני מפיבושת בהלכה ועליו אמר שלמה בחכמתו (משלי כג טו)

reproaches,] David was rewarded and Kilab came forth from him and R. Jochanan said: "His name was not Kilab but Daniel; why then was he called Kilab? Because he reproached Mephi-bosheth in matters of Halacha, and concerning him (Kilab) Solomon said in his wisdom (Pr. 23, 15.) My son, if thy heart be wise, my heart shall rejoice, even mine. And it is also said (Ib. 27, 11.) Become wise, my son, and cause my heart to rejoice that I may give an answer to him that reproacheth me." Why, did David call himself pious? Is it not written (Ps. 27, 13.) Unless I had to see the goodness of the Lord in the land of life, and we are taught in the name of R. Jose, "Why is the word Lulei (unless) dotted? David said before the Holy One, praised be He! 'Sovereign of the universe, I assuredly trust in Thee, knowing that Thou wilt properly reward the just when the time shall come [in the future world], but I doubt whether I shall have a share in them,' [Hence we infer that David did not consider himself a pious man.]" He was afraid because of the sin, as R. Jacob b. Ide said; for R. Jacob b. Ide raised the following contradictory question: "It is written (Gen. 28, 15.) And behold, I, (God) am with thee, (Jacob), and will keep thee withersoever thou goest. And it is written (Ib. 32, 8.) And Jacob was greatly afraid and he felt distressed. [Why was he afraid after the Lord promised to be with him?] Jacob said: 'Perhaps there is some cause of sin which will prevent the fulfillment of His promise;' as we have been taught: 'It is said (Ex. 15, 16.) Till thy people pass over, O Lord, till this people pass over, which Thou hast purchased. Till thy people pass over, O Lord: refers to the first entrance, [into the land of Israel]; Till this people pass over which Thou

בני אם חכם לבך ישמח לבי גם אני ואומר (שם כז יא) חכם בני ושמח לבי ואשיבה חורפי דבר. ודוד היכי קרי לנפשיה חסיד והא כתיב (תהלים כז יג) לולא האמנתי לראות בטוב ה׳ בארץ חיים ותנא משמיה דרבי יוסי למה נקוד על לולא אמר דוד לפני הקב״ה רבש״ע מובטח אני בך שאתה משלם שכר טוב לצדיקים לעתיד לבא אבל איני יודע אם יש לי חלק ביניהם אם לאו שמא יגרום החטא כדרבי יעקב בר אידי דרבי יעקב בר אידי רמי כתיב (בראשית כח טו) והנה אנכי עמך ושמרתיך בכל אשר תלך וכתיב (שם לב ח) ויירא יעקב מאד אמר שמא יגרום החטא כדתניא (שמות טו טז) עד יעבור עמך ה׳ עד יעבור עם זו קנית, עד יעבור עמך ה׳ זו ביאה ראשונה עד יעבור עם זו קנית זו ביאה שניה מכאן אמרו חכמים ראויים היו ישראל ליעשות להם נס בימי עזרה כדרך שנעשה להם בימי יהושע בן נון אלא שגרם החטא:

hast purchased; refers to the second entrance [in the days of Ezra]. From this, declared the sages, it can be inferred that Israel was to be brought in [into the land of Israel] during the days of Ezra by the same miracles through which they entered the first time, in the days of Joshua ben Nun, but Israel's sins prevented the fulfillment of this."

(Ib. b) We are taught: The sages made a fence to their words [to protect their ordinances], lest a man coming from the field in the evening, would say: "I will go home, eat a little, drink a little, and sleep a while and then I will read Sh'm'a and pray the evening service." In the meantime he will fall asleep and sleep through the whole night without having read the Sh'm'a or prayed. But [in order to prevent this they say:] "A man coming from the field in the evening shall enter the synagogue, and if he be accustomed to read the Scripture, let him do so; or if he be able to study traditional law, let him do that. After this, he should read the Sh'm'a and pray; then he can eat his meal and recite the Aftermeal Benediction. He who transgresses the words of the wise, deserves the penalty of death." Why docs the Baraitha use the expression here that "He who transgresses the words of the wise is worthy of the penalty of death," and not use it in any other place? If you wish, you may say, because here the force of sleep puts him beyond his own control [and if he is not strongly warned against it, he may transgress the command even though he really desires to fulfill it]; and if you please, you may say, because it is the intention [of the Baraitha] to reverse the opinion of those who say that the evening service is only

(ע״ב) תניא חכמים עשו סייג לדבריהם כדי שלא יהא אדם בא מן השדה בערב ואומר אלך לביתי ואוכל קימעא ואשתה קימעא ואישן קימעא ואח״כ אקרא ק״ש ואתפלל וחוטפתו שינה ונמצא ישן כל הלילה אבל אדם בא מן השדה בערב נכנס לבהכ״נ אם רגיל לקרות קורא ואם רגיל לשנות שונה וקורא ק״ש ומתפלל ואוכל פתו ומברך וכל העובר על דברי חכמים חייב מיתה. מאי שנא בכל דוכתא דלא חייב מיתה ומאי שנא הכא דקתני חייב מיתה. איבעית אימא משום דאיכא אונס שינה ואי בעית אימא לאפוקי ממ״ד תפלת ערבית רשות קמ״ל דחובה. אמר מר קורא ק״ש ומתפלל מסייע ליה לר' יוחנן דאמר ר״י איזהו בן עולם הבא זה הסומך גאולה לתפלה של ערבית רבי יהושע ב״ל אומר תפלות באמצע תקנום במאי קא מיפלגי איבעית אימה קרא איבעית אימה סברא, איבעית אימא סברא דרבי יוחנן סבר גאולה מאורתא נמי הוה אלא גאולה מעלייתא לא הוי אלא עד צפרא ורבי יהושע ב״ל סבר כיון דלא הוי אלא

optional it tells us, therefore, [by its warning,] that it is obligatory. The master said [above]: "He reads the Sh'm'a and prays (the evening service)" This is in support of [the view of] R. Jochanan, who was accustomed to say: "Who is sure to have a share in the world to come? He, who, immediately after the benediction of Geula, says the prayer of the Eighteen Benedictions at the evening service." R. Joshua b. Levi said: "The Eighteen Benedictions were ordained to be said in the middle." On what do they base their difference of opinion? If you please, you may say on a Biblical passage, and if you please, you may say on common sense. As to reason, R. Joshua holds that the redemption (of Egypt) commenced on the evening (towards the fifteenth of Nisan) although the real redemption did not take place until the morning, [therefore the Ge-ula which indicates the redemption should be said immediately before the Eighteen Benedictions in the evening also]; but R. Joshua b. Levi holds that as long as the real redemption did not take place until the morning then the redemption of the evening matters little. As to the Biblical passage they differ in the interpretation of the passage. (Deu. 6, 7.) And when thou lieth down, and when thou riseth up, (referred to Sh'm'a). R. Jochanan holds: "We compare Lying down [at evening] to arising [in the morning] for the reason that just as the reading of the Sh'm'a in the morning comes before the prayer, so, in the evening, the reading of the Sh'm'a comes first also, and then the prayer of the Eighteen Benedictions." R. Joshua holds: "We compare the reading of the Sh'm'a when lying down to the reading of the Sh'm'a when arising, for the reason that

מצפרא לא הוי גאולה מעלייתא ואי בעית אימא קרא ושניהם מקרא אחד דרשו דכתיב (דברים ו ז) בשכבך ובקומך רבי יוחנן סבר מקיש שכיבה לקימה מה קימה ק״ש ואח״כ תפלה אף שכיבה נמי ק״ש ואחר כך תפלה רבי יהושע ב״ל סבר מקיש שכיבה לקימה מה קימה ק״ש סמוך למטתו אף שכיכה נמי ק״ש סמוך למטתו מתיב מר בריה דרבינא בערב מברך שתים לפניה ושתים לאחריה ואי אמרת בעי לסמוך הא לא קא סמך גאולה לתפלה והא בעי למימר השכיבנו אמרי כיון דתקינו רבנן השכיבנו כגאולה אריכתא דמיא דאי לא תימא הכי שחרית היכי מצי סמיך והא אמר רבי יוחנן בתחלה אומר (תהלים נא יז) ה' שפתי תפתח ולבסוף הוא אומר (שם יט טו) יהיו לרצון אמרי פי אלא התם כיון דתקינו רבנן למימר ה' שפתי תפתח כתפלה אריכתא דמי הכא נמי כיון דתקינו רבנן למימר השכיבנו כגאולה אריכתא דמיא:

just as in the morning the Sh'm'a is read close upon rising so is the Sh'm'a of the evening read just before lying down." The following objection was raised by Mar b. Rabina: "We have learned (in a Mishnah) 'In the evening, he says two benedictions before the Sh'm'a and two after the Sh'm'a.' If the Eighteen Benedictions should be said immediately after Ge-ula, then the Benedictions of Hash-ki-benu, prevents his having the Ge-ula, (the first one after Sh'm'a) closely after the Eighteen Benedictions?" Since the Rabbis ordained that Hash-ki-benu is to be said [between Ge-ula and the Eighteen Benedictions] then it is considered as one long benediction; for if we do not say so, then in the morning how can we say the Eighteen Benedictions immediately after the Ge-ula? Has not R. Jochanan said: "He should first say, O Lord, open Thou my lips, and my mouth shall declare thy praise (Ps. 51, 17), and then proceed with the Eighteen Benedictions; and at the conclusion he should say. May the words of my mouth, and the meditation of my heart be acceptable before Thee, O Lord, my rock and my redeemer, (Ib. 19, 15)." But since the Rabbis ordained that the passage [O Lord, open my mouth, etc.] be said, it is considered one long prayer (part of the eighteen benedictions), so in this instance also, since the Rabbis ordained that the Hash-ki-benu be said between Ge-ula and the Eighteen Benedictions, it is considered a part of Ge-ula

R. Elazar b. Abina said: "He who recites Te-hila l' David (Ps. 145) three times a day may be sure of an inheritance in the world to come." What is the reason? Shall I say because that particular chapter is arranged

אמר רבי אלעזר בר אבינא כל האומר (תהלים קמה א) תהלה לדוד שלש פעמים בכל יום מובטח לו שהוא בן העולם הבא מאי טעמא

alphabetically? Then why not prefer chapter 119 Ps., which has an arrangement of eight repetitions of each letter of the alphabet? Is it because it has the verse Thou openeth Thy hand and satisfieth the demands of all Thy creatures. [it influences men to be benevolent]? If so, then why not the Great Hallel? in which also is written (Ib. 136, 25.) He giveth food to all flesh. Because Tehila l' David has the advantages of both; [is arranged alphabetically and influences men to be benevolent].

R. Jochanan said: "Why is the letter Nun missing in the [alphabetical course of] Ashrei? Because the letter Nun is used for bad tidings. It is said (Amos 5, 2.) She is fallen (Nafla) and will not rise again, the virgin of Israel." In Palestine they interpret [this prophecy of Amos as good tidings] thus: She is fallen and will not fall again! Rise! virgin of Israel! R. Nachman b. Isaac said: "Even so, David indicates [the prophecy of] the Nun for the purpose of strengthening Israel, through a holy vision; for he says (Ps. 145, 14.) The Lord upholdeth all who are fallen (Noflim)."

R. Elazar b. Abina said further: "Much more is said [regarding the actions] of Michael than is said of Gabriel; for in describing Michael, it is written (Is. 6, 6.) Then flew unto me one of the Seraphim. Whereas in describing Gabriel it is written (Dan. 9, 21.) The man Gabriel whom I had seen in the vision at the beginning, came flying swiftly." And whence do we know that the word Echad (one) [mentioned by Isaiah] refers to Michael? R. Jochanan said: "We derive it from the word Echad which occurs in both passages; it is written here (Is. 6, 6.) One of the Seraphim and it is written there (Dan. 10, 13.) But Michael, one of the chief princes, came to help me. [Just as in the latter case] the word Echad (one) is applied to Michael, so also in the former case does Echad (one) apply to Michael]." In a Baraitha it was taught: "Michael [reaches his destination] with one [flight]; Gabriel with two; Elijah with four and the angel of death with eight; but during an epidemic the angel of death reaches [his destination] with one [flight]."

(Fol. 5a) R. Levi b. Chama, in the name of Simon b. Lakish said: "At all times let man stir up his good inclination against the evil inclination), for it is said (Ps. 4, 5.) Tremble, and sin not. If he conquers it (the evil inclination) it is well, but if he does not, then he should study the Torah; for we read, (Ib.) Commune with your heart. If it goes away, then it is well, but if not he should then read the Sh'm'a; for it is said (Ib.) Upon your bed. If he conquers it, then it is well, but if not, he should then remind himself of the day of death, for it is written. And be still Selah (to the end)." R. Isaac said: "Whoever reads the Sh'm'a when on his bed is considered [protected] as if he were holding a two-edged sword in his hand, for it is written (Ps. 149, 6.) The exalted praises (of God) are in their mouths and the two-edged sword in their hands." How does he infer this? Mar Zutra and according to others, R. Ashi, said: "From the beginning of that passage (Ib. ib. 5.) Let the pious be joyful in glory; let them, sing aloud upon their beds; and it is written after this The exalted praise of God is in their mouths and a two-edged sword in their hands." Furthermore, said R. Isaac: Whoever reads the Sh'm'a on his bed [before sleep],

הראשונים בא לעזרני. תנא מיכאל באחת גבריאל בשתים אליהו בארבע ומלאך המות בשמונה ובשעת המגפה באחת:

(דף ה) אמר ר' לוי בר חמא אמר רשב"ל לעולם ירגיז אדם יצ"ט על יצ"ה שנא' (תהלים ד ה) רגזו ואל תחטאו. אם נצחו מוטב. ואי לא יעסוק בתורה שנאמר אמרו בלבבכם. אם נצחו מוטב אי לא יקרא ק"ש שנאמר על משכבכם. אם נצחו מוטב ואי לא יזכיר לו יום המיתה שנאמר ודומו סלה. אמר ר' יצחק כל הקורא ק"ש על מטתו כאילו אוחז חרב של שתי פיות בידו שנאמ' (שם קמט ו) רוממות אל בגרונם וחרב פיפיות בידם מאי משמע אמר מר זוטרא ואיתימא רב אשי מרישיה דענינא דכתיב יעלזו חסידים בכבוד ירננו על משכבותם וכתיב בתריה רוממות אל בגרונם וחרב פיפיות בידם. ואמר רבי יצחק כל הקורא ק"ש על מטתו מזיקין בדילים ממנו שנאמר (איוב ה ז) ובני רשף יגביהו עוף ואין עוף אלא תורה שנאמר (משלי כג ה) התעיף עיניך בו ואיננה ואין רשף אלא מזיקין שנאמר (דברים

will cause the departure of all evil spirits; for it is said (Job 5, 7.) And the sons of fire take up their flight. By Uf (flight) is meant nothing else but the Torah, as it is said (Pr. 23, 5.) When thou letteth merely thine eyes fly over it (i. e., if thou learneth the Torah superficially), it is no more. And reshef (fire) means nothing else but evil spirits; as it is said (Deu. 32, 24.) Devoured with burning heat and with bitter deadly disease."

Furthermore, said R. Levi b. Chama, in the name of Resh Lakish: "What is meant by the passage (Ex. 24, 12.) And I will give thee the tablets of stone, with the law and the Commandments, which I have written to teach them? i.e, the tablets of stone, refers to the ten commandments; the Torah, refers to the Bible; the commandments, refers to the Mishnah; which I hare written, refers to the Prophets and Hagiographa; to teach them, refers to the Gemara; whence we infer that — all were given unto Moses on Mt. Sinai."

R. Simon b. Lakish said: "Whoever studies the Torah will prevent affliction from coming upon him, for it is said (Job 5, 7.), And the sons of fire take up their flight. By Uf (flight) is meant nothing else but the Torah, as it is said (Pr. 23, 5.) When thou letteth merely thine eye fly over it (i.e., if you study the Torah by merely glancing over it with your eyes), it is no more, (you will easily forget it). And Reshef (fire) means nothing else but affliction, as it is said (Deu. 32, 24.) Devoured with evil spirits." "Aye." exclaimed R. Jochanan, "even the school children know this! for it is said, (Ex. 15. 2.5.) And he said, if thou wilt deligently hearken unto the voice of the Lord and wilt do what is riqht in His eyes, etc. But it means thus: Upon him who is capable of studying the Torah, but does not do so the Holy One, praised be He! will bring repulsive suffering which will greatly disturb him; for it is said (Ps. 39, 3.) I was dumb in deep silence, I was quite still even from speaking good, but my pain greatly disturbed me. By tob (good) is meant nothing else but the Torah, for it is said (Pr. 4, 2.) For good doctrine do I give, etc." R. Zeira, and some say, R. Chanina b. Papa, said: "Come and see that the custom of the Holy One. praised be He! is not like the custom of mortal men. The custom of mortal men is that if a man sell a valuable thing to his fellow-man, the seller is sorry and only the buyer is happy; but the custom of the Holy One, praised be He! is not so. He bestowed the Torah on Israel and He rejoiced, for it is said (Ib. 4, 2.) For good doctrine do I give thee." Raba, and according to others R. Chisda, said: "If a man see that troubles are coming unto him, let him search his deeds, for it is said, (Lam. 3, 40) Let us search through and examine our ways and let us return unto the Lord. If he has investigated and found nothing wrong, then let him attribute it to a neglect of the study of the Torah. for it is said (Ps. 94, 12.) Happy is the man whom Thou admonisheth, O Lord, and teacheth out of Thy Torah. But if he investigated and did not find [neglect of the study of the Torah] then it is known that his affliction is the cause of God's love, for it is said (Pr. 3, 12.) Because whomsoever the Lord loveth He admonisheth." Raba, in the name of R. Sechorah, who quoted R. Huna, said: "Whomsover the Holy One, praised be He! loveth. He afflicteth, for it is said (Is. 53, 10.) But the Lord was pleased to crush him through disease. We might think that, even

(תהלים לט ג) נאלמתי דומיה החשיתי מטוב וכאבי נעכר. ואין טוב אלא תורה שנאמר (משלי ד ב) כי לקח טוב נתתי לכם וגו'. אמר ר' זירא ואיתימא רבי חנינא בר פפא בוא וראה שלא כמדת הקדוש ברוך הוא מדת בשר ודם. מדת בשר ודם אדם מוכר חפץ לחבירו מוכר עצב ולוקח שמח. אבל הקב"ה אינו כן נתן להם תורה ושמח שנאמר כי לקח טוב נתתי לכם וגומר. אמר רבא ואיתימא רב חסדא אם רואה אדם שיסורין באין עליו יפשפש במעשיו. שנאמר (איכה ג) נחפשה דרכינו ונחקורה פשפש ולא מצא יתלה בבטול תורה שנא' (תהלים צט יב) אשרי הגבר אשר תיסרנו יה ומתורתך תלמדנו ואם תלה ולא מצא בידוע שיסורין של אהבה הן שנאמר (משלי ג יב) כי את אשר יאהב ה' יוכיח. אמר רבא אמר רב סחורה אמר רב הונא כל שהקדוש ברוך הוא חפץ בו מדכאו ביסורין שנאמר (ישעיה נג י) וה' חפץ דכאו החלי יכול אפילו לא קבלן מאהבה תלמוד לומר (שם) אם תשים אשם נפשו. מה אשם לדעת אף יסורין לדעת ואם קבלם עליו מאהבה מה שכרו (שם) יראה זרע יאריך ימים ולא עוד אלא שתלמודו מתקיים בידו שנאמר (שם) וחפץ ה' בידו יצלח. פליגי בה רבי יעקב בר אידי ור' אחא בר חנינא חד אמר אלו הם יסורין של אהבה כל שאין להם בטול תורה שנאמר (תהלים

if he does not accept the affliction with resignation. It is therefore said (Ib.) When his soul hath brought the trespass-offering, i. e., just as a guilt offering must come with his acknowledgement, so also must this be accepted with resignation. And if he accept it with love what will be his reward? Then shall he see (his) seed live many days, (Ib.) and moreover his learning shall endure with him, as is said (Ib.) And the pleasure of the Lord shall prosper in his hand." As to affliction, there is a difference of opinion between R. Jacob b. Ide and R. Acha b. Chanina. One holds that all such affliction which does not prevent one from studying the Torah is one of love, for it is said (Ps. 94, 12.) Happy is the man whom Thou admonisheth, O Lord, and teacheth from Thy Torah; and the other holds that such affliction which does not prevent one from praying is one which comes from love, for it is said (Ps. 66, 20.) Blessed he God who hath not removed my prayer nor His kindness from me. R. Abba, the son of R. Chiya b. Abba, said: "Thus said my father (R. Chiya) in the name of R. Jochanan; 'Both of these afflictions are the kind which come from love, for it is written (Pr. 3, 12.) Because whomsoever the Lord loveth He admonisheth; But what do we learn [from the passage] Thou teacheth him of the Torah. Do not read Tlamdenu (that he should be able to study the Torah); but read it Tlamdainu (Out of Thy Torah, Thou teacheth us) i. e., we learn from thine Torah [that one who is punished by God should be happy] namely, through the rule of a fortiori concerning the tooth and the eye; that if the loss of a tooth or an eye [stricken out by the master] which affects only one member of the human body, frees the slave, how much more then are afflictions, which affect the

צד יב) אשרי הגבר אשר תיסרנו יה ומתורתך תלמדנו וחד אמר אלו הם יסורין של אהבה כל שאין להם בטול תפלה שנאמר (שם סו כ) ברוך אלהים אשר לא הסיר תפלתי וחסדו מאתי. אמר ליה רבי אבא בריה דרבי חייא בר אבא הכי אמר אבא א״ר יוחנן אלו ואלו יסורין של אהבה הן שנאמר (משלי ג יב) כי את אשר יאהב ה'. יוכיח אלא מה תלמוד לומר ומתורתך תלמדנו אל תקרא תלמדנו אלא תלמדנו דבר זה מתורתך תלמדנו קל וחומר משן ועין מה שן ועין שהוא אחד מאבריו של אדם עבד יוצא בהם לחירות יסורין שממרקין כל גופו של אדם לא כל שכן והיינו דרשב״ל, דאמר רשב״ל נאמר ברית במלח ונאמר ברית ביסורין נאמר ברית במלח דכתיב (ויקרא ב יג) ולא תשבית מלח ברית ונאמר ברית ביסורין דכתיב (דברים כח מט) אלה דברי הברית מה ברית האמור במלח, מלח ממתקת את הבשר, אף ברית האמור ביסורין, יסורין ממרקין כל עונותיו של אדם:

whole human body, capable of cleaning one of evil.'" And that is meant by R. Simon b. Lakish, for he said: "It is said Convenant (Brith) in connection with the word salt, and it is said Convenant (Brith) in connection with the word affliction. Covenant by salt — as it is written (Lev. 2, 13.) Thou shalt not suffer the salt of the covenant (Brith)! Covenant by affliction — as it is written (Deu. 28, 49.) These are the words of the covenant. (Brith) Just as the covenant of the salt was made to sweeten meat, so the covenant of affliction was made to cleanse man of all iniquities."

We are taught that R. Simon b. Jochai said: "Three precious gifts the Holy One, praised be He! bestowed on Israel, and none of them was bestowed without affliction. The gifts are, the Torah, Palestine and the world to come. How do we learn that the Torah was given with affliction? It is written (Ps. 94, 12.) Happy is the man whom Thou admonisheth, O Lord, and from Thy Torah, Thou teacheth him. Whence do we learn that Palestine was given with affliction? It is written (Deu. 8. 5.) Thou shalt consider in thy heart, that as a man chasteneth his son, so the Lord, thy God, chasteneth thee. Immediately following are the words For the Lord, thy God, bringeth thee into a good land, Whence do we learn the world to come was given with affliction? It is written (Pr. 6, 23.) For the commandment is a lamp, and the Torah is a light, and the way of life is to administer correction."

תניא רבי שמעון בן יוחאי אומר שלש מתנות טובות נתן הקב״ה לישראל וכולם לא נתנן אלא על ידי יסורין, אלו הן: תורה, ארץ ישראל והעולם הבא. תורה מניין שנאמר, אשרי הגבר אשר תיסרנו יה ומתורתך תלמדנו; ארץ ישראל, דכתיב (דברים ח ה) כי כאשר ייסר איש את בנו ה׳ אלהיך מיסרך, וכתיב בתריה, כי ה׳ אלהיך מביאך אל ארץ טובה; העולם הבא, דכתיב (משלי ו כג) כי נר מצוה ותורה אור ודרך חיים תוכחות מוסר:

A disciple recited before R. Jochanan: "Whoever occupies himself with the study of the Torah and with the practice of loving kindness and (Ib. b.) buries his children

תני תנא קמיה דרבי יוחנן, כל העוסק בתורה ובגמילות חסדים (ע״ב) וקובר את בניו מוחלין לו על כל עונותיו אמר ליה רבי יוחנן בשלמא תורה

[during his life] will have all his sins forgiven." "It is right," said R. Jochanan to him, "in the cases of the Torah and of charity; for it is written (Pr. 16, 6.) Through kindness is iniquity atoned for. Chesed (Kindness) means the practice of loving kindness as it is said (Ib. 21, 21.) He that pursueth righteousness and Kindness (Chesed). Emeth (Truth), means the Torah, for it is said (Ib. 23, 23.) Buy the truth (emeth) and sell it not) but as to the one, who buries his children whence do we learn it?" An old gentleman taught R. Jochanan, in. the name of R. Simon b. Jochai: "We infer this [through the rule of analogy] from the word, 'iniquity' (Avon). It is written here: Through kindness and truth is iniquity (Avon) atoned for, and it is written (Jer. 32, 18.) Inflicts the iniquities (Avon) of the fathers unto the bosoms of their children after them. [Just as the former Avon refers to atones, so does the latter]." R. Jochanan said: "Leprosy and [burying] children are not to [be considered among] the afflictions which come from love [of God]." And is not leprosy an affliction which comes from love? Have we not been taught: "Whoever is afflicted with one of these four forms of leprosy should deem it nothing else but an altar of forgiveness." "Aye," R. Joachanan answered, "it is true that it is an altar of forgiveness, but it is not an affliction which comes from the love of God; and if you wish, you may say that one statement refers to those who dwell in Babylon, and the other refers to those who dwell in Palestine; and if you wish, you may say that one statement deals with leprosy in a hidden place, and the other deals [with leprosy] in an open place." And [death of] children, you say, is not from the affliction of love? How shall we construe

וגמילות חסדים דכתיב (שם טז ו) בחסד ואמת יכופר עון חסד זו גמילות חסדים שנאמר (שם כא כא) רודף צדקה וחסד ימצא חיים צדקה וכבוד. אמת זו תורה שנאמר (שם כג כג) אמת קנה ואל תמכור אלא קובר את בניו מנין תנא ליה ההוא סבא משום ר׳ שמעון בן יוחאי אתיא עון עון כתיב הכא בחסד ואמת יכופר עון וכתיב התם (ירמיה לב יח) ומשלם עון אבות אל חיק בניהם אחריהם. אמר רבי יוחנן נגעים ובנים אינן יסורין של אהבה. ונגעים לא והא תניא, כל מי שיש בו אחד מד׳ מראות נגעים הללו אינן אלא מזבח כפרה מזבח כפרה הוו יסורין של אהבה לא הוו אב״א הא לן והא להו ואב״א הא בצנעא והא בפרהסיא. ובנים לא היכי דמי אי לימא דהוו ליה ומיתו והאמר רבי יוחנן דין גרמא דעשיראה ביר אלא הא דלא הוו ליה כלל והא דהוו ליה ומיתו:

this case? Shall we say that he had children but they died, then my objection is, that R. Jochanan himself said, "This is the bone of my tenth son whom I have buried." [Should we then believe that the affliction of such a great man as R. Jochanan was not affliction caused by the love of God?] But the statement of R. Jochanan refers to the case where there were no children born, and the latter deals with a case where there were born, but died during the parents' lifetime.

(Ib. b) R. Jochanan once became ill, and R. Chanina came to visit him. "Do you love these afflictions?" R. Chanina asked him. "I desire neither them nor their rewards," he answered. R. Chanina then said "Give me your hand." Thereupon R. Jochanan gave him his hand and he [R. Chanina] made him well. Why did not R. Jochanan make himself well without the aid of R. Chanina? [Did it not happen that] when R. Chiya b. Abba once became sick, he was visited by R. Jochanan, who asked him, "Do you love the afflictions," and when the answer came, "[I love] neither them nor their rewards," R. Jochanan asked for his hand and made him well. [Why could he not do the same for himself?] I will tell thee. A prisoner cannot liberate himself from his prison. R. Elazar once became sick. R. Jochanan came to visit him and saw that he was sleeping in a dark room. Whereupon R. Jochanan uncovered his own arm and immediately the room grew light. R. Jochanan then noticed that R. Elazar was weeping. "Why art thou weeping?" asked R. Jochanan. "Is it because thou hast not learned sufficiently of the Torah? Behold we are taught (in a Mishnah) 'No matter whether one [offers] much or little, only the intentions of his heart shall count for the

(ע״ב) רבי יוחנן חלש על לגביה ר׳ חנינא אמר ליה חביבין עליך יסורין אמר ליה לא הן ולא שכרן אמר ליה הב לי ידך יהב ליה ידיה ואוקמיה ואמאי לוקים ר׳ יוחנן לנפשיה דהא רבי חייא בר אבא חלש ועל לגביה רבי יוחנן ואמר ליה חביבין עליך יסורין אמר ליה לא הן ולא שכרן אמר ליה הב לי ידך יהב ליה ידא ואוקמיה וליקום איהו לנפשיה אמרי אין חבוש מתיר את עצמו מבית האסורין. רבי אלעזר חלש על לגביה רבי יוחנן חזא דהוה קא גני בבית אפל גלייה לדרעיה ונפל נהורא חזייה דהוה קא בכי רבי אלעזר אמר ליה אמאי קא בכית אי משום תורה דלא אפשת שנינו אחד המרבה ואחד הממעיט ובלבד שיכוין לבו לשמים. ואי משום מזוני לא כל אדם זוכה לשתי שלחנות אי משום בני דין גרמא דעשיראה ביר. א״ל להאי שופרא דבלי בעפרא קא בכינא אמר ליה על דא ודאי קא בכית ובכו תרוייהו. אדהכי והכי אמר ליה חביבין עליך יסורין אמר ליה לא הן

sake of Heaven.' Is it because you are in need and poor? [Do you know that] not everyone deserves two tables (in this world and the world to come). Is it because of trouble from your children? Here is a bone of my tenth son [whom I have buried — hence you are not the only one who has such troubles]." "I weep," said R. Elazar to him, "for that beauty which will decay in the earth." "For that," said R. Jochanan, "you really ought to weep," and both wept. "Do you love the afflictions?" R. Jochanan meanwhile asked of him. "[I love] neither them nor their rewards," answered R. Elazar. "Then give me your hand." R. Elazar did so and was made well. R. Huna had four hundred barrels of wine which had turned into vinegar. On hearing of his misfortune, R. Juda, brother of R. Sala the pions, accompanied by Rabbis, or as some say, R. Ada b. Ahaba, accompanied by Rabbis, came to visit him. "Let the master," said they, "investigate his affairs." "What!" said he. "Do you believe me to have been guilty of wrong-doing?" "Shall we then," responded they, "suspect the Holy One. praised be He! of executing judgment unjustly?" R. Huna then said, "If you have heard aught against me [don't conceal it] tell it to me." So they said to him, "We heard that the master allows his tenant no share in the wines [when they are pruned]." "Aye,' said R. Huna, "he has stolen all the produce of my vineyards and has left nothing for me." "There is a maxim." they replied, "that whoever steals from a thief smells of theft." "If so," said he, "I promise to give him his share." Thereupon according to some the vinegar turned to wine again, and according to others, the price of vinegar rose to the price of wine.

ולא שכרן א"ל הב לי ידך יהב
ליה ידיה ואוקמיה. רב הונא
תקיפו ליה ארבע מאה דני
דחמרא על לגביה ר' יהודה
אחוה דרב סלא חסידא ורבנן.
ואמרי לה רב אדא בר אהבה
ורבנן אמרו ליה לעיין מר
במליה אמר להו ומי חשידנא
בעינייכו אמרי ליה מי חשיד
קודשא בריך הוא דעביד דינא
בלא דינא. אמר להו אי איכא
מאן דשמיע עלי מילתא לימא
אמרי ליה הכי שמיע לן דלא
יהיב מר שיבשא לאריסיה
אמר להו מי קא שביק לי מידי
מיניה הא קא גניב ליה כוליה
אמרי ליה היינו דאמרי אינשי
בתר גנבא גנוב וטעמא טעים
אמר להו קבילנא עלי
דיהיבנא ליה איכא דאמרי
הדר חלא והוה חמרא ואיכא
דאמרי אייקר חלא ואזדבן
בדמי דחמרא:

It is taught that Abba Benjamin says: "I was always sorry for two things, that my prayer should be in front of my bed, and my bed should be placed between the north and the south." My prayer should be in front of my bed. What is meant by 'in front of my bed'? Shall I say it means to pray near the bed? Has not R. Juda said in the name of Rab, and according to others it was R. Joshua b. Levi who said: "Whence do we learn that he who prays shall have nothing between him and the wall? It is said (Is. 38, 2.) Then did Hezekiah turn his face to the wall, and prayed unto the Lord." [Hence we see, that a man ought not to pray before his bed.] Do not say 'Before the bed,' but say 'Immediately after rising.' And what does he mean by 'My bed shall be placed between the north and the south'? This refers to what R. Chama the son of R. Chanina and according to others R. Isaac said: "He who places his bed between the south and the north will have male children; as it is said (Ps. 17, 14.) And whose belly thou fillest with thy hidden treasury they will be satisfied with sons." Rab. Nachman b. Isaac said: "It will also prevent his wife from having a miscarriage; for it is written here. Thou fillest their belly, and it is written there (Gen. 25, 24.) And when her days to he delivered were fulfilled." It was taught that Abba Benjamin says: "Two entered the synagogue to pray; one of them finished his prayer first and went out without waiting for his friend; will his prayer be torn to pieces, as it is said (Job 18, 4.) He teareth himself in his anger: shall for thy sake the earth be forsaken? And moreover he causes [by his action] the Shechina to depart from Israel, as it is said (Ib. ib. ib.) And shall the Tzur move away out of His place? And the word Tzur, refers only

תניא אבא בנימין אומר על ב' דברים הייתי מצטער כל ימי על תפלתי שתהא לפני מטתי ועל מטתי שתהא נתונה בין צפון לדרום. על תפלתי שתהא לפני מטתי מאי לפני מטתי אילימא לפני מטתי ממש והאמר רב יהודה אמר רב ואיתימא ריב"ל מנין למתפלל שלא יהא דבר חוצץ בינו לבין הכותל שנאמר (ישעיה לח ב) ויסב חזקיהו פניו אל הקיר ויתפלל אל ה'. לא תימא לפני מטתי אלא אימא סמוך למטתי. ועל מטתי שתהא נתונה בין צפון לדרום דאמר רבי חמא בר' חנינא ואמרי לה אמר רבי יצחק כל הנותן מטתו בין צפון לדרום הוויין ליה בנים זכרים שנאמר (תהלים יז יד) וצפונך תמלא בטנם ישבעו בנים. רב נחמן בר יצחק אמר אף אין אשתו מפלת נפלים כתיב הכא וצפונך תמלא בטנם וכתיב התם (בראשית כה כד) וימלאו ימיה ללדת. תניא אבא בנימין אומר שנים שנכנסו להתפלל וקדם א' מהם להתפלל ויצא ולא המתין לחבירו טורפין לו תפלתו בפניו שנאמר (איוב יח ד) טורף נפשו באפו הלמענך תעזב ארץ ולא עוד אלא שגורם לשכינה שתסתלק מישראל שנאמר (שם) ויעתק צור ממקומו. ואין צור אלא הקב"ה שנא' (דברים לב יח) צור ילדך תשי. ואם המתין לו מה שכרו (דף ו) אמר רב יוסי בר' חנינא זוכה לברכות הללו שנא' (ישעי' מח יח) לוא

to the Holy One, praised be He! as it is said (Deu. 32, 18.) Of the Rock (Tzur) that begot thee thou wast unmindful." And if he waits for his friend what shall his reward be? (Fol. 6a) R. Jose the son of R. Chanina said: "He will be worthy of the following blessings which are said (Is. 48, 18.) Oh, that thou hadst but listened to my commandments! Then would have been as a river thy piece. and as the waves of the sea, thy prosperity." We are taught that Abba Benjamin says: "The prayers of men are not heard [by God] save only when they come from the synagogue, for it is written (I Kin. 8, 28.) To listen, unto the song of Thy praise and unto Thy prayer, i.e., in the place where songs of praise are said, there should be the place of prayer." Rabin b. R. Ada said in the name of R. Isaac: "Whence do we learn that God frequents the synagogue? It is said (Ps. 82, 1.) God standeth in the Congregation of God; whence do we learn that when ten men are praying together the Sheehina rests with them? It is said (Ib.) God standeth in the congregation of God; whence do we learn that when three are sitting and discharging judgment, the Sheehina rests with them? It is said (Ib.) In the midst doth He judge. And whence do we learn that when two are sitting together and studying the Torah. the Sheehina is with them? It is said (Malachi 3, 16.) Then conversed they that feared the Lord, one with another; and the Lord listened and heard it, and there was written a book of remembrance before him for those who feared the Lord and for those who respect his name." What should be understood by the words. And for those who respect His name? R. Ashi said: "Even when one intended to observe a commandment but was accidentally prevented from doing

הקשבת למצותי ויהי כנהר שלומך וגו' ויהי כחול זרעך וגו'. תניא אבא בנימין אומר אין תפלתו של אדם נשמעת אלא בבית הכנסת שנאמר (מלכים א ח':כ"ח) לשמוע אל הרנה ואל התפלה במקום רנה שם תהא תפלה אמר רבין בר רב אדא אמר רבי יצחק מנין שהקב"ה מצוי בבהכ"נ שנאמר (תהלים פב א) אלהים נצב בעדת אל. ומנין לעשרה שמתפללין ששכינה עמהם שנאמר אלהים נצב בעדת אל. ומנין לשלשה שיושבין בדין ששכינה עמהם שנאמר (שם) בקרב אלהים ישפוט, ומנין לשנים שיושבין ועוסקין בתורה ששכינה עמהם שנאמר(מלאכי ג טז) אז נדברו יראי ה' איש אל רעהו ויקשב ה' וישמע ויכתב ספר זכרון לפניו ליראי ה' ולחושבי שמו. מאי ולחושבי שמו אמר רב אשי אפילו חשב אדם לעשות מצוה ונאנס ולא עשאה מעלה עליו הכתוב כאילו עשאה. ומנין לאחד שיושב ועוסק בתורה ששכינה עמו שנאמר (שמות כ כד) בכל המקום אשר אזכיר את שמי אבוא אליך וברכתיך וכי מאחר דאפי' חד תרי מיבעיא. תרי מיכתבן מלייהו בספר הזכרונות חד לא מיכתבן מליה בספר הזכרונות. וכי מאחר דאפי' תרי תלתא מבעיא. מהו דתימא דינא שלמא בעלמא הוא ולא אתיא שכינה קמ"ל דדין נמי היינו תורה. וכי מאחר דאפילו תלתא עשרה

so, it is credited to him as if he had actually observed it." And whence do we learn that even if one sits and studies the Torah, the Sheehina is with him? It is said (Ex. 20, 24.) In every place where I shall permit my name to be mentioned, I will come unto thee and I will bless thee. Now let us see, since we know that the Sheehina is even with one, why is it necessary to infer that it rests with two? Because if two study together the Sheehina inscribes their words in the book of remembrances; for one, however, it does not inscribe his words in the book of remembrances. Since we know that when two study, the Sheehina is with them, why do we need any inference for three? Because we should not think that discharging judgment is merely bringing peace and nothing else, and the Sheehina therefore is not with them. It informs us then that discharging judgment is as important as the Torah: and since we know that the Sheehina is with three, why do we need the inference concerning ten? Because in the case of ten people, the Sheehina precedes, but for three, the Sheehina does not appear until the three are together.

R. Abin b. R. Ada, in the name of R. Isaac, said: "Whence do we learn that the Holy One, praised be He! lays Tephilin? It is said (Is. 62, 8.) Sworn hath the Lord by His right hand and by the arm of His strength. By His right hand, is meant the Torah, for it is said (Deu. 33, 2.) From His right hand, He gave a fiery law unto them; and by His strength, is meant Tephilin; as it is said (Ps. 29, 11.) The Lord will give strength unto His people. How do we know that the Tephilin are a strength to Israel? It is said (Deu. 28, 10.) And all the nations of the earth shall see, that Thou art

מיבעיא. עשרה קדמא שכינה ואתיא. תלתא עד דיתבי:

אמר רבי אבין בר רב אדא אמר רבי יצחק מנין שהקדוש ב"ה מניח תפילין שנאמר (ישעיה סב ח) נשבע ה' בימינו ובזרוע עוזו ואין ימינו אלא תורה שנא' (דברים לג ב) מימינו אש דת למו ואין עוזו אלא תפילין שנאמר (תהלים כט יא) ה' עוז לעמו יתן. ומנין שהתפילין עוז הם לישראל דכתיב (דברים כח י) וראו כל עמי הארץ כי שם ה' נקרא עליך ויראו ממך. ותניא רבי אליעזר הגדול אומר אלו

called by the name of the Lord, and they shall be afraid of Thee; and we are also taught that R. Eliezer, the Great, says 'This (the above verse) means the Tephilin of the head." R. Nachman b. Isaac said to R. Chiya b. Abin: "What is written in the Tephilin of the Sovereign of the universe?" "It is written," he answered, "Who is like thy people Israel, the only nation." (I Chr. 17, 21.) "And does the Holy One, praised be He! praise himself with the glory of Israel?" "Yea, for it is written (Deu. 26, 17.) Thou hast this day acknowledged the Lord, etc., and the Lord hath acknowledged thee, this day, i.e., the Holy One, praised be He! said unto Israel 'You have made me the only object of love in the world — as it is written (Deu. 6, 4.) Hear, O Israel, the Lord our God, is one God; I will therefore make you the only object of love in the world — as it is written (I Chr. 17, 21.) And who is like thy people, Israel the only nation'" R. Acha, the son of Raba, said to R. Ashi: "You may be right concerning one section of the Tephilin, what about the remaining sections?" "In the remaining sections," [said R. Ashi] "are. For what great nation is there (Deu. 4, 7); And what great nation (Ib. ib.); Happy art thou, O Israel! (Ib. 33, 29); Or hath a God essayed, (Ib. 4, 34.) So that he may set thee, the highest (Ib. 26, 19)." "If so then there are more than four sections?" "But," [said he], "Or what great nation is there. And what great nation, both being practically [in meaning] alike, are one section; Happy art thou Israel, and For what part of a nation, are another section; Or hath a God essayed, is the third section; and So that He may set thee the highest, is the fourth section; and all these verses are written and [put together into one section which is] placed also in the Tephilin of the

תפילין שבראש. אמר ליה רב נחמן בר יצחק לרב חייא בר אבין הני תפילין דמארי עלמא מה כתיב בהו (הנכון כפי פירוש הרשב״א) א״ל (דה״א יז כא) ומי כעמך ישראל גוי אחד. ומי משבח קוב״ה בשבחייהו דישראל אין דכתיב (דברים כו יז) את ה' האמרת היום וה' האמירך היום אמר להם הקב״ה לישראל אתם עשיתוני חטיבה אחת בעולם ואני אעשה אתכם חטיבה אחת בעולם, אתם עשיתוני חטיבה (פי' ציור אחד בעולם כלומר דבר הנכר שאין כמותו) אחת בעולם דכתיב (שם ו) שמע ישראל ה' אלהינו ה' אחד ואני אעשה אתכם חטיבה אחת בעולם דכתיב ומי כעמך ישראל גוי אחד בארץ. א״ל רב אחא בריה דרבא לרב אשי תינח בחד ביתא בשאר בתי מאי א״ל (דברים ד ז) כי מי גוי גדול ומי גוי גדול (שם לג כט) אשריך ישראל (שם ד לד) או הנסה אלהים (שם כו יט) ולתתך עליון אי הכי נפישי להו טובא בתי אלא כי מי גוי גדול ומי גוי גדול דדמיין להדדי בחד ביתא אשריך ישראל ומי כעמך, בחד ביתא. או הנסה אלהים, בחד ביתא, ולתתך עליון בחד ביתא וכולהו כתיבי באדרעיה:

hand.

Rabin b. R. Ada in the name of R. Isaac said: "Whoever frequents the synagogue [daily] and misses one day, the Holy One, praised be He! inquires about him; for it is written (Is. 50, 10.) Who is among you, that feareth the Lord, that hearkeneth to the voice of His servant? Though he has walked in darkness and had no light, let him trust in the name of the Lord; i.e., if he went to perform a meritorious deed [and was therefore absent from synagogue] there will be light unto him; but if his absence is due to personal business, then there will be no light unto him for he should have placed his trust in God." R. Jochanan said: When the Holy One, praised be He! enters the synagogue and does not find ten [men] present, His anger is immediately stirred, as it is said (Is. 50, 2.) Why did I come and no man was there, did I call with none to answer."

R. Chelbo said, in the name of R. Huna: "The God of Abraham will help him who chooses a regular place for his prayers and when he dies, people will say of him, 'Woe, humble one! Woe pious! one of the real disciples of our father Abraham!' And whence do we know that Abraham had appointed a certain place [for his prayers]? For it is written (Gen. 19, 27.) And Abraham rose early in the morning to the place where he had stood before the Lord. And the word Omad (stood) refers to prayer, as it is said (Ps. 106, 30.) And Phineas stood and prayed." R. Jochanan in the name of R. Simon b. Jochai said: "He who designates a certain place for prayer, will cause all his enemies to fall before him. for it is said (II Sam. 7, 10.) I have procured a place for my people, Israel, and I have

(ע״ב) אמר רבין בר רב אדא אמר רבי יצחק כל הרגיל לבא לבית הכנסת ולא בא יום אחד הקב״ה משאיל בו שנאמר (ישעיה נ׳) מי בכם ירא ה׳ שומע בקול עבדו אשר הלך חשכים ואין נוגה לו אם לדבר מצוה הלך נוגה לו ואם לדבר הרשות הלך אין נוגה לו יבטח בשם ה׳ מאי טעמא משום דהוה לו לבטוח בשם ה׳ ולא בטח. אמר רבי יוחנן בשעה שהקב״ה בא בבית הכנסת ולא מצא בה עשרה מיד הוא כועס. שנאמר (שם נ ב) מדוע באתי ואין איש קראתי ואין עונה:

אמר ר׳ חלבו אמר רב הונא כל הקובע מקום לתפלתו אלהי אברהם (יהיה) בעזרו. וכשמת אומרין לו אי עניו אי חסיד מתלמידיו של אברהם אבינו. ואברהם אבינו מנא לן דקבע מקום דכתיב (בראשית יט כז) וישכם אברהם בבקר אל המקום אשר עמד שם את פני ה׳. ואין עמידה אלא תפלה שנא׳ (תהלים קו ל) ויעמוד פינחס ויפלל (עוד להלן בפרק זה) א״ר יוחנן משום רשב״י כל הקובע מקום לתפלתו אויביו נופלים תחתיו שנאמר (ש״ב ז י) ושמתי מקום לעמי ישראל ונטעתיו ושכן תחתיו ולא ירגז עוד ולא יוסיפו בני עולה

planted them, that they may dwell in a place of their own, and be no more troubled; and that the children of wickedness shall not afflict them any more as heretofore." R. Huna raised the following contradictory question: "It is written (in them), and it is written (Chr. 17, 9.) [of the same thing] Lechalotho (to destroy them). At the beginning the wicked merely afflicted Israel but later they tried to destroy Israel."

R. Chelbo in the name of R. Huna said: "He who leaves the synagogue should not hurry." "This," says Abaye, "is only When he leaves, but on going to [the synagogue] it is meritorious to hasten, as it is said (Hos. 6, 3.) Let us know and hasten to serve the Lord." R. Zeira said: "At first when I saw the Rabbis hurrying to the session [of learning] on the Sabbath I thought to myself, 'The Rabbis profane the Sabbath.' But after I heard of what R. Tanchum said in the name of R. Joshua b. Levi: 'Always shall a man run to study, even though on the Sabbath, as it is said (Ib. 11, 10.) They shall follow after the Lord when, He will roar like a lion,' I, too, began to run." R. Zeira said: "The [chief] reward for attending a lecture lies in running" [to it, i.e., anxiety to hear it]. Abaye said: "The [chief] merit in attending the public lecture before a holiday [when the laws concerning the holidays are explained] lies in being pressed [on account of the crowd]." Raba said: "The [chief] merit for studying Halacha is in obtaining a full explanation of it." R. Pappa said: "The [chief] merit of attending a funeral is the silence." R. Zutra said: "The [chief] merit for observing a feast day is charity." R. Shesheth said: "The [chief] merit of a funeral address is in the lifting up [the voice in lamentation]." R. Ashi said: "The [chief] merit in attending a wedding festival is the words [of entertainment]."

R. Chelbo in the name of R. Huna said: "Whoever prays with his back turned to the synagogue is to be called wicked, as it is said (Ps. 12, 9.) On every side do the wicked walk." Abaye said: "This refers only to one who does not turn his face towards the synagogue but if he does turn his face towards the synagogue it does not matter even if his back is towards the worshipers." There was one man who prayed with his back turned to the synagogue; Elijah happened to pass by. It seemed to Elijah that the man prayed in the manner of an Arabian merchant, and he said to him: "Art thou standing before thy Master as if there were two dominions?" Thereupon Elijah drew his sword and killed the man.

R. Jochanan and R. Elazar both said: "When a man must apply for help to his fellow-men, his face changes like [the worm called] Kerum; as it is said (Ps. 12, 9.) Like a worm, so is the cheapness of the sons of men." What is Kerum? When R. Dimi came he related that among the sea-coast towns, there is a certain worm, the name of which is 'Kerum', and when the sun shines upon him, he changes into various colors. R. Ami and R. Ashi both say: "He [who has to apply for charity] is as if two judgments were passed upon him — those of fire and water, as it is said (Ps. 66, 12.) Thou hast caused man to ride on our heads; we entered into fire and into water."

R. Chelbo in the name of R. Huna said further: "A man shall always be strict in the observance of the Mincha service, for Elijah,

אמר רב הונא כל המתפלל אחורי בית הכנסת נקרא רשע שנאמר (תהלים יב ט) סביב רשעים יתהלכון כרום זלות לבני אדם אמר אביי לא אמרן אלא דלא מהדר אפיה לבי כנשתא אבל מהדר אפיה לבי כנישתא לית לן בה. ההוא גברא דקא מצלי אחורי בי כנישתא ולא מהדר אפיה לבי כנישתא חלף אליהו אידמי ליה כטייעא א״ל כדו בר קיימת קמי מרך שלף ספסירא וקטליה:

רבי יוחנן ורבי אליעזר דאמרי תרווייהו כיון שנצרך אדם לבריות פניו משתנות ככרום שנא' כרום זלות לבני אדם מאי כרום כי אתא רב דימי אמר עוף אחד יש בכרכי הים ושמו כרום וכיון שחמה זורחת עליו מתהפך לכמה גוונין. רבי אמי ורבי אסי דאמרי תרווייהו כאילו נדון בשתי דינין אש ומים. שנאמר (שם סו יב) הרכבת אנוש לראשנו באנו באש ובמים:

אמר רב הונא לעולם יזהר אדם בתפלת המנחה שהרי אליהו לא נענה אלא בתפלת

the Prophet, was answered only at the Mincha service, as it is said (I Kin. 18, 36-37.) And it came to pass at (the time of) the offering of the perpetual evening sacrifice (Mincha) that Elijah the Prophet came near, and said: Answer me, O Lord, answer me, i. e., answer my prayer that a fire descend from Heaven, and answer me that they shall not say it was an act of magic." R. Jochanan said: "In the evening service also [shall a man pay heed], for it is said (Ps. 141, 2.) May my prayers be valued as incense before Thee; lifting up of my hands as the evening offering." R. Nachman b. Isaac said: "To the morning service also [shall a man pay heed,] for it is said (Ps. 5, 4.) O Lord, in the morning do Thou hear my voice."

Further said R. Chelbo in the name of R. Huna: "He who does not cheer the bridegroom, whose wedding feast he has enjoyed, transgresses against the five voices (the passage where voice is mentioned five times) (Jer. 33, 11.) The voice of gladness, the voice of joy, the voice of the bridegroom and the voice of the bride, the voice of those who say Praise ye the Lord of Hosts." And if he does cheer him, what will his reward be? R. Simon b. Lakish said: "He will merit the Torah, which was given with five voices, as it is said (Ex. 19, 16.) And it came to pass on the third day, when it was morning, that there were thunders, and the voice of the cornet, etc.. And the voice of the cornet was, etc., And God answered him with a loud voice." R. Abuhu said: ["To cheer the bridegroom is considered meritorious] as if he brought a thanksgiving offering; for it is said (Jer. 33, 11.) Of those that bring thanksgiving offering unto the house of the Lord." R. Nachman b. Isaac said: "It is as if he

המנחה שנאמר (מ"א יח לו - לז) ויהי בעלות המנחה ויגש אליהו הנביא ויאמר וגו' ענני ה' ענני. ענני שתרד אש מן השמים וענני שלא יאמרו מעשה כשפים הם. רבי יוחנן אמר אף בתפלת ערבית שנאמר (תהלים קמא ב) תכון תפלתי קטרת לפניך משאת כפי מנחת ערב רב נחמן בר יצחק אמר אף בתפלת שחרית שנאמר (שם ה ד) ה' בקר תשמע קולי:

ואמר רבי חלבו אמר רב הונא כל הנהנה מסעודת חתן ואינו משמחו עובר בה' קולות שנאמר (ירמיה לג יא) קול ששון וקול שמחה קול חתן וקול כלה קול אומרים הודו. ואם משמחו מה שכרו אמר ריב"ל זוכה לתורה שנתנה בה' קולות שנאמר (שמות יט טז) ויהי ביום השלישי וגו' ויהי קולות וגו'. וקול שופר וגו'. ויהי קול השופר וגו'. והאלהים יעננו בקול וגו'. איני והכתיב (שם) וכל העם רואים את הקולות. אותן קולות דקודם מתן תורה הוו. רבי אבהו אומר כאילו הקריב תודה שנאמר (ירמיה לג יא) מביאים תודה בית ה' רב נחמן בר יצחק אמר כאילו בנה אחת מחורבות ירושלים שנא' (שם) כי אשיב את שבות הארץ כבראשונה אמר ה':

had rebuilt one of the ruins of Jerusalem, for it is said (Ib.) For I will cause their captivity to return, as at the first, saith the Lord."

R. Chelbo in the name of R. Huna also said: "Whoever has fear of God, his words will be heard;" as it is said (Ecc. 12, 13.) The end of the matter is, let us sum up the whole; fear God, and keep His commandments, for this is the whole [duty of] man." What is meant by For this is the whole duty of man. R. Elazar said: "The Holy One, praised be He! said 'The whole world would not have been created if not for him [who fears God].'" R. Abba b. Cahana said: "This [fear of God] is equal in importance to that of the whole world put together." R. Simon b. Azai, and according to some, R. Simon b. Zoma said: "The whole world would not have been created if not for the purpose of being host to him (who fears God)."

ואמר ר' חלבו אמר רב הונא כל אדם שיש בו יראת שמים דבריו נשמעים שנאמר (קהלת יב יג) סוף דבר הכל נשמע את האלהים ירא ואת מצותיו שמור כי זה כל האדם. מאי כי זה כל האדם אמר ר' אלעזר אמר הקב"ה כל העולם כולו לא נברא אלא בשביל זה רבי אבא בר כהנא אמר שקול זה כנגד כל העולם כולו ר"ש בן עזאי ואמרי לה ר"ש בן זומא אומר כל העולם כולו לא נברא אלא לצוות לזה:

R. Chelbo in the name of R. Huna further said: "He who knows that his friend is accustomed to greet him, shall try to greet him first, for it is said (Ps. 34, 15.) Seek peace and pursue it, and when one responds not to a greeting he receives, he is to be called robber, as it is said (Is. 3, 14.) But ye who have eaten up the vineyard; the plunder of the poor is in your houses." [What have the poor that they were plundered of? Nothing but their greeting.]

ואמר רבי חלבו אמר רב הונא כל שיודע בחבירו שהוא רגיל ליתן לו שלום יקדים לו שלום שנאמר (תהלים לד טו) בקש שלום ורדפהו ואם נתן לו ולא החזיר נקרא גזלן. שנאמר (ישעיה ג יד) ואתם בערתם הכרם גזלת העני בבתיכם:

(Fol. 7a) R. Jochanan said in the name of R. Jose b. Zimra: "Whence do we know that the Holy One, praised be He! prayeth? It is said (Is. 56, 7.) Even these will I bring to my holy mountain, and make them joyful in my house of prayer. It does not say in their [house of] prayer, but in my [house of] prayer. We learn from this that the Holy

(דף ז) אמר רבי יוחנן משום רבי יוסי בן זמרא מנין שהקב"ה מתפלל שנאמר (שם נו ז) והביאותים אל הר קדשי ושמחתים בבית תפלתי תפלתם לא נאמר אלא תפלתי מכאן שהקדוש ברוך הוא מצלי. מאי מצלי

One, praised be He! prays." What doeth He pray? R. Zutra b. Tubia, in the name of Rab, said: "[Thus He prayeth] 'May it be my will that my mercy overcome my anger; and let my compassion rule over my attributes [of Justice] that I may deal with my children in attributes of kindness; and out of regard to them may I overlook Judgment.' " It is taught that Rabbi Ishmael b. Elisha said: "Once, when I entered tlie Holy of Holies to burn the incense, I saw the Lord of all Hosts sitting on a high and exalted throne, and He said to me 'Ishmael, my son, bless me!' I replied, 'Sovereign of the Universe! may it be Thy will that Thy mercy overcome Thy anger, and Thy compassion may overrule Thy other attributes; let Thy conduct toward Thy children be with the attribute of loving kindness and enter inside the line of justice; and, out of regard to them mayest Thou overlook Judgment!' The Lord shook His head at me" [as a sign confirming my prayer]. By this R. Ishmael wants to teach us that the blessing of a common man shall not be lightly esteemed. R. Elazar said in the name of R. Chanina: "Never shall the blessing of even a common man be considered insignificant in your eyes; for two great men of their generation were blessed by simple men and their blessings were fulfilled. They are: David and Daniel — David was blessed by Aravnah, as it is written (IE Sam. 24, 23.) And Aravnah said unto the king. May the Lord thy God receive thee favorably. Daniel was blessed by King Darius; as it is written (Dan. 6, 17.) May thy God whom thou dost worship continually, truly deliver thee."

R. Jochanan in the name of R. Jose said: "Whence do we learn that we must not attempt to appease a man at the moment of his excitement? It is written (Ex. 33, 14.) My presence shall walk before you, and I will give thee rest, i.e., the Holy One, praised be He! said unto Moses. "Wait for me until my excitement shall subside and I shall then give thee rest.' " Is wrath [to be ascribed] to the Holy One — praised be He? Yea! As it is taught; And a God who is angry every day (Ps. 7, 12). And how long does His anger last? For a moment. And how long lasts a moment? One fifty-eight thousand eight hundred and eighty-eighth part of an hour; and this is meant by the word Regga (moment); and no creature is able to determine that exact moment [when the anger arises] except Bilam the wicked, for it is written (Num. 24, 16.) And knoweth the knowledge of the most High. How is it possible? If he did not know even the temperament of his animal, how could he acquire a knowledge of the Most High? We must therefore say that he knew how to determine the exact hour in which the Holy One, praised be He! is angry. And this is meant by the prophet who said to Israel (Micha 6, 5.) O my people, do but remember what Balak the king of Moab resolved in order to know the gracious benefits of the Lord. What is meant by The gracious benefits of the Lord. R. Elazar said: "Thus said the Holy One, praised be He! unto Israel. 'Do but remember how many gracious benefits I bestowed unto ye, that I kept myself back from becoming angry during all the days of Bilam, the wicked; for my anger might have inflicted a great misfortune upon them [in that generation].' And this is meant by Bilam when he said. (Num. 23, 8.) How shall I denounce, whom God hath not denounced? And how shall I defy, when the Lord hath not defied?" And how long endureth His anger?

לג יד) פני ילכו והניחותי לך. אמר ליה הקב"ה למשה המתן לי עד שיעברו פנים של זעם ואניח לך. ומי איכא ריתחא קמיה דקודשא בריך הוא אין דתניא (תהלים ז יב) ואל זועם בכל יום וכמה זעמו רגע. וכמה רגע אחד מחמשת רבוא ושמונת אלפים ושמונה מאות ושמונים ושמונה בשעה וזו היא רגע ואין כל בריה יכולה לכוין אותה השעה חוץ מבלעם הרשע דכתיב ביה (במדבר כד טז) ויודע דעת עליון. השתא דעת בהמתו לא הוה ידע דעת עליון הוי ידע אלא מלמד שהיה יודע לכוין אותה שעה שהקב"ה כועס בה. והיינו דאמר להו נביא לישראל (מיכה ו ה) עמי זכר נא מה יעץ בלק מלך מואב. למען דעת צדקות ה' מאי למען דעת צדקות ה' אמר רבי אלעזר אמר להם הקב"ה לישראל דעו כמה צדקות עשיתי עמכם שלא כעסתי בימי בלעם הרשע שאלמלי כעסתי לא נשתייר משונאיהם של ישראל שריד ופליט והיינו דקאמר ליה בלעם לבלק (במדבר כג ח) מה אקוב לא קבה אל ומה אזעום לא זעם ה' מלמד שכל אותם הימים לא זעם. וכמה זעמו רגע. וכמה רגע אמר רבי אבין ואי תימא רבי אבינא רגע כמימריה ומנא לן דרגע רתח שנא' (תהלים ל ו) כי רגע באפו חיים ברצונו ואי בעית אימא מהכא (ישעיה כו כ) חבי כמעט רגע עד יעבור זעם. ואימת רתח אמר אביי

A Regga (moment). How long does a Regga last? R. Abin and according to some R. Abina said: "A Regga lasts as long as it takes to utter it." And whence do we learn that God is angry? It is said (Ps. 30, 6.) For His anger is momentary, (but) life rests upon his favor. And if you wish I say from this (Is. 26, 20.) Hide thyself but for about a moment, until anger passeth away. And when is He angry? Abaye said: "During the first three hours of the day, when the crest of the cock becomes white and he stands on one leg." But the cock stands like that all the time? At all times it has red stripes [in the white crest], but in that particular hour there are no red stripes whatsoever. A certain heretic was in the neighborhood of R. Joshua b. Levi, and annoyed him exceedingly, questioning him about various passages. One day R. Joshua b. Levi took a cock, tied it to his bed and watched it, thinking that as soon as he would notice the sign, he would curse the heretic. But before the time came, sleep overtook him. So he said: "I learn from this [incident] that it is not proper to do such a thing: And he is beneficent in all His work, it is written (Ps. 145, 17.) and it is also written (Pr. 17, 26.) Punishment, even to the just, is not good." It was taught in the name of R. Meier: "At the time when the sun rises and all the heathen Kings of the East and West, with their crowns upon their heads, prostrate themselves before the sun, there-upon the Holy One, praised he He! immediately becomes angry."

Further said R. Jochanan in the name of R. Jose: "One chastisement in the heart of man (self reproach) is better than many lashes, as it is said (Hos. 2, 9.) And she will pursue her lovers, then will she say, 'I will go and return

בהנך תלת שעי קמייתא כי חוורא כרבלתא דתרנגולא וקאי אחד כרעא כל שעתא ושעתא נמי קאי הכי כל שעתא אית ביה שורייקי סומקי בההיא שעתא לית ביה שורייקי סומקי. ההוא מינאה דהוה בשיבבותיה דריב"ל הוה קא מצער ליה טובא בקראי יומא חד שקל תרנגולא ואוקמיה בין כרעיה דערסא ועיין ביה סבר כי מטא ההיא שעתא אלטייה כי מטא ההיא שעתא נייס אמר שמע מיניה לאו אורח ארעא למעבד הכי (תהלים קמה יז) ורחמיו על כל מעשיו כתיב וכתיב (משלי יז כו) גם ענוש לצדיק לא טוב. תנא משמיה דרבי מאיר בשעה שהחמה זורחת וכל מלכי מזרח ומערב מניחין כתריהם בראשיהם ומשתחוים לחמה מיד כועס הקדוש ברוך הוא:

ואמר ר' יוחנן משום רבי יוסי טובה מרדות אחת בלבו של אדם יותר מכמה מלקיות שנאמר (הושע ב ט) ורדפה את מאהביה וגו' ואמרה

to my first husband; for if was better with me then than now.'" Resh Lakish said: "It is better than one hundred stripes, as it is said (Pr. 17, 10.) A reproof penetrateth more deeply into a wise man than a hundred lashes into a fool."

Further, said R. Jochanan in the name of R. Jose: "Three things did Moses request of the Holy One, praised be He! and they were all granted unto him. He asked that the Sheehina shall dwell in Israel and it was granted, as it is said (Ex. 33, 16.) Is it not in that because Thou goest with us? He asked that the Sheehina might not dwell with heathens and it was granted to him, as it is said (Ib.) So shall we be distinguished, I and thy people. He asked that the Holy One, praised be He! make known His ways, and it was granted to him, as it is said (Ib, ib. 18.) And he said, let me see, I beseech Thee, Thy glory, i. e., he said before the Holy One, praised be He! 'Sovereign of the universe, why is there a righteous man who prospers while another righteous person suffers? Some wicked person prospers while another wicked person suffers?' He answered him: 'Moses! the righteous person that prospers is righteous himself, and the son of a righteous one; the righteous one that suffers" is righteous himself but the son of a, wicked one [he suffers for the sins of his parents]; the wicked person who prospers is wicked himself but the son of a righteous person, and the wicked person who suffers is wicked himself and the son of a wicked one.'" The Master said above, "The righteous person that prospers is righteous himself and the son of a righteous one; the righteous one that suffers is righteous himself but the son of a wicked one." Is this so? Behold! It is

אלכה ואשובה אל אישי הראשון כי טוב לי אז מעתה. וריש לקיש אמר יותר ממאה מלקיות, שנאמר (משלי יז י) תחת גערה במבין מהכות כסיל מאה:

ואמר רבי יוחנן משום רבי יוסי שלשה דברים בקש משה מלפני הקב"ה ונתן לו. בקש שתשרה שכינה על ישראל ונתן לו שנא' (שמות לג טז) הלוא בלכתך עמנו. בקש שלא תשרה שכינה על עובדי עבודת כוכבים ונתן לו שנאמר (שם) ונפלינו אני ועמך בקש להודיעו דרכיו של הקב"ה ונתן לו שנאמר (שם לג יח) הודעני נא את דרכך. אמר לפניו רבונו של עולם מפני מה יש צדיק וטוב לו ויש צדיק ורע לו. יש רשע וטוב לו ויש רשע ורע לו. אמר לו משה צדיק וטוב לו צדיק בן צדיק. צדיק ורע לו צדיק בן רשע. רשע וטוב לו רשע בן צדיק. רשע ורע לו רשע בן רשע. אמר מר צדיק וטוב לו צדיק בן צדיק. צדיק ורע לו צדיק בן רשע. איני והא כתיב (שמות כ ה) פוקד עון אבות על בנים וכתיב (דברים כד טז) ובנים לא יומתו על אבות (סנהדרין פ"ג). ורמינן קראי אהדדי. ומשנינן לא קשיא הא כשאוחזין מעשה אבותיהם בידיהם. הא כשאין אוחזין מעשה אבותיהם בידיהם. אלא הכי קאמר ליה. צדיק וטוב לו צדיק גמור צדיק ורע לו צדיק שאינו גמור. רשע וטוב לו רשע שאינו גמור. רשע ורע לו רשע גמור.

written (Ex. 20, 5.) Visiting the iniquities of the fathers upon the children; and it is written (Deu. 24, 16.) Fathers shall not be put to death for the children, and we have asked the question as to the contradiction of these two passages, and answered; there is no difficulty. One passage refers to those who continue the [wicked] deeds of their parents, and the other passage refers to those who do not continue the [wicked] deeds of their parents. [Hence we see that a righteous man, even if the son of a wicked man does not suffer?] But we must say that He said thus to him: "A righteous one who prospers, is one who is perfectly righteous; a righteous one who suffers, is not a perfectly righteous one; a wicked one who prospers, is one not really wicked; a wicked one who suffers, is one grossly wicked." And this [saying of Rabbi Jochanan] differs from that of R. Meier, for R. Meier said: "Two requests were granted to Moses and one was not granted, for it is said (Ex. 33, 19.) And I will be gracious to whom I will be gracious, although he does not deserve it; And I will show mercy to whom I will show mercy, although he does not deserve it." And He said: Thou, canst not see my face. (Ib.) R. Joshua b. Karcha said: "Thus said the Holy One, praised be He! unto Moses: 'When I was willing [to reveal myself] thou wast unwilling (didst hide thy face); now when thou art willing [to see me] I am not willing [to reveal myself].'" And this differs from the opinion of R. Samuel b. Nachmeini who quoted R. Jonathan; for R. Samuel b. Nachmeini said in the name of Jonathan: "On account of three things Moses earned the merit of the following three things; viz., for And Moses hid his face, (Ib. 3, 6.) he earned the merit of A shining face; for He

ופליגא דר״מ דאמר רבי מאיר שתים נתנו לו ואחת לא נתנו לו שנאמר (שמות לג יט) וחנותי את אשר אחון אף על פי שאינו הגון ורחמתי את אשר ארחם אע״פ שאינו הגון: ויאמר לא תוכל לראות את פני (שמות לג יט). תנא משמיה דרבי יהושע בן קרחה כך א״ל הקב״ה למשה כשרציתי לא רציתי עכשיו שאתה רוצה איני רוצה. ופליגא דרבי שמואל בר נחמני א״ר יונתן דאמר רבי שמואל בר נחמני אמר רבי יונתן בשכר ג׳ זכה לג׳ בשכר (שם ג ו) (עיקרים מ״ב פכ״ב) ויסתר משה פניו זכה לקלסתר פנים. בשכר כי ירא זכה לוייראו מגשת אליו בשכר מהביט זכה לותמונת ה׳ יביט. (שם לג כג) והסירותי את כפי וראית את אחורי אמר ר ב חמא בר ביזנא אמר ר״ש חסידא מלמד שהראה הקדוש ברוך הוא למשה קשר של תפילין:

was afraid (Ib.) he earned the merit of, And they were afraid to come nigh unto him (Ib. 34, 30.); and for To look up to God (Ib. 3, 6.) he earned the merit of. And the similitude of the Lord doth he behold (Num. 12, 8)." [Hence it shows that he was rewarded for hiding his face and differing with R. Joshua B. Karcha]. And then I will remove my hand, and thou shalt see my back; but my face shall not be seen (Ex. 33, 23). R. Chama b. Bizua in the name of R. Simon the Pious said: "This means that the Holy One, praised be He! showed to Moses the knot of the Tephilin (Philacteries)."

(Ib. b) R. Jochauan in the name of R. Simon b. Jochai said: "Since the day the Holy One, praised be He! created the world there was no man who called the Holy One, praised be He! 'Lord' (Adon) until Abraham came and called him 'Lord,' for it is said (Gen. 15, 8.) And he said Lord God, whereby shall I know that I shall inherit it?" Rab said "Daniel also would not have been answered were it not for the sake of Abraham, for it is said (Dan. 9, 17.) And now listen, O our God! to the prayer of thy servant, for the sake of the Lord; — 'for Thy sake' he [Daniel] ought to have said? But [he prayed] for the sake of Abraham, who called you Lord." Again said R. Jochanan in the name of R. Simon b. Jochai: "Since the day when the Holy One, praised be He! created the world, there was no man who thanked the Holy One, praised be He! until Leah came and thanked Him, as it is said (Gen. 29, 35.) This lime will I thank the Lord." What is the meaning of being called Reuben? R. Elazar said: "Leah said, 'See the difference between my son and the son of my father-in-law (Esau); whereas my father-in-law's son sold his birthright to

(ע״ב) אמר רבי יוחנן משום רבי שמעון בן יוחאי מיום שברא הקדוש ברוך הוא את העולם לא היה אדם שקראו להקדוש ברוך הוא אדון עד שבא אברהם וקראו אדון שנא׳ (בראשית טו ח) ויאמר אדני אלהים במה אדע כי אירשנה. אמר רב אף דניאל לא נענה אלא בשביל אברהם שנאמר (דניאל ט יז) ועתה שמע אלהינו אל תפלת עבדך ואל תחנוניו והאר פניך אל מקדשך השמם למען אדני למענך מיבעי ליה אלא למען אברהם שקראך אדון. ואמר רבי יוחנן משום רשב״י מיום שברא הקב״ה את עולמו לא היה אדם שהודה להקב״ה עד שבאת לאה והודתו שנאמר (בראשית כט לה) הפעם אודה את ה׳. ראובן א״ר אלעזר אמרה לאה ראו מה בין בני לבן חמי דאלו בן חמי אע״ג דמדעתיה זבנה לבכירותיה דכתיב (שם כה לג) וימכור את בכורתו ליעקב חזי מה כתיב ביה (שם כז

Jacob of his own accord, as it is written (Gen. 25, 33.) And he sold his right of first-horn unto Jacob, yet what happened? As it is written (Ib. 27, 41.) And Esau hated Jacob, and it is also written (Ib. ib. 36.) And he said, hath he been therefore named Jacob, because he hath supplanted me these two times; but my son, although it was against his will that Joseph took from him the birthright, as it is written (I Chr. 5, 1.) But when he defiled his father's bed was his birth-right given unto the sons of Joseph; yet he never envied him, for it is written (Gen. 37, 21.) And when Reuben heard it he delivered him out of their hands.'" Why was she named Ruth? R. Jochanan said "Be cause she merited that from her shall come forth David, who satisfied the Holy One, praised be He! with songs and praises." And whence do we derive that the name is the cause? R. Elazar said: "It is said (Ps. 46, 9.) Come, look at the deeds of the Lord, who hath made desolation on the earth. Do not read it Shamoth (desolation), but read Shemoth (names)."

Further said E. Jochanan in the name of R. Jose: "Every utterance which came forth from the mouth of the Holy One, praised be He! for good purpose even when upon condition, was never retracted." Whence do we derive this? From our Teacher Moses, as it is said (Deu. 9, 14.) Let me alone, and I may destroy them, and blot out their names from under the heavens, and I will make of thee a nation mightier and more numerous than they; and although Moses invoked mercy concerning this thing and succeeded in annuling that decree, yet it [the promise. And I will make thee a nation mightier and more numerous] was fulfilled to his children,

מא) וישטטום עשו את יעקב וכתיב (שם כז לו) ויאמר הכי קרא שמו יעקב ויעקבני זה פעמים ואלו בני אף על גב דעל כרחיה שקלה יוסף לבכירותיה מיניה דכתיב (דה״א ה א) ובחללו יצועי אביו ניתנה בכורתו ליוסף אפילו הכי לא איקנא ביה דכתיב (בראשית לז כא) וישמע ראובן ויצילהו מידם. רות (ב״ב פ״ק) מאי רות א״ר יוחנן שזכתה ויצא ממנה דוד שריוהו להקב״ה בשירות ותשבחות ומנא לן דשמא גרים. אמר רבי אלעזר דאמר קרא (תהלים מו ט) לכו חזו מפעלות ה׳ אשר שם שמות בארץ אל תקרי שמות אלא שמות:

ואמר רבי יוחנן משום רבי יוסי כל דבור ודבור שיצא מפי הקב״ה לטובה אפילו על תנאי לא חזר בו. מנא לן ממשה רבינו שנאמר (דברים ט יד) הרף ממני ואשמידם ואמחה את שמם ואעשה אותך לגוי עצום ורב ממנו. ואע״ג דבעי משה רחמי עלה דמלתא ובטלה אפ״ה אוקמיה בזרעיה שנאמר (דה״א כג טו-טז) ובני משה גרשום ואליעזר ויהיו בני אליעזר רחביה הראש וגו׳ ובני רחביה רבו למעלה וגו׳. ותני רב יוסף למעלה מס׳

as is said (I Chr. 23, 15-16.) The sons of Moses were Gershon, and Eliezer, and the sons of Eliezer were Rechabyah, the chief, the sons of Rechabyah became exceedingly great in number, and R. Joseph taught they were more than sixty myriads. This is inferred from the two similar words, Rabu, Rabu: It is written here. They were exceedingly great in number (Rabu), and it is written there (Ex. 1, 7.) They were fruitful and exceedingly great in number (Vayirbu).

(Ib. b) Further said R. Jochanan in the name of R. Simon b. Jochai: "A degenerate child in a man's house is worse than the war of Gog and Magog, for it is said (Ps. 3, 1.) A song of David, when he fled from before Abshalom, his son. Immediately after this is written. Lord! How numerous are my assailants! How many that rise up against me, while of the war of Gog and Magog it is written (Ib. 2, 1.) Wherefore do nations rage and people meditate vain things? But How numerous are my assailants is not stated [in connection with the war of Gog and Magog]." A song of David, when he fled from Abshaalom his son (Ib.) It should have been said, A lamentation of David? R. Simon b. Jochai said: "Unto what can David's incident be likened? Unto a man against whom a large note was brought forth to be paid; before he paid it he felt grieved and sorrowful, but after he had paid it, he rejoiced. So was David — since the Holy One. praised be He! said to him (II Sam. 12, 11.) Behold! I will raise up against thee evil out of thy own house; he felt grieved, for he feared it would be a slave or a bastard who would have no mercy on him. But when he saw it was Abshalom [his own son] he was glad and composed a song."

רבוא. אתיה רביה רביה. כתיב הכא רבו למעלה וכתיב התם (שמות א ז) פרו וישרצו וירבו:

(ע״ב) ואמר ר׳ יוחנן משום רשב״י קשה תרבות רעה בתוך ביתו של אדם יותר ממלחמת גוג ומגוג שנא׳ (תהלים ג א) מזמור לדוד בברחו מפני אבשלום בנו וכתיב בתריה ה׳ מה רבו צרי רבים קמים עלי ואלו גבי מלחמת גוג ומגוג כתיב (שם ב) למה רגשו גוים ולאמים יהגו ריק ואלו מה רבו צרי לא כתיב. מזמור לדוד בברחו מפני אבשלום בנו מזמור לדוד קינה לדוד מיבעי׳ ליה. א״ר שמעון בן אבישלום למה הדבר דומה לאדם שיצא עליו שטר חוב קודם שפרעו היה עצב לאחר שפרעו שמח אף כאן דוד כיון שאמר לו הקב״ה (ש״ב יב יא) הנני מקים עליך רעה מביתך היה עצב אמר שמא עבד או ממזר הוא דלא חייס עלי כיון דחזא דאבשלום הוא שמח משום הכי אמר מזמור:

Further said R. Jochanan in the name of R. Simon b. Jochai: "It is permitted to quarrel with the wicked in this world, because it is said (Pr. 28, 4.) They that forsake the Torah praise the wicked, but those who observe the Torah contend with them." We also have a Baraitha to the same effect. R. Dostai b. Mathun says: "It is permitted to quarrel with the wicked in this world; as it is said (Pr. 28, 4.) They that forsake the Torah praise the wicked, but those who observe the Torah contend with them; and if some one should whisper to you saying: 'Behold! it is written (Ps. 37, 1.) Of David! Do not fret thyself because of the evil-doers.' Tell him that he whose heart smites him [who has no clear conscience] says so, for the real meaning of the passage is: Do not compete with the evil-doers, i.e., to be among evil-doers; And neither be thou envious against the workers of iniquity, to be like them. And it is also said (Pr. 23, 17.) Let not thy heart be envious against sinners, but in the fear of the Lord (remain) at all times." Is that so? Behold! R. Isaac said: "If you see a wicked man upon whom fortune smiles, do not quarrel with him, for it is said (Ps. 10, 5.) Prosperous are his ways at all times; and moreover, he always wins by law, as it is said (Ib.) Far aloof (remain) Thy punishments from him; and moreover, he sees [revenge] in his enemies, as it is said (Ib.) All his assailants, he puffeth at them." There is no difficulty [in understanding this]; one deals with secular affairs and the other deals with divine affairs, and, if you wish, you may say both passages deal with divine affairs and there is no difficulty; for one deals with a wicked man upon whom fortune smiles, and the other with the wicked man upon whom fortune does not smile; and, if you wish, you

ואמר רבי יוחנן משום ר"ש בן יוחאי מותר להתגרות ברשעים בעולם הזה שנאמר (משלי כח ד) עוזבי תורה יהללו רשע ושומרי תורה יתגרו בם. תניא נמי הכי רבי דוסתאי בר מתון אומר מותר להתגרות ברשעים בעולם הזה שנאמר עוזבי תורה יהללו רשע ואם לחשך אדם לומר והכתיב (תהלים לז א) לדוד אל תתחר במרעים אמור לו מי שלבו נוקפו אומר כן אלא אל תתחר במרעים להיות כמרעים ואל תקנא בעושה עולה להיות כעושה עולה ואומר (משלי כג יז) אל יקנא לבך בחטאים כי אם ביראת ה' כל היום. איני והא אמר רבי יצחק אם ראית רשע שהשעה משחקת לו אל תתגרה בו שנאמר (תהלים י ה) יחילו דרכיו בכל עת. ולא עוד אלא שזוכה בדין שנאמר (שם) מרום משפטיך מנגדו. ולא עוד אלא שרואה בצריו שנאמר (שם) כל צורריו יפיח בהם. לא קשיא הא במילי דידיה הא במילי דשמיא. ואי בעית אימא הא והא במילי דישמיא ולא קשיא הא ברשע שהשעה משחקת לו הא ברשע שאין השעה משחקת לו. ואי בעית אימא הא והא ברשע שהשעה משחקת לו ולא קשיא הא בצדיק גמור הא בצדיק שאינו גמור דאמר רב הונא מאי דכתיב (חבקוק א יג) למה תביט בוגדים תחריש כבלע רשע צדיק ממנו. וכי רשע בולע צדיק והכתיב (תהלים לז לג) ה' לא יעזבנו בידו וכתיב (משלי יב

may say both deal with a wicked man upon whom fortune smiles; yet there is no difficulty, for one deals with a perfectly righteous man and the other with one who is not righteous throughout; for R. Huna said: "What means the passage (Habakuk 1, 13.) Wherefore wilt thou look upon those that deal treacherously: be silent when the wicked swallows us him that is more righteous than he? How can it be possible that a wicked man should swallow up a righteous man? Behold! It is written (Ps. 37, 33.) The Lord will not leave him in his hand, and it is written (Pr. 12, 21.) No wrong can come unawares to the righteous! We must therefore say: "One, more righteous than he is, the wicked person does destroy, but he cannot destroy the perfectly righteous man." And, if you wish, you may say that when fortune smiles upon a man, it is different [and even one perfectly righteous should not fret at him].

Again said R. Jochanan in the name of R. Simon b. Jochai: "The obedience [to the law] is more important than the study; for it is said (II Kings 3, 11.) Here is Elisha the son of Shaphat, who poured water on the hand of Elijah. Poured, is said, not Studied; from this we infer that obedience [to the law] is more important than the study." ...

R. Isaac said to R. Nachman: "Why did not the master come to the synagogue to pray?" "Because I was not feeling well," answered R. Nachman. "The master should have gathered ten in his house and then prayed," said R. Isaac. "It was too hard a task for me," said R. Nachman. "If so," remarked R. Isaac, "then why did not the master direct the Sexton to inform him when the public pray?

כא) לא יאונה לצדיק כל און אלא צדיק ממנו בולע צדיק גמור אינו בולע. ואיב"א שעה משחקת לו שאני:

ואמר ר' יוחנן משום רשב"י גדולה שימושה של תורה יותר מלמודה שנא' (מ"ב ג יא) פה אלישע בן שפט אשר יצק מים ע"י אליהו למד לא נאמר אלא יצק מלמד שגדולה שמושה יותר מלמודה:

אמר ליה רבי יצחק לרב נחמן מאי טעמא לא אתי מר לבי כנשתא לצלויי אמר ליה לא יכילנא אמר ליה לכנפי למר עשרה וליצלי. אמר ליה טריחא לי מלתא ולימא ליה מר לשליחא דצבורא ליתי ולידעי למר בעידנא דמצלי צבורא. אמר ליה מאי כולי האי. אמר ליה דאמר רבי

[so that he might pray at that time?]" "Why are you so particular about it?" asked R. Nachman, "Because," said R. Isaac, "R. Jochanan in the name of R. Simon b. Jochai said: (Fol. 8a) 'What is meant by the passage (Ps. 69, 14.) But as for me, I direct my prayer unto Thee, O Lord, in a time of favor. When is it a time of favor? It is when the community at large prays.'" R. Jose, the son of Chanina said: "We infer it from this, (Isa. 49, 8.) Thus hath said the Lord, in the time of favor have I answered thee." R. Chanina said: "We derive it from this, (Job 36, 5.) Behold, God is mighty and despiseth no one, and it is written (Ps. 55, 19.) He delivered my soul in peace from the battle against me; for in multitudes are they (contending) with me." We have also a Baraitha to the same effect, R. Nathan said: "Whence do we know that the Holy One, praised be He! despiseth not the prayers of a community? It is written (Job 36, 5.) Behold God, many He doth not despise, and it is written (Ps. 55, 19.) He delivereth my soul in peace from the battle against me; for in multitudes, etc., i.e., the Holy One, praised be He! says: 'When any one occupies himself with the study of the Torah and the practice of loving kindness I consider as if he delivered me and my children from the nations.' "

R. Levi said: "Whoever has a synagogue in his town, and does not go there to pray, is to be called a wicked neighbor, as it is said (Jer. 12, 14.) Thus hath said the Lord against all my wicked neighbors; moreover by his actions he causes exile to himself and his children, as it is said (Ib.) I will pluck them out of their land, and the house of Judah will I pluck out from the midst of them." They told R. Jochanan. that there are aged people in

יוחנן משום ר׳ שמעון בן יוחאי (דף ח) מ״ד (תהלים סט יד) ואני תפלתי לך ה׳ עת רצון אימתי עת רצון בשעה שהצבור מתפללים. ר׳ יוסי בר׳ חנינא אמר מהכא (ישעיה מט ח) כה אמר ה׳ בעת רצון עניתיך. רבי אחא בר חנינא אמר מהכא (איוב לו ה) הן אל כביר ולא ימאס. וכתיב (תהלים נה יט) פדה בשלום נפשי מקרב לי כי ברבים היו עמדי. תניא נמי הכי רבי נתן אומר מנין שאין הקב״ה מואס בתפלתן של רבים. שנאמר הן אל כביר לא ימאס וכתיב פדה בשלום נפשי מקרב לי וגו׳. אמר הקב״ה כל העוסק בתורה ובגמילות חסדים ומתפלל עם הצבור מעלה אני עליו כאלו פדאני לי ולבני מבין עכו״ם ומזלות:

אמר רבי לוי כל מי שיש לו בית הכנסת בעירו ואינו נכנס שם להתפלל נקרא שכן רע שנאמר (ירמיה יב) כה אמר ה׳ על כל שכני הרעים הנוגעים בנחלה אשר הנחלתי את עמי את ישראל. ולא עוד אלא שגורם גלות לו ולבניו שנאמר (שם) הנני נותשם מעל אדמתם ואת בית יהודה אתוש מתוכם.

Babylon, and he remarked wonderingly, "It is written (Deu. 11, 21.) In order that your days may be multiplied, and the days of your children in the land which the Lord swore unto your fathers, but not outside of Palestine." But when he was informed [of the fact] that they come early to the synagogue, and leave it late, then he said: "Aye, it is this which helps them, as R. Jochanan b. Levi said unto his children, 'Come early and remain late in the synagogue, in order that you may live long.'" R. Acha the son of R. Chanina said: "From what Biblical passage [do we learn this]? Happy is the man that hearkeneth unto me, watching day by day at my gates, waiting at the posts of my doors (Pr. 8, 34), and after this is written. For he who finds me, finds life." R. Chisda said: "A man shall always enter two doors to the synagogue." What does he mean by "two doors"? He means that a man should wait as long as it takes to walk the length of two doors, and then begin to pray.

For this shall every pious one pray unto Thee at the time when Thou mayest be found (Ps. 32, 6). R. Chanina said: "L-eth Metzo, (At the time when thou mayest be found) alludes [to the time when one is about to take a] wife, as it is written (Pr. 18, 22.) Whoso hath found a wife hath found happiness." In Palestine, when a man married he was asked Matzah (found), or Motzei (find). Matzah, as it is written (Pr. 18, 22.) Whoso hath found (Matza) a wife hath found happiness; Motzei, as it is written (Ecc. 7, 26.) And I find (Motzei) the woman more bitter than death. R. Nathan said: "L-eth Metzo, refers to the Torah, as it is written (Pr. 8, 35.) For he who findeth me (the Torah), findeth life." R.

אמרי ליה לרבי יוחנן איכא סבי בבבל תמה ואמר (דברים יא כא) למען ירבו ימיכם וימי בניכם על האדמה כתיב אבל בחוצה לארץ לא. כיון דאמרי ליה מקדמי ומחשכי לבי כנישתא. אמר היינו דאהני להו כדאמר רבי יהושע בן לוי לבניו קדימו וחשיכו ועיילו לבי כנישתא כי היכי דתוריכו חיי. אמר רבי אחא ברבי חנינא מאי קראה (משלי ח לד) אשרי אדם שומע לי לשקוד על דלתותי יום יום לשמור מזוזות פתחי וכתיב בתריה כי מוצאי מצא חיים. אמר רב חסדא לעולם יכנס אדם ב' פתחים בבית הכנסת ב' פתחים ס"ד אלא אימא שיעור ב' פתחים ואחר כך יתפלל:

(תהלים לב ו) על זאת יתפלל כל חסיד אליך לעת מצוא א"ר חנינא לעת מצוא זו אשה שנא' (משלי יח כב) מצא אשה מצא טוב. (יבמות פ"ה) במערבא כי נסיב איניש אתתא אמרי ליה הכי מצא או מוצא מצא דכתיב מצא אשה מצא טוב ויפק רצון מה'. מצא דכתיב (קהלת ז כו) ומוצא אני מר ממות את האשה. רבי נתן אומר לעת מצוא זו תורה דכתיב (משלי ח לה) כי מוצאי מצא חיים. רב נחמן בר יצחק אמר לעת מצוא זו מיתה שנאמר (תהלים סח כא) למות תוצאות. תניא נמי

Nachman b. Isaac said: "L-eth Metzo, means [the time of] death, as it is written (Ps. 68, 21.)The escape from death." We have also a Baraitha to the same effect: There are nine hundred and three kinds of deaths in the world, as it is said (Ib.) The escape from death (Totzaoth). The numerical value of the word Totzaoth, amounts to nine hundred and three; the hardest of all deaths is croup, and the easiest of all is the divine kiss; croup is like a thorn in a ball of wool, which [if one tries to tear loose] lacerates backward (in the opposite direction of the knots); others say as the gushing water at the entrance of a canal [when the sluice bars are raised]; the kiss referred to is like the extraction of a hair from milk. R. Jochanan said: "L-eth Metzo, refers to the grave." R. Chanina said: "Where is the Biblical passage to prove it? (Job 3, 22.) Who would rejoice, even to exulting, who would he glad could they but find a grave." Rabba b. R. Shila said: "Thus it is that people say: 'Man ought to pray for peace even to the last clod of earth thrown on his grave.' " Mar Zutra said: "L-eth Metzo, refers to the necessity of living in a place where there are sanitary conditions." The sages of Palestine [upon hearing all the opinions in explaining the above passage] remarked that Mar Zutra's opinion is the best of all.

Raba said to Rafram b. Papa: "Speak to us, Master, of those excellent things you said in the name of R. Chisda in reference to the synagogue." "This is what R. Chisda said," said [Rafram] to him: " 'What is the meaning of the passage (Ps. 87, 2.) The Lord loveth the gates of Zion more than all the dwellings of Jacob. The Lord loveth the gates that are marked with the signs of Halacha (laws) more than the synagogues and the houses of study.' and this agrees with R. Chiya b. Ami who said, in the name of Ulla: 'Since the destruction of the Temple, nothing has remained to the Holy One, praised be He! in His world, but four cubits of the Halacha [where it is studied].' " Abaye said: "At first I was accustomed to study in the house and pray in the synagogue, but since I heard what R. Cliiya b. Ami said in the name of Ulla, that since the destruction of the Temple, nothing has remained to the Holy One, praised be He! in his world but four cubits of the Halacha, I never prayed but where I studied.'" K. Ami and R. Assi, although they both had twelve synagogues in Tiberia, still did not pray elsewhere but between the pillars where they had studied. R. Chiya b. Ami, in the name of Ulla said: "A man shall always live in the same place where his teacher lives, for as long as Shimi b. Geira lived, solomon did not marry Pharaoh's daughter." Behold, we are taught that a man shall not live in the same place with his teacher! This is not difficult to explain, for the former deals with a disciple who bends before (obeys) his teacher, and the latter deals with a disciple who does not bend before (obey) his teacher. Another thing said R. Chiya b. Ami, in the name of Ulla: "He who enjoys life through the labor of his hand, is greater than he who fears God, for concerning the man who fears God, it is written (Ps. 112, 1.) Happy is the man who feareth the Lord; while concerning the man who enjoys the labor of his hand, it is written (Ib. 128, 2.) When thou eateth of the labor of thy hands: (then) wilt thou be happy, and it shall be well with thee. — Wilt thou be happy, in this world. And it shall be well with thee, in the world to come; but concerning the one who fears God it is not

חייא בר אמי משמיה דעולא מיום שחרב בהמ"ק אין לו להקב"ה בעולמו אלא ארבע אמות של הלכה בלבד. ואמר אביי מריש הוה גריסנא בגו ביתא ומצלינא בבי כנישתא כיון דשמענא להא דאמר ר' חייא בר אמי משמיה דעולא מיום שחרב בית המקדש אין לו להקב"ה בעולמו אלא ד' אמות של הלכה בלבד לא הוה מצלינא אלא היכא דגריסנא. רב אמי ורב אסי אע"ג דהוו להו תליסר בי כנישתא בטבריא לא מצלו אלא ביני עמודי היכא דהוו גרסי. אמר רבי חייא בר אמי משמיה דעולא לעולם ידור אדם במקום רבו שכל זמן ששמעי בן גרא קיים לא נשא שלמה את בת פרעה. והתניא אל ידור לא קשיא הא דכייף ליה הא דלא כייף ליה. ואמר רבי חייא בר אמי משמיה דעולא גדול הנהנה מיגיעו יותר מירא שמים דאלו גבי ירא שמים כתיב (שם קיב א) אשרי איש ירא את ה'. ואלו גבי נהנה מיגיעו כתיב (שם קכח ב) יגיע כפיך כי תאכל אשריך וטוב לך. אשריך בעולם הזה וטוב לך לעולם הבא. ולגבי ירא שמים לא כתיב ביה וטוב לך:

said, And it shall be well with thee."

(Ib. b) Raba said to his children (by way of advice): "When you cut meat don't cut it on your hand." — Some attribute this to the danger in cutting into the hand and others to the spoiling of the meat. — "And you should not sit down on the bed of an Armenian, and do not pass behind the synagogue at the time the community is praying." Regarding the bed of an Armenian, some say is meant not to go to sleep without the Sh'm'a which resembles an Armenian bed, and according to others, it means not to marry a proselyte. And, according to others, it means a real Armenian and refers to the incident that happened to R. Papa. R. Papa visited an Armenian and she brought him out a bed bidding him to sit on it. R. Papa refused and said to her: "I shall not sit on it unless thou wilt lift up the bed and show me what is under it." She did so and he noticed a dead child was uader the bed. Since than the sages said: "A man shall not sit on the bed of an Armenian." "Do not pass the rear of the synagogue while the community is praying;" this supports the opinion of R. Joshua b. Levi, who said: "A man has no right to pass behind the synagogue while the community is praying."

We are taught that R. Akiba says: "For three things do I admire the Medians: when they carve meat, they do it on the table; when they kiss, they do so only upon the hand; and when they keep counsel, they do so only in the field." R. Ada b. Ahaba said: "What Biblical passage indicates [that consultation should be held only in the field]? And Jacob sent and called Rachel and Leah to his flock (Gen. 31, 8)."

(ע״ב) אמר להו רבא לבניה כשאתם חותכים בשר אל תחתכו על גב היד. א״ד משום סכנה. וא״ד משום קלקול סעודה. ואל תשבו על מטת ארמית. ואל תעברו אחורי בית הכנסת בשעה שהצבור מתפללין. אל תשבו על מטת ארמית. איכא דאמרי לא תגנו בלא ק״ש. וא״ד דלא תנסבו גיורתא. וא״ד ארמית ממש ומשום מעשה דרב פפא. דרב פפא אזל לגבי ארמית הוציאה לו מטה אמרה לו שב. אמר לה איני יושב עד שתגביהי את המטה. הגביהה את המטה ומצאו שם תינוק מת. מכאן אמרו חכמים אסור לישב על מטת ארמית. ואל תעברו אחורי בית הכנסת בשעה שהצבור מתפללין מסייע לה לריב״ל דאמר ריב״ל אסור לו לאדם שיעבור אחורי בהכ״נ בשעה שהצבור מתפללין:

תניא אמר רבי עקיבא בג׳ דברים אוהב אני את המדיים כשחותכים את הבשר אין חותכין אלא על גב השלחן. כשנושקין אין נושקין אלא על גב היד. וכשיועצין אין יועצין אלא בשדה. אמר רב אדא בר אהבה מאי קרא (בראשית לא ח) וישלח יעקב ויקרא לרחל וללאה השדה אל צאנו:

(Fol. 9a) R. Abba said: "All agree that the deliverance of Israel out of Egypt took place in the evening, as it is said (Deu. 16, 1.) Did the Lord, thy God, bring thee forth out of Egypt by night; and [they also agree] that they did not leave [Egypt] before the next morning, as it is said (Num. 33, 3.) On the morrow after the Passover sacrifice, the children of Israel went out with a high hand, but they differ as to the meaning of Chipazon (In haste, Ex. 12, 11). R. Elazar b. Azariah holds that Chipazon (In haste), refers to the Egyptians who [after realizing the plague of the first-born] hurried the children of Israel to leave; and R. Akiba holds Chipazon (In haste), refers to the Israelites [who were in haste to leave]." We have also a Baraitha to the same effect: Did the Lord, thy God, bring thee forth out of Egypt by night (Deu. 16, 1). "Did they really go out at night? Behold! it was in the morning, for it is said (Num. 33, 3.) On the morrow after the Passover sacrifice, did the children of Israel go out with a high hand. We must therefore say that the beginning of the deliverance was in the evening."

(דף ט) אמר ר׳ אבא הכל מודים כשנגאלו ישראל ממצרים לא נגאלו אלא בערב שנאמר (דברים טז א) הוציאך ה׳ אלהיך ממצרים לילה. וכשיצאו לא יצאו אלא ביום שנאמר (במדבר לג ג) ממחרת הפסח יצאו בני ישראל ביד רמה. על מה נחלקו על שעת חפזון דר״א ב״ע סבר מאי חפזון חפזון דמצרים ור״ע סבר מאי חפזון חפזון דישראל. תניא נמי הכי הוציאך ה׳ אלהיך ממצרים לילה וכי בלילה יצאו והלא לא יצאו אלא ביום שנאמר ממחרת הפסח יצאו בני ישראל ביד רמה אלא מלמד שהתחילה להם גאולה מבערב:

Speak. (I beg thee) in the ears of the people (Ex. 11, 2). It was said in the school of R. Janai: "The word Nah, means nothing else but request; the Holy One, blessed be He! said unto Moses. 'I pray thee go and tell them (Israel) that I request of them they shall ask from the Egyptians silver vessels and golden vessels, lest that righteous one (Abraham) shall not say, Aye, the decree, (Geu. 13, 13.) And they will make them serve and they will afflict them, was indeed fulfilled for them; but [the other half of the decree] And afterwards shall they go out with great substance was not fulfilled.'

(שמות יא ב) דבר נא באזני העם וגו׳ אמרי דבי רבי ינאי אין נא אלא לשון בקשה אמר לו הקב״ה למשה בבקשה ממך לך ואמור להם בבקשה מכם שאלו ממצרים כלי כסף וכלי זהב שלא יאמר אותו צדיק (בראשית טו יג) ועבדום וענו אותם קיים בהם (שם) ואחרי כן יצאו ברכוש גדול לא קיים בהם. אמרו לו ולואי שנצא בעצמנו. משל לאדם שהיה חבוש בבית האסורים והיו אומרים לו בני אדם מוציאין אותך למחר מבית

[When Moses informed Israel of this] they said to Him: 'O that we might go out ourselves.'" This may be likened unto a man detained in prison, who when told by the people that he would be set free the next morning and would receive a large sum of money, said to them: "I pray of you, take me out immediately; that is all I wish." And they caused to give unto them, what they required (Ib.). R. Ami said: We infer from this, that it was given to them against their will." Some say against the will of the Egyptians, and others say against the will of the Israelites; those who say against the will of the Egyptians, infer this from (Ps. 68, 13.) Yet she that tarried at home (Egypt that tarried at home), divided the spoil; and those that say against the will of the Israelites, because of the burden of carrying them; And they emptied out Egypt. (Ib.) R. Ami said: "We learn from this that they left her (Egypt) like a net without grain," and Resh Lakish said: "They left her like a depth without fishes."

I will be that I will be (Ex. 3, 14). The Holy One, praised be He! said unto Moses, "Go and tell Israel that I was with you during this subjugation and I will be with you during the next subjugation." So Moses said unto Him: "Sovereign of the Universe, is not the affliction terrible enough when it is really present [without telling of it beforehand]?" Whereupon the Holy One, praised be He! said unto Moses: "Then go and tell, 'I will be,' sent me unto you." Answer me, O Lord, answer me (I Kings 18, 37). R. Abuhu said: "Why did Elijah say twice, Answer me? We infer from this that Elijah said, before the Holy One, praised be He! 'Sovereign of the Universe, answer me that a fire shall come

האסורים ונותנים לך ממון הרבה ואמר להם בבקשה מכם הוציאוני מיד ואיני מבקש כלום. (שמות יב לו) וישאילום אמר רבי אמי מלמד שהשאילום בעל כרחם. א״ד בעל כרחם דמצרים. וא״ד בעל כרחם דישראל. מ״ד בעל כרחם דמצרים דכתיב (תהלים סח יג) ונות בית תחלק שלל. ומאן דאמר בעל כרחם דישראל משום משוי. (שמות יב לו) וינצלו את מצרים. (פ׳ ע״פ) אמר רב אמי מלמד שעשאוה כמצודה שאין בה דגן. ור״ל אמר עשאוה כמצולה שאין בה דגים:

(שמות ג יד) אהיה אשר אהיה א״ל הקב״ה למשה לך אמור להם לישראל אני הייתי עמכם בשעבוד זה ואני אהיה עמכם בשעבוד גליות. אמר לפניו רבש״ע דיה לצרה בשעתה. אמר לו הקב״ה לך אמור להם (שם ג יד) אהיה שלחני אליכם. (מ״א יח לז) ענני ה׳ ענני אמר רבי אבהו למה אמר אליהו ענני ב׳ פעמים. מלמד שאמר אליהו לפני הקב״ה רבונו של עולם ענני שתרד אש מן השמים ותאכל כל אשר על המזבח. וענני שתסיח דעתם כדי שלא יאמרו מעשה כשפים הם

down from Heaven and consume everything that is upon the altar; and answer me, to remove from their mind that they shall not think it was the result of sorcery,' as it is said (lb.) Thou hast turned their hearts back again.":

Let us see: The passage (Ps. 19, 15.) May the words of my mouth he acceptable, can be explained in the past tense, and it may be explained in the future tense. Why then have the Rabbis decided to say it after the Eighteen Benedictions and not before? R. Juda, the son of R. Simon b. Pazi, said: "Because David did not say this verse until after he had said eighteen chapters, therefore did the Rabbis decree [to say it] after the Eighteen Benedictions." Is it after eighteen? Behold! it is after nineteen? Aye! the first two chapters, viz., Happy is the man, and Wherefore do heathens rage, are only one chapter, for R. Juda, the son of R. Simon b. Pazi, said: "One hundred and three chapters were uttered by David, and he did not say Hallelujah until he had contemplated the downfall of the wicked; as it is said (Ps. 104, 35.) Let the sinners be taken completely out of the earth, and let the wicked be no more; Bless the Lord, O my soul. Hallelujah! Instead of one hundred and three, we ought to say, one hundred and four? but we infer this, that Blessed is the man, and Why do the heathens rage, are but one psalm. (Fol. 10a) As R. Samuel b. Nachmeini in the name of R. Jonathan said: 'Every chapter that was beloved by David, he began and concluded it with the word, Happy; It began with Happy is the man (Ps. 1, 1), and ended with Happy are all they that put treir trust in Him (Ib. 2, 10).' [This proves that the first two chapters are one]."

שנאמר (שם) ואתה הסיבות את לבם אחורנית:

מכדי האי (תהלים יט טו) יהיו לרצון אמרי פי משמע לבסוף ומשמע מעיקרא דבעינן למימר. מאי טעמא תקינו רבנן לאחר שמונה עשרה ברכות (כיון דמיניה יליף סמיכות גאולה לתפלה שפיר טפי לאומרו מעיקרא. מהרש״א) לימרו מעיקרא. אמר רב יהודה בריה דרבי שמעון בן פזי הואיל ולא אמרו דוד אלא לאחר שמונה עשרה פרשיות לפיכך תקינו רבנן לאחר שמונה עשרה ברכות. הני תמני סרי תשסרי הויין. אשרי האיש ולמה רגשו גוים חדא פרשתא היא. דאמר רבי יהודה בריה דרבי שמעון בן פזי מאה וג׳ פרשיות אמר דוד ולא אמר הללויה עד שראה במפלתן של רשעים שנאמר (תהלים קד לה) יתמו חטאים מן הארץ ורשעים עוד אינם ברכי נפשי את ה׳ הללויה. הני מאה ושלש מאה וארבע הוויין. אלא שמע מינה אשרי האיש ולמה רגשו חדא פרשה היא. דאמר (דף י) רשב״ג אמר רבי יוחנן כל פרשה שהיתה חביבה על דוד פתח בה באשרי וסיים בה באשרי פתח באשרי דכתיב (תהלים א א) אשרי האיש. וסיים באשרי דכתיב (שם ב י) אשרי כל חוסי בו:

There were some highwaymen in the neighborhood of R. Meier who annoyed him so much that he once prayed that they should die; but his wife Baruriah said to him: "How do you justify this? [such prayer?] Is it because, it is written (Ps. 104, 35.) Let sin be consumed [which you understand to mean that the wicked should be destroyed]; behold is it then written The sinners? It is written sin! Besides, read the last part of this verse And the wicked will be no more. Pray, therefore [on their behalf], that they may be led to repentance and the wicked will be no more." He did pray for them and thereupon they were led to repent. A Sadduce once asked R. Abuhu: "It is written (Ps. 3, 1.) A psalm of David when he fled from his son, Abshalom, and it is written (Ib. 57, 1.) By David a Michtam, when he fled from Saul. Let us see, which event occurred first? Was it not the incident with Saul? Why then is it written last? "Aye," R. Abuhu said to him, "you, who do not recognize the rule of contiguous passages find this difficult, but to us who recognize the rule of contiguous passages, it is not at all difficult; for R. Jochanan said: "What is the Biblical proof for the rule of contiguous passage? It is said (Ps. 111, 8.) They are well supported forever and eternally they are framed in truth and uprightness. Why is the story of Abshalom placed near the chapter of Gog and Magog? If one should ask you, 'Is it possible that a slave (Gog and Magog) shall rebel against his master (God)?' answer him: 'How is it possible that a son shall rebel against liis own father? Yet, it did so happen (with Abshalom); so is this also possible.' "

R. Shimi b. Ukba, and some say Mar Ukba, frequented the house of R. Simon b. Pazi.,

הנהו בריוני דהוו בשבבותיה דר״מ והוו קא מצערי ליה טובא הוה קא בעי ר״מ רחמי עלייהו דלימותו. אמרה ליה ברוריה דביתהו מאי דעתיך משום דכתיב (שם קד לה) יתמו חטאים. מי כתיב חוטאים חטאים כתיב ועוד שפיל לסיפיה דקרא ורשעים עוד אינם כיון דיתמו חטאים ורשעים עוד אינם אלא בעי רחמי עלייהו דלהדרי בתשובה ורשעים עוד אינם. בעא רחמי עלייהו והדרי בתשובה. א״ל ההוא צדוקי לר׳ אבהו כתיב (תהלים ג א) מזמור לדוד בברחו מפני אבשלום בנו וכתיב (שם נז א) לדוד מכתם בברחו מפני שאול במערה הי מעשה הוה ברישא מכדי מעשה דשאול הוה ברישא ליכתוב ברישא. אמר ליה אתון דלא דרשיתון סמוכים קשיא לכו אנן דדרשינן סמוכים לא קשיא לן דא״ר יוחנן סמוכים מן התורה מנין שנא׳ (שם קיא ח) סמוכים לעד לעולם עשויים באמת וישר למה נסמכה פרשת אבשלום לפרשת גוג ומגוג שאם יאמר לך אדם כלום יש עבד שמורד ברבו אף אתה אמור לו כלום יש בן שמורד באביו אלא הוה. הכא נמי הוה:

רב שימי בר עוקבא ואמרי לה מר עוקבא הוה שכיח קמיה

who was accustomed to arrange Agadah before R. Joshua b. Levi, and asked R. Simon b. Pazi: "What is the meaning of the passage (Ps. 103, 1.) Praise the Lord, O my soul, and all that is within me (praise) His Holy name." "Come and see,"' said R. Simon b. Pazi to him, "how the custom of the Holy One, praised be He! differs from the custom of frail man! The custom of frail man is to form a shape on the wall but he can put into it neither breath nor soul, nor entrails nor bowels, but the Holy One, praised be He! is not so. He forms a shape within a shape (creates a body within a body) and puts into it breath, soul, entrails and bowels, and it is this that Hannah means when she said (I Sam. 2, 2.) There is none holy like the Lord; for there is none besides Thee, and there is not any rock like our Lord. What is meant by Ein Tzur Keloheinu? It means that there is no shaper like our Lord." And what does it mean by For there is none besides Thee? R. Juda b. Menassya said: "Do not read Ein Biltecha (none besides Thee), but read Ein Lebalathecha (nothing could wear you out), for the nature of the Holy One, praised be He! is not like the nature of frail man. The works of frail man wear out their maker, but the Holy One, praised be He! is not so. He wears out his work." "You did not quite understand my question," said R. Shimi b. Ukba to R. Simon b. Pazi, "what I Intended to ask was this: Five times did David say Bless the Lord, O my soul; in reference to what was it said?" "He said it," [replied R. Simon b. Pazi] "in reference to the Holy One, praised be He! and in reference to the soul, for just as the Holy One, praised be He! filleth the entire world, so does the soul fill the entire body; just as the Holy One, praised be He! seeth, but cannot be seen, so does the soul

דר' שמעון בן פזי והוה מסדר אגדתא קמיה דרבי יהושע בן לוי א״ל מ״ד (שם קג א) ברכי נפשי את ה' וכל קרבי את שם קדשו. א״ל בא וראה שלא כמדת הקב״ה מדת ב״ו מדת ב״ו צר צורה על גבי הכותל ואינו יכול להטיל בו רוח ונשמה קרבים ובני מעיים. והיינו דאמרה חנה (ש״א ב ב) אין קדוש כה' כי אין בלתך ואין צור כאלהינו. מאי אין צור כאלהינו אין צייר כאלהינו. מאי כי אין בלתך. אמר רב יהודה בר מנסיא אל תקרי כי אין בלתך אלא אין לבלותך. שלא כמדת הקב״ה מדת ב״ו. מדת ב״ו מעשה ידיו מבלין אותו והקב״ה מבלה מעשיו אמר ליה אנא הכי קא אמינא לך הני ה' ברכי נפשי כנגד מי אמרן דוד. לא אמרן אלא כנגד הקב״ה וכנגד נשמה. מה הקב״ה מלא כל העולם אף נשמה מלאה את כל הגוף. מה הקב״ה רואה ואינו נראה, אף נשמה רואה ואינה נראית, מה הקב״ה זן את כל העולם כולו אף נשמה זנה את כל הגוף. מה הקב״ה טהור אף נשמה טהורה. מה הקב״ה יושב בחדרי חדרים אף נשמה יושבת בחדרי החדרים יבא מי שיש בו חמשה דברים הללו וישבח למי שיש בו חמשה דברים הללו:

see, but cannot be seen; just as the Holy One, praised be He! feedeth the entire world, so does the soul feed the entire body; just as the Holy One, praised be He! is pure, so is the soul pure; and just as the Holy One, praised be He! dwelleth in a place secret from all, so does the soul dwell in a secret place; therefore, let that (the soul) which possesses these five attributes come and praise Him, to whom these five attributes belong."

R. Hamnuna said: "What means the passage (Ecc. 8, 1.) Who is like the wise? And who knoweth (as well) the explanation of a thing? i. e., who is like the Holy One, praised be He! who knoweth how to compromise 'between two righteous men, between (King) Hezekiah and Isaiah? Hezekiah said, Isaiah ought to come to me for we find that Elijah went to Ahab, as it is said (I Kings 18, 2.) And Elijah went to show himself unto Ahab; and Isaiah said Hezekiah ought to come to me (to pay me a visit), just as we find that Jehoram, the son of Ahab went to Elisha. What did the Holy One, praised be He! do? He brought affliction on Hezekiah, and then said to Isaiah: 'Go and visit the sick,' as it is said (Isaiah, 38, 1.) In those days Hezekiah fell sick unto death; and there came unto him Isaiah, the son of Amotz, the Prophet, and said to him: Thus hath the Lord said. Give thy charge to thy house for thou Shalt die and not live." What is meant by Thou shalt die and not live? [if he will die, he will surely not live]. Thou shalt die in this world, and thou shalt not live in the world to come. "Why so severe a punishment?" asked Hezekiah. "Because," said Isaiah, "thou hast not married." "Aye," said Hezekiah, "it was because I foresaw through the Divine Spirit,

אמר רב המנונא מאי דכתיב (קהלת ח א) מי כהחכם ומי יודע פשר דבר. מי כהקב"ה שיודע לעשות פשרה בין שני צדיקים בין חזקיהו לישעיהו. חזקיהו אמר ליתי ישעיהו גבאי דהכי אשכחן באליהו דאזיל לגבי אחאב שנאמר (מ"א יח ב) וילך אליהו להראות אל אחאב. ישעיהו אמר ליתי חזקיהו גבאי דהכי אשכחן ביהורם בן אחאב דאזיל לגבי אלישע. מה עשה הקב"ה הביא יסורין על חזקיהו ואמר לו לישעיהו לך ובקר את החולה. שנאמר (ישעיה לח א) בימים ההם חלה חזקיהו למות ויבא אליו ישעיהו בן אמוץ הנביא ויאמר כה אמר ה' צבאות צו לביתך כי מת אתה ולא תחיה וגו' מאי כי מת אתה ולא תחיה מת אתה בעולם הזה ולא תחיה לעולם הבא. אמר ליה מאי כולי האי אמר ליה משום דלא עסקת בפריה ורביה. א"ל משום דחזאי לי ברוח הקודש דנפקי מנאי בנין דלא מעלה אמר ליה בהדי כבשי דרחמנא למה לך מאי דמפקדת אבעי לך למעבד

that bad children will come forth from me." "What have you to do with, the secret of the Almighty? Whatever you are commanded to do, you ought to fulfill, and whatever pleases the Holy One, praised be He! let Him do." "If so,'" said Hezekiah, "then give me thy daughter, Perhaps thy merits combined with mine will prove effective to bring forth good children." "But," said Isaiah, "it has already been decreed that you must die." "Aye, son of Amotz," exclaimed Hezekiah, "finish thy prophecy and go forth! for thus have I a tradition from the house of my father's father (David): 'Even if the sword already touches the throat, yet should a man not refrain from praying for mercy.' " It has been taught that R. Jochanan and R. Elazar both say, "Even if the sword already touches the throat, yet should a man not refrain from praying for mercy, as it is said (Job 13, 15.) Lo, though he slay me yet will I trust in Him (Ib. b)." Soon after this it is said Then did Hezekiah turn his fare toward the Kir, and prayed to the Lord (Is. 38, 2). What is meant by Kir? R. Simon b. Lakish said: "It means from the chamber of his heart, as it is said (Jer. 4, 19.) My bowels, my bowels! I am shaken at the very chambers (Kiroth), of my heart." R. Levi said: "It means concerning the chamber; he (Hezekiah) said before the Holy One, praised be He! 'Sovereign of the Universe, if for the Shunamith who prepared only one little chamber [for Elisha], Thou hast saved the life of her son, then how much more [should you help me], for the sake of my father (Solomon) who covered the whole Temple with silver and gold?' " Remember now, that I have walked before Thee in truth and with an undivided heart and have done what is worthy in thine eyes (Ib.). What means And have done what is

ומה דניחא קמיה קודשא בריך הוא לעביד. אמר ליה השתא הב לי ברתך אפשר דגרמא זכותא דידי ודידך ונפקי מנאי בני דמעלי. אמר ליה כבר נגזרה עליך גזרה אמר ליה בן אמץ כלה נבואתך וצא כך מקובלני מבית אבי אבא אפילו חרב חדה מונחת על צוארו של אדם אל ימנע עצמו מן הרחמים. איתמר נמי רבי יוחנן ורבי אלעזר דאמרי תרוייהו אפילו חרב חדה מונחת על צוארו של אדם אל ימנע עצמו מן הרחמים שנאמר (איוב יג טו) הן יקטלני לו איחל. (ע״ב) מיד (ישעיה לח ב) ויסב חזקיהו פניו אל הקיר ויתפלל אל ה'. מאי קיר. א״ר שמעון בן לקיש מקירות לבו שנאמר (ירמיה ד יט) מעי מעי אוחילה קירות לבי וגו'. רבי לוי אמר על עסקי הקיר. אמר לפניו רבונו של עולם ומה שונמית שלא עשתה אלא קיר אחת קטנה החיית את בנה אבי אבא שחפה את ההיכל כלו בכסף וזהב על אחת כמה וכמה. (ישעיה לח ג) זכר נא את אשר התהלכתי לפניך באמת ובלב שלם והטוב בעיניך עשיתי. מאי והטוב בעיניך עשיתי. אמר רבי יהודה אמר רב שסמך גאולה לתפלה. ר' לוי אמר שגנז ספר רפואות:

worthy in thine eyes? R. Juda in the name of Rab said: "He was always careful to say the Eighteen Benedictions immediately after the benediction of Ge-ula." R. Levi said: "He hid the book of remedies [so that the sick should pray to God to invoke His mercy, and not depend merely on medicinal help]."

R. Jochanan said in the name of R. Jose b. Zimra: "He who depends [for God's help] upon his own merits will [finally] be raised through the merits of others, but he who depends upon others' merits will [finally] be helped because of his own merits. Moses, who depended upon the merits of others, as it is said (Ex. 32, 13.) Remember Abraham, Isaac and Israel, Thy servants, was raised because of his own merits, as it is said (Ps. 106, 23.) He therefore spoke of destroying them, had not Moses, his chosen, stood in the breach before Him. Hezekiah depended upon his own merits, as it is written (Is. 38, 3.) Remember now that I have walked before Thee, but was [finally] raised through the merits of others, as it is said (II Kings 19, 34.) And I will shield the city to save it, for my own sake, and for the sake of David, my servant." And this is [the interpretation] of R. Joshua b. Levi. For R. Joshua b. Levi said: "What is the meaning of the passage (Is. 38, 17.) Behold, for in peace I had great bitterness, i.e., even when the Holy One, praised be He! sent peace unto him, yet he felt bitter [since it was done because of the merits of others]."

Further said R. Jose, the son of R. Chanina, in the name of R. Eliezer b. Jacob: "A man should never stand upon an elevated place while praying, but upon a low place shall he stand and pray, as it is said (Ps. 130, 1.) Out

א"ר יוחנן משום רבי יוסי בן זמרא כל התולה בזכות עצמו תולין לו בזכות אחרים. וכל התולה בזכות אחרים תולין לו בזכות עצמו. משה תלה בזכות אחרים שנאמר (שמות לב יג) זכור לאברהם ליצחק ולישראל עבדיך תלו לו בזכות עצמו שנאמר (תהלים קו כג) ויאמר להשמידם לולי משה בחירו וגו. חזקיה תלה בזכות עצמו דכתיב (ישעיה לח ג) זכר נא את אשר התהלכתי לפניך תלו לו בזכות אחרים שנאמר (מ"ב יט לד) וגנותי אל העיר הזאת להושיעה למעני ולמען דוד עבדי. והיינו דריב"ל דאמר ריב"ל מאי דכתיב (ישעיה לח יז) הנה לשלום מר לי מר. אפילו בשעה ששיגר לו הקב"ה שלום מר הוא לו:

ואמר רבי יוסי בר' חנינא משום רבי אליעזר בן יעקב אל יעמוד אדם במקום גבוה ויתפלל אלא במקום נמוך ויתפלל שנאמר (תהלים קל א) ממעמקים קראתיך ה'.

of the depth have I called Thee. O Lord." We have also a Baraitha to the same effect: "A man should never stand either upon a chair or upon a bench nor upon an elevated place while praying, but upon a low place shall he stand and pray because pride cannot exist before the Lord, as it is written (Ib.) Out of the depth have I called Thee, O Lord, and it is also written (Ib. 102, 1.) A prayer of the afflicted, when he is overwhelmed." Again said R. Jose, the son of R. Chanina in the name of R. Eliezer b. Jacob: "He who prays should keep his feet straight (one near the other), for it is said (Ez 1, 8.) Their feet were straight feet." And R. Jose, the son of R. Chanina, in the name of R. Eliezer b. Jacob, said further: "What means the passage (Lev. 19, 26.) Ye shall not eat upon the blood? Ye shall not eat before ye pray on behalf of your blood (life)." R. Isaac said in the name of R. Jochanan, who spoke in the name of R. Jose, the son of R. Chanina, who in turn, quoted R. Eliezer b. Jacob: "Concerning one who eats and drinks, and then prays, of him the passage says: (I Kin. 14, 9.) And me hast thou cast behind thy back. Do not read Geivecha (thy back) but read it Geiyecha (thy pride), i. e., the Holy One, praised be He! said: 'Only after this one had become haughty [through eating] he took upon himself the Heavenly Kingdom.'"

(Fol. 12b) Rabba b. Chinena, the Senior, in the name of Rab, said further: "Whoever is able to pray for mercy on behalf of his friend and does not pray, is to be called a sinner; as it is said (I Sam. 12, 23.) Moreover as for me, far be it from me that I should sin against the Lord by ceasing to pray in your behalf." Raba said: "If he who is the sick be a great man, his friend should pray for him until he

תנ"ה לא יעמוד אדם לא על גבי כסא ולא על גבי שרפרף ולא במקום גבוה ויתפלל אלא במקום נמוך ויתפלל, לפי שאין גבהות לפני המקום שנאמר ממעמקים קראתיך ה' וכתיב (שם קב א) תפלה לעני כי יעטוף. ואמר רבי יוסי בר' חנינא משום ראב"י המתפלל צריך שיכוין את רגליו שנאמר (יחזקאל א ח) ורגליהם רגל ישרה. ואמר רבי יוסי בר' חנינא משום רבי אליעזר בן יעקב מאי דכתיב (ויקרא יט כו) לא תאכלו על הדם. לא תאכלו קודם שתתפללו על דמכם. אמר רבי יצחק אמר ר' יוחנן אמר רבי יוסי ברבי חנינא משום ראב"י כל האוכל ושותה ואח"כ מתפלל עליו הכתוב אומר (מ"א יד ט) ואותי השלכת אחרי גוך. אל תקרי גוך אלא גאיך. אמר הקב"ה לאחר שנתגאה זה קבל עליו מלכות שמים:

(יב ע"ב) ואמר רבה בר חיננא סבא משמיה דרב כל שאפשר לו לבקש רחמים על חבירו ואינו מבקש נקרא חוטא שנא' (ש"א יב כג) גם אנכי חלילה לי מחטוא לה' מחדול להתפלל בעדכם. אמר רבא אם תלמיד חכם הוא צריך שיחלה עצמו עליו. מאי טעמא אילימא משום

himself is worn out." What is the reason? Shall we say because it is written (Ib. 22, 8.) And there is none who sickens for me nor informeth me? Perhaps this refers only to a King? But we learn it from this, (Ps. 35, 13.) But as for me, when they were sick, my clothing was sackcloth. Further said Rabba b. Chinena, the Senior, in the name of Rab: "He, who after committing a transgression, feels ashamed, will be forgiven of all his sins, as it is said (Ez. 16, 63.) In order that thou mayest remember, and feel ashamed and never open thy mouth any more because of thy shame. When I forgive thee for all that thou hast done saith the Lord God." Perhaps a community [to which that refers] is different? But we learn from this, (I Sam. 28. 15.) And Samuel said unto Saul, Why hast thou disquieted me? And Saul answered, I am greatly distressed for the Philistines make war against me, and God has departed from me and hath not answered me any more, neither by the agency of the prophets, nor by means of dreams: therefore I have called thee, that thou mayest make known unto me what I shall do. And he fails to mention the Urim and Tummim; he was ashamed to mention these because he killed all the priests of Nob who performed that rite. And whence do we learn that his sins were forgiven by Heaven? It is said (Ib.) And Samuel said unto Saul, to-morrow shalt thou and thy sons be with me, and R. Jochanan said: "With me, means in my abode." And the other Rabbis say from this [it is derived that God forgave his sin], (II Sam. 21, 6.) And we will hang them up unto the Lord in Gibas of Saul, the chosen of the Lord. i.e., A Bath Kol (heavenly voice) went forth and said "The chosen of the Lord."

דכתיב (שם כב ח) ואין חולה מכם עלי ואין גולה את אזני. דלמא מלך שאני. אלא מהכא (תהלים לה יג) ואני בחלותם לבושי שק. ואמר רבה בר חיננא סבא משמיה דרב כל העושה דבר עבירה ומתבייש בה מוחלין לו על כל עונותיו שנאמר (יחזקאל טז סג) למען תזכרי ובשת ולא יהיה לך עוד פתחון פה מפני כלמתך בכפרי לך לכל אשר עשית נאם ה׳ אלהים. דלמא צבור שאני. אלא מהכא (ש״א כח טו) ויאמר שמואל אל שאול למה הרגזתני להעלות אותי וגו׳ ויאמר שאול צר לי מאד ופלשתים נלחמים בי וה׳ סר מעלי ולא ענני עוד גם ביד הנביאים גם בחלומות ואקראה לך להודיעני מה אעשה. ואילו אורים ותומים לא קאמר משום דקטליה לנוב עיר הכהנים. ומנין דאחילו ליה מן שמיא שנאמר (שם) ויאמר שמואל אל שאול מחר אתה ובניך עמי. וא״ר יוחנן עמי במחיצתי. ורבנן אמרי מהכא (ש״ב כא ו) והוקענום לה׳ בגבעת שאול בחיר ה׳. יצאתה בת קול ואמרה בחיר ה׳:

It was taught that Ben Zoma said to the sages: "Is it truly so that the Exodus from Egypt will be mentioned [as a miraculous incident] after Messiah will come? Has not the prophet long ago said (Jer. 23, 7.) Therefore, behold, days are coming, saith the Lord, when they shall no more say, as the Lord liveth, who hath brought up the children of Israel out of the Land of Egypt; But as the Lord liveth, who hath brought up, and who hath led forth the seed of the house of Israel out of the north country, and out of all countries whither I had driven them." "This," said the sages, "is intended to mean, not that the memory of the redemption of Egypt will be removed from its place (entirely extinct), but that the latter redemption will be the principal consideration and the redemption of Egypt the secondary. Just as it is said (Gen. 35, 10.) Thy name shall not be called any more Jacob, but Israel shall be thy name. (Fol. 13a.) It means not that the name Jacob will entirely fall into disuse, but that Israel shall be the principal name and Jacob the secondary. And this is meant by the passage (Is. 43, 18.) Remember not the former things, and ancient events regard no more. Remember not former things, alludes to the present subjugation, and ancient events regard no more, refers to the redemption of Egypt." Behold, I will do a new thing; now shall it spring forth (Ib. ib. 10). R. Joseph recited a Baraitha that this alludes to the war of Gog and Magog. It is likened to a man who while walking on the road met a wolf from whom he escaped, and as he was exulting over the miracle of the wolf, he met a lion and also escaped him. He exulted over his escape from the lion, forgetting the miracle of the escape from the wolf. He then

תניא אמר להם בן זומא לחכמים וכי מזכירים יציאת מצרים לימות המשיח והלא כבר נאמר (ירמיה כג ז) הנה ימים באים נאם ה' ולא יאמרו עוד חי ה' אשר העלה את בני ישראל מארץ מצרים כי אם חי ה' אשר העלה ואשר הביא את זרע בית ישראל מארץ צפונה ומכל הארצות אשר הדחתים שם. אמרו לו לא שתעקר יציאת מצרים ממקומו אלא שתהא שעבוד מלכיות עיקר ויציאת מצרים טפל לו. כיוצא בו אתה אומר (בראשית לה י) לא יקרא שמך עוד יעקב כי אם ישראל יהיה שמך. (דף יג) לא שיעקר יעקב ממקומו אלא ישראל עיקר ויעקב טפל לה וכן הוא אומר (ישעיה מג יח) אל תזכרו ראשונות וקדמוניות אל תתבוננו אל תזכרו ראשונות זו שעבוד גליות, וקדמוניות אל תתבוננו זו יציאת מצרים. (שם) הנני עושה חדשה עתה תצמח. תני רב יוסף זו מלחמת גוג ומגוג. משל למה"ד לאדם שהיה מהלך בדרך ופגע בו זאב וניצול ממנו והיה מספר והולך מעשה זאב. פגע בו ארי וניצול ממנו והיה מספר והולך מעשה ארי. פגע בו נחש וניצול ממנו שכח מעשה שניהם והיה מספר והולך מעשה נחש אף כך ישראל צרות אחרונות משכחות הראשונות:

met a serpent and also escaped. He forgot all the former escapes and exulted over the miracle of the serpent. Thus it is with Israel; the later troubles make them forget the earlier ones.

Abram, the same is Abraham. (I Chr. 1, 27.) i.e., at first he was the father (progenitor) of Aram but later he became the father (progenitor) of the entire world. And Sarai, the same is Sarah (Ib.), i,e., at first she was a princess of her own nation but later she became a princess of the entire world. Bar Kappara recited: "Whoever calls him Abram instead of Abraham transgresses a positive commandment, for it is said (Gen. 17, 5.) But thy name shall be Abraham." R. Eliezer said: "He transgresses the prohibitory law which says: (Ib. ib. ib.) Neither shall thy name any more be called Abraham." But according to this, if one calls Sarai instead of Sarah, would you also say [that he transgresses the positive law]? Nay: In this case the Holy One, praise be He! said to Abraham only: As for Sarai thy wife, thou shall not call her name Sarai. but Sarah shall her name be. But according to this, if one calls Jacob "Jacob" instead of Israel, should we also say [that he transgresses the positive law]? Nay: The latter is different because the Scripture itself repeats his name later as Jacob, for it is written (Ib. 46, 2.) And God said to Israel in the vision of the night saying "Jacob, Jacob." R. Jose b. Abin and according to others R. Jose b. Zebida raised the following contradiction: Thou art indeed the Lord the (true) God, who didst choose Abram (Neh. 9, 7). [Hence he calls; him Abram]? There the prophet renewed the praises of the Lord by referring to the past [when Abraham's name was still Abram].

אברם הוא אברהם (פסוק הוא בדה״א א) בתחלה נעשה אב לארם ולבסוף נעשה אב לכל העולם כלו. שרי היא שרה בתחלה נעשית שרי לאומתה ולבסוף נעשית שרה לכל העולם כולו. תני בר קפרא כל הקורא לאברהם אברם עובר בעשה. שנאמר (בראשית יז ה) והיה שמך אברהם. רבי אליעזר אומר עובר בלאו שנאמר (שם) ולא יקרא עוד את שמך אברם. אלא מעתה הקורא לשרה שרי הכי נמי. התם הקדוש ברוך הוא אמר לאברהם (שם) שרי אשתך לא תקרא את שמה שרי כי שרה שמה. אלא מעתה הקורא ליעקב יעקב הכי נמי. שאני התם דהדר אהדריה קרא דכתיב (שם מו ב) ויאמר אלהים לישראל במראות הלילה ויאמר יעקב יעקב. מתיב רבי יוסי בר אבין ואיתימא רב יוסי בר זבידא (נחמיה נו ב) אתה הוא ה׳ האלהים אשר בחרת באברם. אמר ליה התם נביא הוא דקא מסדר לשבחיה דרחמנא מאי דהוה מעיקרא:

Chapter 2

R. Joshua b. Karcha said: "Why is the section of Sh'm'a recited before the section of V'haya im, Shamo'a? Because one should first take upon himself the yoke of the Heavenly Kingdom [Hear O Israel, the Lord our God, is one God], and then he can take upon himself the yoke of the commandments [referred to in the second chapter]. And why is V'haya im Shamo'a recited before Vayomer? Because V'haya treats of meritorious deeds that are to be performed day and night, and Vayomer treats of [Tzitzith] a religious act that is to be observed only in daytime."

(Ib. b) We have been taught that Sumchus says: "Whoever prolongs the utterance of the word Echad, shall have his days and years prolonged for him." R. Acha b. Jacob said: [He should prolong the utterance] of the Daleth [the D of Echad], R. Ashi said: "But he should not hurry the utterance of the Cheth [the ch of Echad]." R. Jeremiah sitting before R. Chiya b. Abba noticed that he prolonged it (the Echad) considerably; so he said to him: "If you prolong it enough to acknowledge His Kingdom in Heaven and on earth and at the four corners of the world, it suffices; it is not necessary to prolong it longer than that."

(Fol. 14a) Rab said: "Whoever greets his friend before he has prayed is considered as if he had built a heathenish altar, for it is said (Is. 2, 22.) Withdraw yourselves from man whose breath is in his nostrils; for what is he to be esteemed. Do not read Bameh (for

אמר ר׳ יהושע בן קרחה למה קדמה פרשת שמע לוהיה אם שמוע. כדי שיקבל עליו עול מלכות שמים תחלה ואח״כ מקבל עליו עול מצות. והיה אם שמוע לויאמר. שוהיה אם שמוע נוהג בין ביום ובין בלילה ויאמר אינו נוהג אלא ביום בלבד:

(ע״ב) תניא סומכוס אומר כל המאריך באחד מאריכין לו ימיו ושנותיו. אמר ר׳ אחא בר יעקב ובדלי״ת. א״ר אשי ובלבד שלא יחטוף בחי״ת. רבי ירמיה הוה יתיב קמיה דרבי חייא בר אבא חזייה דהוה מאריך טובא א״ל כיון דאמליכתיה למעלה ולמטה ולארבע רוחות השמים תו לא צריכת:

(דף יד) אמר רב כל הנותן שלום לחברו קודם שיתפלל כאלו עשאו במה שנאמר (ישעיה ב כב) חדלו לכם מן האדם אשר נשמה באפו כי במה נחשב הוא אל תקרי

what) but read Bamah (a heathen altar)." Samuel explains it, with what right didst thou pay thy regard to him [whom you greeted] and not to God? R. Shesheth raised the following objection: [We have been taught in a Mishnah] "Between the sections he may salute a respectable man and answer," [and the Sh'm'a is before the Eighteen Benedictions and yet one is allowed to salute a respectable man]. R. Abba explained that Rab deals with a man who visits his neighbor for the sole purpose of greeting him before he has prayed [therefore it is wrong, but the Mishnah refers to one who happened to meet his neighbor]. R. Jonah in the name of R. Zeira said: "Whoever greets his friend before he has prayed [is considered as if he] has erected a heathen altar." Questioned by his disciples whether he really meant 'a, heathen altar,' he replied: "I meant that 'it is prohibited,'" as R. Ide b. Abin, who said in the name of R. Isaac b. Assian: "It is prohibited to greet a friend and to go out to business before one has prayed, for it is said (Ps. 85, 14.) Righteousness will go before him." Further said R. Ide b. Abin, in the name of R. Isaac b. Assian: "For him who prays first and then goes to his undertakings, the Holy One, praised be He! will fulfill his desires, for it is said (Ib.) Righteousness will go before him, and will (level) the way by its steps."

R. Jonah in the name of R. Zeira said: "He who passed seven nights [in succession] without dreaming, is to be called wicked, for it is said (Pr. 19. 23.) And he (that hath it) shall abide satisfied: he shall not be visited with evil. Do not read Sabea (satisfied) but read Sheba (seven)." R. Acha, the son of R. Chija and the grandson of R. Abba, said to him, "Thus had said R. Chiya in the name of R. Jochanan: 'He who goes to sleep after he has satisfied himself with the words of the Torah will never be the recipient of bad tidings, as it is said (Ib.) And he [that hath it] shall abide satisfied, he shall not be visited with evil.' "

(Ib. b) Ulla said: "Whoever reads the Sh'm'a without wearing Tephilin, is like one who testifies falsely against himself." R. Chiya b. Abba in the name of R. Jochanan says: "It is as if he had offered a burnt offering without the meal offering, or a sacrifice without the accompanying wine offering." R. Jochanan said: "He who desires to take upon himself the yoke of the Heavenly Kingdom perfectly (Fol. 15a) must first ease himself, wash his hands, lay Tephilin, read the Sh'm'a and pray [the Eighteen Benedictions]: this is the perfect acknowledgment of the Heavenly Kingdom." R. Chiya b. Abba said: "Whoever eases himself, washes his hands, lays Tephilin, reads the Sh'm'a and prays [the Eighteen Benedictions], is considered as having built an altar and offered a sacrifice upon it, for it is said (Ps. 26. 6.) I will wash in purity mine hands, and I will compass thy altar. O Lord." Raba said unto him (R. Chiya b. Abba): "Does not the master consider the washing of the hands just as if he bathed? For it is written I will wash in purify [which indicates for the whole body], and it is not written I wash my hands."

Further said R. Chama, son of R. Chanina: (Fol. 16a) "Why have Tents been placed near Streams? As is written (Num. 24. 6.) As streams are they spread forth, as gardens by the river's side, as tents which the Lord hath planted, etc. To teach you that just as

רבי חייא אמר רבי יוחנן כל המשביע עצמו מדברי תורה ולן אין מבשרין אותו בשורות רעות. שנאמר ושבע ילין בל יפקד רע:

(ע"ב) אמר עולא כל הקורא קריאת שמע בלא תפילין כאילו מעיד עדות שקר בעצמו. ורבי חייא בר אבא אמר רבי יוחנן כאילו הקריב עולה בלא מנחה וזבח בלא נסכים. אמר רבי יוחנן הרוצה שיקבל עליו עול מלכות שמים שלמה (דף טו) יפנה ויטול ידיו ויניח תפילין ויקרא ק"ש ויתפלל וזו היא מלכות שמים שלמה. א"ר חייא בר אבא אמר רבי יוחנן כל הנפנה ונוטל ידיו ומניח תפילין וקורא ק"ש ומתפלל מעלה עליו הכתוב כאילו בנה מזבח והקריב עליו קרבן שנאמר (תהלים כו ו) ארחץ בנקיון כפי ואסובבה את מזבחך ה'. אמר ליה רבא לא סבר לה מר כאילו טבל דכתיב ארחץ בנקיון ולא כתיב ארחיץ כפי:

ואמר רבי חמא בר' חנינא למה נסמכו (דף טז) אהלים, לנחלים דכתיב (במדבר כד ו) כנחלים נטיו כגנות עלי נהר כאהלים נטע וגו'. לומר לך מה נחלים מעלים את האדם מטומאה לטהרה אף אהלים

streams render an impure man pure, so tents [where the Torah is studied] lift up man from the scale of guilt to the scale of merit."

Our Rabbis taught: "Only three are called Patriarchs (Abraham, Isaac, and Jacob), and only four are called mothers (Sarah, Rebecca, Rachael, and Leah)." Why is this so? Shall I say because we do not know [after these] whether one is a descendant of Reuben or of Simon: if so then as to the mothers: we also do not know whether one is a descendant of Leah or Rachael? But, it is because these are highly notable [and deserve to be called fathers and mothers], but those succeeding them are not so notable.

(Ib. b) R. Elazar said: "What means the passage (Ps. 63, 4.) Thus I will bless Thee while I live; in Thy name will I lift up my hands? i.e., Thus will I bless Thee, refers to the Sh'm'a, In Thy name will I lift up my hands, refers to the prayer of the Eighteen Benedictions; and for him who does so, says the passage (Ib. ib. 5.) As with fat and marrow shall my soul be satisfied, and moreover he will inherit both this and the future world, as it is said (Ib.) And with joyful lips shall my mouth praise Thee." R. Elazar after he had finished his [daily] prayers made the following prayer: "May it be Thy will, O Lord, our God, that Thou shalt cause to dwell in our lot (midst), love and brotherhood, peace and friendship; and Thou shalt increase our territory with scholars; that Thou shalt cause us to realize into a prosperous end and into hopefulness; that Thou shalt establish our share in Paradise, and direct us in this world by means of good

מעלים את האדם מכף חובה לכף זכות:

תנו רבנן אין קורין אבות אלא לשלשה ואין קורין אמהות אלא לד׳. אבות מ״ט. אילימא משום דלא ידעינן אי מראובן קא אתינן אי משמעון קא אתינן. אי הכי אמהות נמי לא ידעינן אי מרחל קא אתינן אי מלאה קא אתינן. אלא עד הכי חשיבי, טפי לא חשיבי:

(ע״ב) אמר רבי אלעזר מאי דכתיב (תהלים סג ד) כן אברכך בחיי בשמך אשא כפי, כן אברכך, זו קריאת שמע. בשמך אשא כפי זו תפלה, ואם עשה כן עליו הכתוב אומר (שם סג ה) כמו חלב ודשן תשבע נפשי, ולא עוד אלא שנוחל שני עולמים, העולם הזה והעולם הבא שנאמר (שם) ושפתי רננות יהלל פי. רבי אלעזר בתר דמסיים צלותיה אמר הכי יהי רצון מלפניך ה׳ אלהינו שתשכן בפורנו אהבה ואחוה שלום ורעות ותרבה גבולנו בתלמידים ותצליח סופנו אחרית ותקוה ותשים חלקנו בגן עדן ותקננו בחבר טוב ויצר טוב בעולמך ונשכים ונמצא ייחול לבבנו ליראה את שמך ותבא לפניך קורת נפשנו לטובה. רבי יוחנן בתר דמסיים צלותיה אמר הכי יהי

associates and with a good inclination so that when we rise we shall find the inclination of our hearts to fear Thy name, and all the necessities [of our souls and the requirements of our well-being] shall appear before Thee." R. Jochanan after he had finished his prayer made the following prayer: "May it be Thy will, O Lord, our God, that Thou shalt see our shame and shalt look upon our misfortunes and shalt clothe Thyself with Thy mercy and cover Thyself with Thy strength and enwrap Thyself with Thy pity and gird Thyself with Thy gracefulness and let come before Thee the attribute of Thy compassion and Thy meekness." R. Zeira when he had finished his [daily] prayer was wont to make the following prayer: "May it be Thy will, O Lord, our God, that we shall sin no more and we shall not be shamed nor reproached by our parents." Rab Chiya, after he finished Ins [daily] prayer was accustomed to say the following prayer: "May it be Thy will, O Lord, our God, that your Torah shall be our occupation and that we shall not suffer with our heart nor shall our eyes become darkened." Rab, when he had finished his [daily] prayer, would make the following prayer: "May it be Thy will, O Lord, our God, and the God of our fathers, that Thou shalt grant us long life, a life of peace, of good, of blessing, of sustenance, of bodily vigor marked by the fear of Heaven and the dread of sin; a life free from shame and reproach, a life of prosperity and honor, a life wherein shall dwell in us the love of the Torah and the fear of Heaven, a life in which the desires of our hearts be fulfilled for good."

Rabbi when he had finished his [daily] prayer made the following prayer: "May it be Thy

רצון מלפניך ה׳ אלהינו שתציץ בבשתנו ותביט ברעתנו ותתלבש ברחמיך ותתכסה בעוזך ותתעטף בחסידותך ותתאזר בחנינותך ותבא לפניך מדת טובך וענותנותך. רבי זירא בתר דמסיים צלותיה אמר הכי יהי רצון מלפניך ה׳ אלהינו שלא נחטא ולא נבוש ולא נכלם מאבותינו. רבי חייא בתר דמצלי אמר הכי יהי רצון מלפניך ה׳ אלהינו שתהא תורתך אומנותנו ואל ידוח לבנו ואל יחשכו עינינו. רב בתר צלותיה אמר הכי יהר"מ ה׳ אלהינו שתתן לנו חיים ארוכים חיים של שלום חיים של טובה חיים של ברכה חיים של פרנסה חיים של חלוץ עצמות חיים שיש בהם יראת שמים ויראת חטא חיים שאין בהם בושה וכלימה חיים של עושר וכבוד חיים שתהא בנו אהבת תורה ויראת שמים חיים שתמלא לנו את כל משאלות לבנו לטובה:

רבי בתר צלותיה אמר הכי יהי רצון מלפניך ה׳ אלהינו

will, O Lord, my God, "and the God of my fathers, to deliver me from arrogant men and from arrogance; from a bad man, from any mishap, from a bad associate, from a bad inclination, and from a bad neighbor, and from the adversary' that destroyeth; from a severe judgment and from a severe opponent, whether it be a son of the covenant (Jew) or a son not of the covenant;" and although constables were at Rabbi's disposal [yet he prayed to God for help]. R. Safra when he had finished his [daily] prayer made the following prayer: "May it be Thy will, O Lord, our God, to make peace (Fol. 17a) in the heavenly household (the angels) and the household here below on earth; between the scholars who study Thy Torah for its own sake and those who study, not for its own sake [but for selfish ends]; and concerning all those who study it not for its own sake, may it be Thy will that they shall begin to study it for the Torah's sake."

R. Alexandri when he finished his [daily] prayer was wont to say the following prayer: "May it be Thy will, O Lord, our God, that Thou place us in the corner of light [honorable position] and shalt not place us in the corner of obscurity and our hearts shall not suffer nor shall our eyes become darkened." Some say this was the prayer of R. Hamnuna, and R. Alexandri when he finished his [daily] prayer said the following: "Sovereign of all universe! It is revealed and well known to Thee that our desire is to do Thy will. What prevents it but the leaven of the dough (evil inclination) and the subjugation of the exile? May it he Thy will, O Lord, our God, to deliver us from their hands, and we shall return to perform the

ואלהי אבותינו שתצילני מעזי פנים ומעזות פנים מאדם רע ומפגע רע מחבר רע מיצר רע משכן רע ומשטן המשחית מדין קשה ומבעל דין קשה בין שהוא בן ברית ובין שאינו בן ברית ואף על גב דקיימי קצוצי עליה דרבי. רב ספרא בתר דמסיים צלותיה אמר הכי יהי רצון מלפניך ה' אלהינו שתשים שלום (דף יז) בפמליא של מעלה ובפמליא של מטה ובין התלמידים העוסקים בתורתך בין עוסקים לשמה בין עוסקים שלא לשמה וכל העוסקין שלא לשמה יהי רצון מלפניך שיהיו עוסקין לשמה:

רבי אלכסנדרי בתר צלותיה אמר הכי יהי רצון מלפניך ה' אלהינו שתעמידנו בקרן אורה ואל תעמידנו בקרן השכר. ואל ידוה לבנו ואל יחשכו עינינו. איכא דאמרי הא רב המנונא מצלי לה, ורבי אלכסנדרי בתר צלותיה אמר הכי. רבון העולמים גלוי וידוע לפניך שרצונו לעשות רצונך ומי מעכב שאור שבעיסה ושעבוד גליות. יהי רצון מלפניך ה' אלהינו שתכניע מלפנינו ומאחרינו ונשוב לעשות חקי רצונך בלבב שלם. מר בריה דרב הונא בתר צלותיה אמר הכי אלהי נצור לשוני מרע ושפתותי

decrees of Thy will with a perfect heart." Mar, the son of R. Huna, when he had finished his [daily] prayer, would make the following prayer: "O my God! Guard my tongue from evil and my lips from speaking guile. To such as curse me, let my soul be dumb, yea, let my soul be unto all as the dust. Open my heart to Thy Torah, and let my soul pursue Thy commandments. Deliver me from any mishap, from evil inclination, from a bad wife and from evils which break forth and visit the world. If any design evil against me, speedily make their counsel of no effect, and frustrate their designs. Do it for the sake of Thy name; do it for the sake of Thy right hand; do it for the sake of Thy holiness, do it for the sake of Thy Torah; in order that Thy beloved ones may be delivered; O save [me] with Thy right hand and answer me; may the words of my mouth and the meditation of my heart be acceptable before Thee, O Lord, my Rock and my Redeemer."

מדבר מרמה ולמקללי נפשי תדום ונפשי כעפר לכל תהיה פתח לבי בתורתך ובמצותיך תרדוף נפשי ותצילנו מפגע רע מיצר הרע ומאשה רעה ומכל רעות המתרגשות לבוא בעולם, וכל החושבים עלי רעה מהרה הפר עצתם וקלקל מחשבותם. יהיו לרצון אמרי פי והגיון לבי לפניך ה׳ צורי וגואלי:

Raba when he had finished his prayer made the following prayer: "O my God, before I was formed, I was nothing worth; now that I have been formed, I am but as though I had not been formed. Dust am I in my life, how much more so in my death! Behold I am before Thee like a vessel filled with shame and confusion. O may it be Thy will, O Lord, my God, and God of my father, that I may sin no more; as to the sins I have committed, purge them in thine abundant compassion but not by means of affliction and sore disease." This was the confession (Vidui) of R. Hamnuna Zuta on the Day of Atonement.

רבא בתר צלותיה אמר הכי אלהי עד שלא נוצרתי איני כדאי ועכשיו שנוצרתי כאלו לא נוצרתי עפר אני בחיי קל וחומר במיתתי הרי אני לפניך ככלי מלא בושה וכלמה יהי רצון מלפניך ה׳ אלהי שלא אחטא עוד ומה שחטאתי לפניך מרק ברחמיך הרבים אבל לא על ידי יסורים וחלאים רעים. והיינו וידוי דרב המנונא זוטא ביומא דכפורא:

When R. Shesheth fasted after he had finished his usual prayer, he would say the

רב ששת כי הוה יתיב בתעניתא בתר דמצלי אמר

following prayer: "Sovereign of the universe, it is known to Thee that during the time the Holy Temple was in existence, if a man sinned he was to bring an offering of which only its fat and blood was offered upon the altar, yet his sin was expiated; and now I have been sitting in fast, thus causing a diminishing of my fat and blood; may it therefore be Thy will that the amount of my fat and blood thus diminished shall be considered as an offering unto Thee upon the altar and acceptable as such."

R. Jochanan, when he finished the book of Job, would say: "The end of man is to die; the end of an animal is to be slaughtered; all are bound to die; happy is he who has been brought up to study the Torah and put his energy in the Torah; and is a source of pleasure to his Creator; he shall grow with a good name and shall depart from the world with a good name." It is concerning such a man that Solomon said in his wisdom (Ecc. 7, 1.) A good name is better than precious ointment. R. Meier was accustomed to say: "Learn with all thy heart and soul to know my (the Torah's) ways, and to watch upon the gates of my Torah; guard my learning in thy heart and let my fear be before thy eyes; guard thy mouth from all sins, cleanse and purify thyself from all guilts and iniquities and I shall then be with thee in all places." The Rabbis of Jabnai were accustomed to say: "I am a human being; so is my neighbor a human being. My work is in the city and his work is in the field; I rise early to my work and he rises early to his work; as he cannot excel in my work, so can I not interfere in his. Shall I say that I am advancing the cause of learning more than he? We are therefore taught 'Whether one [offers] much or little

הכי רבון העולמים גלוי לפניך בזמן שבית המקדש קיים אדם חוטא ומקריב קרבן ואין מקריבין ממנו אלא חלבו ודמו ומתכפר לו ועכשיו ישבתי בתענית ונתמעט חלבי ודמי יהי רצון מלפניך שיהא חלבי ודמי שנתמעט כאלו הקרבתיו לפניך על גבי המזבח ותרצני:

רבי יוחנן כי הוה מסיים ספרא דאיוב אמר הכי סוף אדם למות וסוף בהמה לשחיטה והכל למיתה הם עומדים אשרי מי שגדל בתורה ועמלו בתורה ועושה נחת רוח ליוצרו וגדל בשם טוב ונפטר בשם טוב מן העולם. ועליו אמר שלמה בחכמתו (קהלת ז א) טוב שם משמן טוב ויום המות מיום הולדו. מרגלא בפומיה דר"מ גמור בכל לבבך ובכל נפשך לדעת את דרכי ולשקוד על דלתי תורתי יום יום נצור תורתי בלבך ונגד עיניך תהיה יראתי. שמור פיך מכל חטא. וטהר וקדש עצמך מכל אשמה ועון. ואני אהיה עמך בכל מקום. מרגלא בפומייהו דרבנן דיבנה אני בריה וחברי בריה. אני מלאכתי בעיר. והוא מלאכתו בשדה. אני משכים למלאכתי והוא משכים למלאכתו. כשם שהוא איננו מתגדר במלאכתי כך אני איני מתגדר במלאכתו. שמא תאמר אני מרבה והוא ממעיט. שנינו אחד המרבה ואחד הממעיט

only the intention of his heart shall be for the sake of Heaven.' " Abaye was accustomed to say: "Man should" always be deliberate for the fear of God (consider in what manner he can serve Him best); reply softly; try to pacify anger, and speak peacefully with his brethren, with his relatives and with every man, even with the heathen; so that he may be beloved in Heaven and below (on the earth) and acceptable by men." It was related of R. Jochanan b. Zakai that never, was he greeted first by any one, even by a heathen; for he always greeted people first. Raba was accustomed to say: "The end of wisdom is repentance and good deeds, lest a man read and study and speak with contempt against his father or mother or teacher, or against those superior to him in wisdom or exceeding in number. For it is said (Ps. 111, 10.) The beginning of wisdom is the fear of God; a good understanding have all they who do God's commands. It does not say Who study God's commands, but Who do God's commands, i.e., to them who do it for God's sake, but not to them who do it for their own sakes. And as for the man who does [study the Torah] not for its own sake, it would have been more satisfactory had he not been created." Rab was wont to say: "The future world will not be like this world. In the future world there will be neither eating nor drinking nor multiplying nor business nor envy nor hatred nor competition; only the righteous will sit with their crowns upon their heads and will enjoy the Divine Glory, as it is written (Ex. 24, 11.) And they saw God and they ate and drank." Our Rabbis taught: "The promise which the Holy One, praised be He! made unto women is much greater than that which He made

ובלבד שיכוין את לבו לשמים. מרגלא בפומיה דאביי לעולם יהא אדם ערום ביראה מענה רך ומשיב חמה ומדבר שלום עם אחיו ועם קרוביו ועם כל אדם. (ס״פ הנזקין וע״ש רש״א) ואפילו עם עובד כוכבים בשוק כדי שיהא אהוב למעלה ונחמד למטה ויהא מקובל על הבריות. אמרו עליו על רבן יוחנן בן זכאי שלא הקדימו אדם שלום מעולם אפילו עובד כוכבים בשוק. מרגלא בפומיה דרבא תכלית חכמה תשובה ומעשים טובים שלא יהא אדם קורא ושונה ובועט באביו ובאמו או ברבו או במי שגדול ממנו בחכמה ובמנין שנאמר (תהלים קיא י) ראשית חכמה יראת ה' שכל טוב לכל עושיהם תהלתו עומדת לעד. ללומדיהם לא נאמר אלא לעושיהם. לעושים לשמה ולא לעושים שלא לשמה וכל העושים שלא לשמה נוח להם שלא נבראו. מרגלא בפומיה דרב לא כהעולם הזה העולם הבא העולם הבא אין בו לא אכילה ולא שתיה ולא פריה ורביה ולא משא ומתן ולא קנאה ולא שנאה ולא תחרות אלא צדיקים יושבים ועטרותיהם בראשיהם נהנין מזיו השכינה שנאמר (שמות כד יא) ויחזו את האלהים ויאכלו וישתו. ת״ר גדולה הבטחה שהבטיחן הקב״ה לנשים יותר מן האנשים שנאמר (ישעיה לב ט) נשים שאננות קומנה, שמענה קולי בנות בוטחות האזנה אמרתי. אמר

unto men. for it is said (Is. 32, 9.) Rise up, ye women that are at ease, hear my voice; Ye careless daughters, give ear unto my speech." Rab said unto E. Chiya: "Wherewith do women [who do not study the Torah] deserve Divine Grace?" "Because," answered he, "they bring their children into school to learn and send their husbands to the house of study, and wait for their return." When the Rabbis departed from the academy of R. Ami, and according to others from the academy of R. Chanina, they were accustomed to say: "Mayest thou see (enjoy) thy existence during thy lifetime, and thy future [reward be reserved] for the life of the world to come, and thy only hope shall be [to endure] for everlasting generations. May thy heart reason with understanding, thy mouth utter wisdom, and thy eyelids shall direct thee straight forward in the Laws, and thine eyes lighten in the enlightenment of the Torah; may thy countenance shine like the brilliant sky; thy lips utter knowledge and thy kidneys rejoice in uprightness, and thy feet run to listen to the words of the Ancient in Days." When the Rabbis departed from the academy of R. Chisda and according to some from the academy of R. Samuel b. Nachmeini, they were in the habit of saying: May our oxen be strong to labor (Ps. 144, 14). Rab and Samuel, and some say R. Jochanan and R. Elazar, [explain the above passage]. One said: "Alupheinu (our oxen), alludes to the Torah and Messubalim (strong to labor), alludes to meritorious deeds;" and the other said "Alupheinu alludes to both the Torah and meritorious deeds, and Messubalim alludes to afflictions." (Ib. b) May there he no breach, (Ib.) i.e., that our following be not like that of Saul's company of whom Do'ag

ליה רב לרבי חייא נשים במאי זכיין. באקרויי בנייהו לבי כנישתא ובאתנויי גברייהו בי רבנן ומנטרן לגברייהו עד דאתו מבי רבנן. כי מפטרי רבנן מבי רבי אמי ואמרי לה מבי רבי חנינא אמרי ליה הכי. עולמך תראה בחייך ואחריתך לחיי העולם הבא ותקותך לדור דורים לבך יהגה תבונה פיך ידבר חכמות ולשונך ירחיש רננות עפעפיך יישירו נגדך עיניך יאירו במאור תורה ופניך יזהירו כזוהר הרקיע שפתותיך יביעו דעת וכליותיך תעלוזנה מישרים ופעמיך ירוצו לשמוע דברי עתיק יומין. כי הוו מפטרי רבנן מבי רב חסדא ואמרי לה מבי רבי שמואל בר נחמני אמרו ליה הכי. (תהלים קמד יד) אלופינו מסובלים. אלופינו מסובלים. רב ושמואל ואמרי לה רבי יוחנן ורבי אלעזר. חד אמר אלופינו בתורה ומסובלים במצות. וחד אמר אלופינו בתורה ובמצות ומסובלים ביסורין. (ע״ב) אין פרץ שלא תהא סיעתנו כסיעתו של שאול שיצא ממנו דואג האדומי. ואין יוצאת שלא תהא סיעתנו כסיעתו של דוד שיצא ממנו אחיתופל. ואין צוחה שלא תהא סיעתנו כסיעתו של אלישע שיצא ממנו גחזי. ברחובותינו שלא יהיה בינינו בן או תלמיד שמקדיח תבשילו ברבים. (ישעיה מו יב) שמעי אלי אבירי לב הרחוקים מצדקה. רב ושמואל ואמרי לה רבי יוחנן ורבי אלעזר. חד אמר

the Adomite was one. Nor land complaint (Ib.), nor shall our following be like that of Elisha of whom Geichazi was one. In our streets (Ib.), i.e., that we may not have a son or a pupil that disgraces his education in public. Hearken unto me, ye stout hearted, that are far from righteousness (Is. 46, 12). Rab and Samuel, and according to others R. Jochanan and R. Elazar, explain the meaning of this passage. One said that this means that the whole world is supported only because of the Lord's righteousness, and those mentioned by Isaiah are sustained on account of their own merits; [hence Isaiah addressed himself to the righteous]; and the others held that the entire world is sustained according to its own merits; and those [mentioned by Isaiah] even of their own merits cannot be sustained, as R. Juda in the name of Rab said; for R. Juda said in the name of Rab: "Every day a Bath Kol (heavenly voice) goes forth from Mount Horeb and says: 'The entire world is sustained by virtue of Chanina my son and as for Chanina my son himself, one Kab of Karob beans is sufficient for his maintenance, from one Friday to another Friday.'" And this disagrees with R. Juda, for R. Juda said: "Who may be called Stout hearted [referred to by Isaiah]? The inhabitants of Gabaya, the fools." And R. Joseph said: "It may be proved by the fact that never was one of them converted to Judaism." R. Ashi said: "Those sons of Matha Mechasia may also be termed Stout hearted, for they observe the praise of the Torah twice a year, yet none of them was converted to Judaism."

כל העולם כולו ניזונין בצדקה והם ניזונין בזרוע. וחד אמר כל העולם כולו ניזונין בזכותן. והם אפילו בזכות עצמן אינן ניזונין. כדרב יהודה אמר רב (תענית וע״ש רש״א) דאמר רב יהודה אמר רב בכל יום ויום בת קול יוצאת מהר חורב ואומרת כל העולם כולו ניזון בשביל חנינא בני וחנינא בני די לו בקב חרובין מערב שבת לערב שבת. ופליגא דרב יהודה דאמר רב יהודה מאן אבירי לב גובאי טפשאי. אמר רב יוסף תדע דהא לא אגייר גיורא מנייהו אמר רב אשי והלין בני מתא מחסיא אבירי לב נינהו דהא קא חזו בשבחא דאורייתא תרי זימני בשתא ולא מנייר גיורא מינייהו :

(Fol. 18a) We are taught that, "A man should not walk in a cemetery while wearing Tephillin (Phylacteries) on his head, or carrying a scroll in his arm and reading it: if he do so he transgresses against what is written (Pr. 17, 5.) Whoso mocketh the poor, blasphemeth his Maker."

Rachaba said in the name of R. Juda who spoke in the name of Rab: "He who sees the [procession of the] dead and does not take part in it transgresses against what is written (Ib.) Whoso mocketh the poor, blasphemeth his Maker." If he does take part what will be his reward? R. Ashi said, "Of such a man, it is said (Ib. 19, 17.) He that hath pity upon the poor lendeth unto the Lord; and also (Ib. 14, 31.) But he that is gracious to the needy honoreth Him" (Fol. 19a) E. Joshua b. Levi said: "He who whispers [with disgraceful intentions] behind the biers of learned men will fall into Gehenna, as it is written (Ps. 125, 5.) But as for those who turn aside into their crooked ways, the Lord shall lead them forth with the workers of wickedness; but peace shall be upon Israel, i.e., even when peace shall be upon Israel, yet shall the Lord lead them forth with the workers of wickedness." Further, said R. Joshua b. Levi: "In twenty-four cases does the court-tribunal excommunicate [a man] for not having paid due respect to the masters of the law [by transgressing their ordinances], and all these cases are mentioned in our Mishnah." R. Elazar asked of him: "Where have they been mentioned?" "Go and find," was the reply. Thereupon R. Elazar went out and sought and found three. "He who whispers behind the biers of learned men; he who disregards the washing of his hands [before meals], and

(דף יח) תניא לא יהלך אדם בבית הקברות ותפילין בראשו וס"ת בזרועו וקורא. ואם עשה כן עובר משום (משלי יז ה) לועג לרש חרף עושהו:

אמר רחבה אמר רב יהודה אמר רב כל הרואה את המת ואינו מלווהו עובר משום (שם) לועג לרש חרף עושהו. ואם לווהו מה שכרו. אמר רבי אסי עליו הכתוב אומר (שם יט יז) מלוה ה' חונן דל (שם יד לא) ומכבדו חונן אביון. (דף יט) אמר רבי יהושע בן לוי כל המספר אחר מטתן של ת"ח נופל בגיהנם שנאמר (תהלים קכה ה) והמטים עקלקלותם יוליכם ה' את פועלי האון שלום על ישראל. אפילו בשעה ששלום על ישראל יוליכם ה' את פועלי האון. תנא דבי רבי ישמעאל אם ראית ת"ח שעבר עבירה בלילה אל תהרהר אחריו ביום שמא עשה תשובה. שמא סלקא דעתך אלא ודאי עשה תשובה. אמר רבה לא אמרן אלא דברים שבגופו אבל בממונא עד דמהדר למריה. ואמר ריב"ל בכ"ד מקומות ב"ד מנדין על כבוד הרב וכולן שנינו במשנתנו. אמר ליה רבי אלעזר היכא א"ל לכי תשכח נפק דק ואשכח תלתא. המספר אחר מטתן של תלמידי חכמים והמזלזל בנטילת ידים והמגיס דעתו כלפי מעלה.

he who behaves haughtily toward Heaven." "He who whispers behind the biers of learned men." What does this mean? It is that which we are taught (in a Mishnah): "He (Akabia b. Mehallalel) also said that a female proselyte and a freed maid-servant are not given the bitter water and the sages say they are. The sages said to him, 'Did this not happen once to a certain Karkmith, a freed maid-slave in Jerusalem, who was made to drink by Shmaya and Abtalion?' He answered them: 'It was for show that they made her drink.' Thereupon the sages placed him under ban, and when he died the court stoned his coffin." Where do we find the reference to one who disregards hand-washing [before meals]? We are taught that R. Juda said: "God forbid [to think] that Akabia b. Mahallalel, who among all Israelites, when the doors of the Temple courtyard were closed, was unequaled in erudition, purity and piety, should have been excommunicated. But to whom then was it done? It was R. Elazar b. Chanoch that was excommunicated for contesting the rule of washing the hands [before the meals], and when he died, the court sent a stone to be put on his coffin; whence we learn that the coffin of him who dies while under ban is to be stoned." And what is he who behaves haughtily towards Heaven? We ere taught that Simon b. Shetaeh sent [word] to Honi the Me'agel: "If thou wert not Honi you should be excommunicated, but what shall I do with thee? since thou art petulant towards God and yet He forgiveth and indulgeth thee like a petted child who is petulant towards his father and is nevertheless forgiven and indulged? To thee may be applied the passage (Pr. 23, 25.) Let (then.) thy father and thy mother rejoice,

המספר אחר מטתן של תלמידי חכמים מאי היא דתנן הוא היה אומר אין משקין לא את הגיורת ולא את המשוחררת וחכמים אומרין משקין. אמר ליה מעשה בכרכמית אחת שפחה משוחררת בירושלים והשקוה שמעיה ואבטליון. אמר ליה דוגמא השקוה. ונדוהו ומת בנדויו וסקלו בית דין את ארונו. המזלזל בנטילת ידים מאי היא דתנן אמר רבי יהודה ח"ו שעקביא בן מהללאל נתנדה שאין העזרה ננעלת על כל אדם מישראל בחכמה ובטהרה וביראת חטא כעקביא בן מהללאל אלא את מי נדו את אלעזר בן חנוך שפקפק בנטילת ידים. ובשמת שלחו ב"ד והניחו אבן גדולה על ארונו ללמדך שכל המתנדה ומת בנדויו בית דין סוקלין את ארונו. המגיס דעתו כלפי מעלה מאי היא. דתנן שלח לו שמעון בן שטח לחוני המעגל צריך אתה להתנדות ואלמלא חוני אתה גוזרני עליך נדוי אבל מה אעשה שאתה מתחטא לפני המקום ועושה לך רצונך כבן שמתחטא לפני אביו ועושה לו רצונו ועליך הכתוב אומר (משלי כג כה) ישמח אביך ואמך ותגל יולדתך:

and let her that hath born thee be glad."

(Fol. 20a) R. Papa asked Abaye: "Why is it that in the preceding generation miracles happened and no miracles happen to us? Is it because they studied more? Behold, during the years of R. Juda, all studied only the order of Nezikin (civil procedure, or damages) while we study all six orders. And when R. Juda reached in the Treatise Uktzin (Stalks), [treating with the law of] 'The woman who pressed vegetables in a pot', or, as some say [to the Mishnab of], 'Olives when pressed with their leaves are [ritually] pure,' he said: 'I notice here the argument of Rab and Samuel [which are beyond my mind].' While we are versed in the treatise of Uktzin in thirteen different ways, yet [when it comes to prayer] as soon as R. Juda had pulled off one of his shoes, rain immediately appeared, and though we afflict ourselves, and keep on crying [for God's help] yet none cares for us." "Do you know why? Abaye said to R. Papa, "because, the former generations were ready to sacrifice their lives to sanctify His name but we are not ready to sacrifice our lives to sanctify His name, as happened once to R. Ada b. Ahaba, who saw a Gentile woman wearing a red headgear-dress while walking in the market place. Believing her to he a Jewess he impatiently tore off her red headgear. It was found that she was a Gentile, and he was fined four hundred zouzim, the value of the dress. He asked the woman what her name was. 'My name is Mathan,' she answered him. 'Mathun, Mathun,' he rejoined, 'is worth four hundred zouzim.'"

(Ib. b) R. Avira expounded, sometimes speaking in the name of R. Ami, and at other times speaking in the name of R. Assi: The ministering angels said before the Holy One, Praised be He! "Sovereign of the universe, it is written in Thy Torah (Deu. 10, 17.) Who shows no favor to persons, and taketh no bribe. Behold Thou showest favors to Israel, for it is written (Num. 6. 26.) The Lord will show His favor unto thee." "Why shall I not favor Israel?" answered He, "for I wrote in my Torah which I gave to them (Deu. 8, 10.) And when thou hast eaten and are satisfied, then shalt thou bless. But they are so particular and careful that even if they eat only as much as the size of an olive or an egg, they also recite the after-meal grace."

(Fol. 21a) E. Juda said, "Whence do we learn that the after-meal grace is a Biblical law? It is written (Ib.) And when thou hast eaten and art satisfied, then shalt thou bless the Lord, thy God. Whence do we learn [that to say] the benediction before beginning the study of the Torah is a Biblical law? It is said (Deu. 32, 3.) When I call on the name of the Lord ascribe ye greatness unto our God."

(Ib. b) R. Ada b. Ahaba said: "Whence do we learn that a single man must not say the Kedusha? It is said (Lev. 22, 32.) So that I may be sanctified among the children of Israel; i.e., everything holy should not be said by less than ten (men)." How does he prove this? Rabanai, the brother of R. Chiya b. Abba explained it: "We deduce it [first] from the words Toch, Toch: it is written here, So that I may be sanctified Betoch (among) the children of Israel, and it is written there (Num. 16, 21.) Separate yourselves Mitoch (from the midst of) the congregation (Eda); [as in the latter case the word Toch in connection with Eda refers to

א״ל משמיה דרבי אסי אמרו מלאכי השרת לפני הקב״ה רבש״ע כתיב בתורתך (דברים י יז) אשר לא ישא פנים ולא יקח שוחד. והלא אתה נושא פנים לישראל דכתיב (במדבר ו כו) ישא ה׳ פניו אליך. אמר להם וכי לא אשא פנים לישראל שכתבתי להם בתורה (דברים ח י) ואכלת ושבעת וברכת את ה׳ אלהיך והם דקדקו על עצמם עד כזית ועד כביצה:

(דף כא) אמר רב יהודה מנין לברכת המזון לאחריה מן התורה שנא׳ (דברים ח י) ואכלת ושבעת וברכת. מנין לברכת התורה לפניה מן התורה שנאמר (שם לב ג) כי שם ה׳ אקרא הבו גדל לאלהינו:

(ע״ב) אמר רב אדא בר אהבה מנין שאין היחיד אומר קדושה שנאמר (ויקרא כב לב) ונקדשתי בתוך בני ישראל כל דבר שבקדושה לא יהא בפחות מעשרה. מאי משמע. דתנא רבנאי אחוה דרבי חייא בר אבא אתיא תוך תוך כתיב הכא ונקדשתי בתוך בני ישראל וכתיב התם (במדבר טז כא) הבדלו מתוך העדה הזאת ואתיא עדה עדה דכתיב התם (שם יד כז) עד מתי לעדה הרעה הזאת. מה להלן עשרה אף כאן עשרה:

ten, so in the former case, the word Toch, although alone, also refers to ten]. Again we deduce [that the latter passage where Toch is mentioned in connection with Eda refers to ten], from the words, Eda, Eda: it is written (Ib. 14, 27.) How long (shall indulgence he given) to this evil Eda (congregation). as that passage [where Eda is mentioned alone] refers to ten (the spies, who were twelve, excluding Joshua and Kaleb) so in the passage where Eda is mentioned in connection with Toch, does it also refer to ten."

(Fol. 24b) R. Abba tried to avoid the sight of R. Juda because he wanted to go to Palestine and R. Juda always said: "Whoever goes up from Babylon to Palestine transgresses the positive law which says (Jer. 27, 22.) Unto Babylon shall they be carried, and there shall they remain until the day that I think of them, saith the Lord." One day R. Abba said I shall go and hear something from him and then I will depart. So he went and found a Tana reciting before R. Juda regarding cleanliness, while praying. (See text.) R. Abba then said, "Were it only for that single thing that I came to listen, it would be sufficient."

(דף כד ע"ב) רבי אבא הוה קא מישתמיט מיניה דרב יהודה דהוה כעי למיסק לארעא דישראל דאמר רב יהודה כל העולה מבבל לארץ ישראל עובר בעשה שנאמר (ירמיה כז כב) בבלה יובאו ושמה יהיו עד יום פקדי אותם נאם ה'. אמר איזיל ואשמע מיניה מילתא מבית וועדא והדר אפיק. אזל אשכחיה לתנא דקתני קמיה דרב יהודה היה עומד בתפלה ונתעטש ממתין עד שיכלה הרוח וחוזר ומתפלל. א"ל אילו לא באתי אלא לשמוע דבר זה דיי:

We have a Baraitha coinciding with R. Chisda's opinion: "If one is walking in filthy alleys, he should not read the Sh'm'a; moreover, even if he were in the middle of his reading and should happen to find himself in a filthy street, he should stop." If he do not stop, what then? R. Meyasha the grandson of R. Joshua b. Levi said: It is of him that the passage says (Ezek. 20, 25.) "Wherefore I gave them also statutes that

תניא כוותיה דרב חסדא היה מהלך במבואות המטונפות לא יקרא קריאת שמע ולא עוד אלא שאם היה קורא ובא פוסק. לא פסק מאי אמר רבי מיאשה בר בריה דרבי יהושע בן לוי עליו הכתוב אומר (יחזקאל כ כה) וגם אני נתתי להם חקים לא טובים ומשפטים בל יחיו בהם. רבי אסי אמר (ישעיה ה יח) הוי

were not good, and ordinances whereby they could not live. R. Assi said from this (Is. 5, 18.) Woe unto those that draw iniquity with the cord of vanity. R. Ada b. Ahaba said from this (Num. 15, 31.) Because the word of the Lord hath he despised. And if he does stop what will his reward be? R. Abuhu said: "To him may be applied the passage (Deu. 32, 47.) And through this thing ye shall prolong your days."

מושכי העון בחבלי השוא. רב אדא בר אהבה אמר מהכא (במדבר טו לא) כי דבר ה' בזה. ואם פסק מה שכרו א"ר אבהו עליו הכתוב אומר (דברים לב מז) ובדבר הזה תאריכו ימים:

Chapter 4

Chapter 4

(Fol. 26b) We are taught (in a Memera)' that R. Jose the son of R. Chanina said: "The daily services were ordained by the Patriarchs (Abraham, Isaac and Jacob)." R. Joshua b. Levi said: "The daily services were ordained to correspond with the [two] perpetual-daily-offerings." We have a Baraitha coinciding with the opinion of R. Jose, the son of R. Chanina, and we have also a Baraitha coinciding with the opinion of R. Joshua b. Levi. As to the support of R. Jose we are taught, "Abraham ordained the morning service, as it is said (Gen. 19, 27.) And Abraham rose up early in the morning to the place where he had stood before the Lord. Omad (stood) refers to nothing else but prayer; for it is said (Ps. 106, 30.) Then stood up (Vaya'amod) Phinehas and offered a prayer. Isaac ordained the afternoon service (Mincha), for it is said (Gen. 24, 63.) And Isaac went out 'Lasuach' in the field towards evening. By the word Lasuach is meant prayer, for it is said (Ps. 102, 1.) A prayer of the afflicted when he is overwhelmed and poureth out before the

(דף כו ע"ב) איתמר רבי יוסי ברבי חנינא אמר תפלות אבות תקנום. רבי יהושע בן לוי אמר תפלות כנגד תמידים תקנום. תניא כוותיה דרבי יוסי ברבי חנינא ותניא כוותיה דרבי יהושע בן לוי. תניא כוותיה רבי יוסי ברבי חנינא אברהם תקן תפלת שחרית שנאמר (בראשית יט כז) וישכם אברהם בבקר אל המקום אשר עמד שם את פני ה' ואין עמידה אלא תפלה שנאמר (תהלים קו ל) ויעמוד פינחס ויפלל יצחק תקן תפלת המנחה שנאמר (בראשית כד סג) ויצא יצחק לשוח בשדה לפנות ערב ואין שיחה אלא תפלה שנא' (תהלים קב א) תפלה לעני כי יעטוף ולפני ה' ישפוך שיחו יעקב תקן תפלת ערבית שנא' (בראשית כח יא) ויפגע במקום וילן שם ואין פגיעה אלא תפלה שנא' (ירמיה ז טז) ואתה אל תתפלל בעד העם הזה ואל תשא בעדם

Lord his complaint (Sicho). Jacob ordained the evening service (Ma'arib), for it is said (Gen. 28, 11.) Vayifg'a upon a certain place, and tarried there all night; by the word Vayifg'a, prayer is meant, for it is said (Jer. 7, 16.) But thou — pray not thou in behalf of this people, nor lift up entreaty or prayer in their behalf, nor make intercession to me (Tifga)." We are taught, coinciding with the opinion of R. Joshua b. Levi: "Why did [the Rabbis] say that the time for the morning service is until noon? Because the perpetual-daily-morning-offering had also its time limited to noon. R. Juda says: Until the fourth hour of the day."

(Fol. 27b) We are taught that R. Eliezer says: "He who prays behind his teacher, he who greets his teacher [without calling him Rabbi], he who opposes his teacher's school [by organizing a separate academy], and who makes statements [in his teacher's name] that he did not hear from his teacher, causes the departure of the Shechinah from Israel." Our Rabbis taught: That once a disciple appeared before R. Joshua and said to him: "Rabbi, is the evening service optional or obligatory?" "Optional," answered R. Joshua. He then came before Rabban Gamaliel and asked the same question: "Is the evening service optional or obligatory?" "Obligatory," was Rabban Gamaliel's answer. "Behold! R. Joshua said to me it is optional!" the disciple remarked. Whereupon Rabban Gamaliel replied, "Wait until the shield bearers (great scholars) enter the house of learning." As soon as the shield bearers entered the house of learning, the inquirer arose and asked, "Is the evening service optional or obligatory?" "Obligatory," responded Rabban Gamaliel. "Is there any one here differing with me on this subject?" inquired Rabban Gamaliel of the scholars. "No," came the answer from R. Joshua. "Behold," interrupted Rabban Gamaliel, "it is said in your name that the service is only optional. Arise Joshua! And let the witness testify against thee!" R. Joshua stood up and said: "Were I alive and he (the witness) dead, I would have been able to deny it, but now, when I am alive and he is alive, how can one living being deny another living being?" So Rabban Gamaliel continued his lecture while R. Josliua remained standing, until all the people moved in excitement and said to Chutzephith the Meturgeman, "Stop!" and he stopped. "How long," said they, "shall we permit R. Joshua to be afflicted and reproached? Last New Year Rabban Gamaliel afflicted and reproached him. In Bechoroth, in the incident of R. Zadok, Rabban Gamaliel annoyed him and now again he reproached and afflicted him; shall we allow such annoyance to be continued? Let us take steps to deprive him of his dignity (of being the Exilareh). But who shall be his successor? Shall we put up R. Joshua? He is his chief opponent [and it would cause him too much aggravation]. Shall we put up R. Akiba? He has no ancestral merits, and may be disposed to Heavenly punishment [through prayers]. Let us therefore choose R. Elazar b. Azaria for he is wise, rich, and the tenth descendant of Ezra. He is wise, and therefore will be able to answer when questioned; he is rich and therefore, if ordered to attend the Emperor's court [of Rome], he will be as well able to do so as Rabban Gamaliel; he is the tenth descendant of Ezra and has therefore ancestral merits, and he (Rabban Gamaliel) will not be able to afflict upon him Heavenly

ועכשיו שאני חי והוא חי היאך יכול החי להכחיש את החי. היה רבן גמליאל יושב ודורש ור' יהושע עומד על רגליו עד שרננו כל העם ואמרו לחוצפית המתורגמן עמוד ועמד. אמרו עד כמה ניצעריה וליזיל. בראש השנה אשתקד צעריה. בבכורות במעשה דר' צדוק צעריה. ה"נ קא מצער ליה. כולי האי ליצעריה וליזיל. תא ונעבריה. מאן נוקים ליה נוקמיה לר' יהושע בעל מעשה הוא. נוקמיה לר"ע דלמא עניש ליה דלית ליה זכות אבות. אלא נוקמיה לר"א בן עזריה דהוא חכם והוא עשיר והוא עשירי לעזרא. הוא חכם דאי מקשי ליה מפרק ליה. הוא עשיר דאי מפלח לבי קיסר האי נמי מצי מפלח כוותיה. והוא עשירי לעזרא דאית ליה זכות אבות ולא מצי עניש ליה אתו ואמרי ליה ניחא ליה למר למיהוי ריש מתיבתא א"ל איזיל ואמליך באנשי ביתאי. אזל ואמליך בדביתהו אמרה ליה (דף כח) דלמא מעבירין לך אמר לה אמרי אינשי לשתמיש יומא חדא בכסא דמוקרא ולמחר ליתבר. אמרה ליה לית לך חוורתא ההוא יומא בר תמני סרי שני הוה אתרחיש ליה ניסא והדרו ליה תמני סרי דארי חוורתא. והיינו דקאמר רבי אלעזר בן עזריה הרי כבן שבעים שנה ולא בן שבעים שנה. תנא אותו היום סלקוהו לשומר הפתח ונתנה רשות לתלמידים ליכנס שהיה ר"ג מכריז ואומר כל ת"ח שאין

punishment." So they came [to R. Elazar b. Azarlia] and said to him: "Is the master willing to become the head of the Academy?" (Fol. 28a.) R. Elazar replied: "I'll go and consult my household." He went and consulted his wife. "Perhaps," said she to him, "they will also depose thee [and you will be disgraced]." "There is a maxim," replied he. "'Use thy precious bowl while thou hast it. even if it be broken the next day.'" "But," said she, "thou hast not any gray hair [and they will not respect thee]." At that time he was but eighteen years of age; thereupon miraculously eighteen of his locks suddenly turned gray. And this R. Elazar b. Azaria meant when he said: "Behold! I am as a man of seventy years of age" but not aged seventy. We are taught that on that day the porter was removed from the door [of the academy], and admission was granted to all students, for, during the administration of Rabban Gamaliel, the announcement was made: "Every scholar whose interior is not like his exterior (who is not pious), shall not enter the academy." On that day many benches were added in the academy. R. Jochanan said: "There is a difference of opinion between Abba Joseph b. Dustoi and the Rabbis; according to one, four hundred benches were added and according to the other, seven hundred benches [were added]." When Rabban Gamaliel noticed the tremendous increase he became discouraged and said to himself, "God forbid, I have perhaps prevented so many from studying the Torah." In a dream was shown to him "white earthen pitchers filled with ashes." But this was shown to him only in order to calm him. We are taught: "On that day the treatise of Edioth was studied in the academy and wherever we find 'On that

תוכו כברו אל יכנס לב"ה ההוא יומא איתוספו כמה ספסלי. אמר רבי יוחנן פליגי בה אבא יוסף בר דוסתאי ורבנן חד אמר איתוסף ת׳ ספסלי וחד אמר ז׳ מאה ספסלי. הוה קא חלשה דעתיה דר"ג אמר דלמא ח"ו מנעתי תורה מישראל אחזו ליה בחלמא חצבי חוורי דמליין קיטמא. ולא היא אלא ליתובי דעתיה הוא דאחזו ליה, תנא עדיות בו ביום נשנית וכל היכא דאמרינן בו ביום ההוא יומא הוה ולא היתה הלכה שהיתה תלויה בב"ה שלא פירשוה ואף רבן גמליאל לא מנע עצמו מבית המדרש אפילו שעה אחת. דתנן בו ביום בא יהודה גר עמוני לפניהם בבית המדרש אמר להם מה אני לבא בקהל. אמר לו רבן גמליאל אסור אתה לבוא בקהל אמר לו רבי יהושע מותר אתה לבוא בקהל אמר לו רבן גמליאל והלא כבר נאמר (דברים כג ד) לא יבא עמוני ומואבי בקהל ה׳. א"ל ר׳ יהושע וכי עמון ומואב במקומן הם יושבין והלא כבר עלה סנחריב מלך אשור ובלבל את כל האומות שנאמר (ישעיה י יג) ואסיר גבולות עמים ועתידותיהם שושיתי ואוריד כאביר יושבים וכל דפריש מרובא פריש. א"ל רבן גמליאל והלא כבר נאמר (ירמיה מט ו) ואחרי כן אשיב את שבות בני עמון וכבר שבו. א"ל רבי יהושע והלא כבר נאמר (עמוס ט יד) ושבתי את שבות עמי ישראל

day,' it means the day on which R. Elazar b. Azaria became the head of the academy. There was no Halacha previously undecided in the academy which was not decided that day. Even Rabban Gamaliel himself, although deposed, did not refrain from attending the academy, as is shown from what we are taught (in a Mishnah): 'On that day Juda the Ammouite, a proselyte, appeared in the academy and asked: 'May I enter the congregation [to marry a Jewess]?' Rabban Gamaliel said unto him: 'Thou art not at liberty to do so,' but R. Joshua said, 'Thou art at liberty to do so.' Rabban Gamaliel then said to R. Joshua, 'Behold it is said (Deu. 23, 4.) An Ammonite ' or Moabite shall not enter the congregation of the Lord!" To this R. Joshua retorted and said, 'Are then these nations still in their native places? Did not Senacherib, the king of Assyria, transplant the nations? As it is said (Is. 10, 13.) I have removed the bounds of the people, and their laid-up treasures have I plundered, etc., therefore, not knowing, we go according to the majority [and the majority are not Ammonites].' 'But,' replied Rabban Gamaliel, 'behold, it is said (Jer. 49, 6.) And afterwards I will bring again the captivity of the children of Ammon, so they must have already returned.' To which R. Joshua rejoined: "Behold it is also said (Amos 9, 14.) And I will bring again the captivity of my people Israel, and these have not returned as yet.' Thereupon the proselyte was immediately permitted to enter the congregation." Then Rabban Gamaliel said to himself: "Since it is so [that R. Joshua's decision was carried], I shall now go and effect a reconciliation with R. Joshua." He thereupon went. When he reached R. Joshua's house, he noticed that the walls of the house were black. "From the

ועדיין לא שבו. מיד התירוהו לבא בקהל. אמר ר"ג הואיל והכי הוא איזיל ואפייסיה לרבי יהושע. כי מטא לביתיה חזינהו לאשיתא דביתיה דמשחרן א"ל מכותלי ביתך אתה ניכר שפחמי אתה א"ל אוי לו לדור שאתה פרנסו שאין אתה יודע בצערן של תלמידי חכמים במה הן מתפרנסין ובמה הם ניזונין. א"ל נעניתי לך מחול לי. לא אשגח ביה. עשה בשביל כבוד אבא איפייס. אמרו מאן ליזיל ולימא להו לרבנן. אמר להו ההוא כובס אנא אזילנא. שלח רבי יהושע לבה"מ מאן דלביש מדא ילבש מדא ומאן דלא לביש מדא יימר למאן דלביש מדא שלח מדייך ואנא אלבשיה. א"ל רבי עקיבא לרבנן מרוקו גלי דלא ליתו עבדי דר"ג וליצערו רבנן. אמר רבי יהושע מוטב דאיקום ואיזיל אנא לגבייהו אתא רבי יהושע טרף אבבא ואמר להו מזה בן מזה יזה. שאיני לא מזה ולא בן מזה יאמר למזה כן מזה מימיך מי מערה ואפרך אפר מקלה:

appearance of the walls of thy house," said Rabban Gamaliel, "it is evident that you are a smith." R. Joshua replied: "Woe unto the age whose leader thou art! for thou knowest not of the cares with which the scholars are occupied and whence they derive their livelihood!" "I have reproached thee, forgive me," Rabban Gamaliel pleaded, but R. Joshua ignored him. "Do it," he again pleaded, "for the sake of the honor of my father's house." R. Joshua then accepted his apology. "Now," they said, "who will go and inform the Rabbis?" [that they had become reconciled.] "I shall go," said a certain laundryman who was there. So R. Joshua sent the following message [through him]: "He who wore the vestment, shall be dressed with it again, and he who has not worn the vestment shall say to him who wore it: 'Take ofT thy priestly cloth, and I shall put it on.'" As soon as R. Akiba was informed of the situation, he said to the Rabbis: "Let all gates [leading to the academy] be closed so that none of Rabban Gamaliel's subordinates shall come and afflict the Rabbis" [in a spirit of revenge for their stand against Rabban Gamaliel]. Meantime R. Joshua said to himself: "It will be much better that I myself shall go and inform them." Accordingly he went and [upon reaching the academy] rapped at the door saying: "Let him sprinkle who is a sprinkler, the son of a sprinkler (a scholar, the son of a scholar); he who is neither himself a sprinkler, nor the son of a sprinkler shall say to him who is a sprinkler and the son of a sprinkler Thy water is plain cave water and thy ashes are plain ashes of a burned cane."

"Hast thou been appeased R. Joshua? said R.

אמר ליה רבי עקיבא רבי

Akiba to him. "What we have done was only for thy sake. If so, then to-morrow you and I shall be at his (Rabban Gamaliers) door early." [And though everything was settled] R. Elazar b. Azaria was not deposed, but from that time on Rabban Gamaliel was to lecture two (Sabbaths while R. Elazar b. Azaria lectured one Sabbath, and it is thus understood, when the master said: "Whose Sabbath was this? That of R. Elazar b, Azaria." The disciple [who asked if the evening service is optional or obligatory] was R. Simon b. Jochai.

(Ib. b) (Mishnah) R. Nechunia b. Hakana, upon entering and leaving the academy was wont to make a short prayer. The Rabbis asked him what kind of a prayer it was? He replied, "When I enter I pray that no stumbling shall happen because of me; and upon leaving, I give praise for my share."

(Gemara) Our Rabbis taught: "Upon entering the house of learning what shall a man pray? 'May it be Thy will, O Lord, my God, that there shall be no stumbling through me and that we shall not stumble over a matter of Halacha, and that my associates shall find rejoicing in me, that I shall not judge as levitically unclean, that which is levitically clean; or as clean, that which is unclean; nor shall my companions stumble over a matter of Halacha and I shall find rejoicing in them.' Upon leaving what shall a man say? 'I give thanks unto thee, O Lord, my God, because thou hast placed my share among those who attended the academy, and hast not placed my share among those who attend the street; they arise early and I arise early [but there is a difference]. They arise early for idle talk, while I arise early for the words of

יהושע נתפייישת כלום עשינו אלא לכבודך למחר אני ואתה נשכים לפתחו. ואפ״ה לא עברוה לרבי אלעזר בן עזריה דהוה דריש רבן גמליאל תרתי שבתא ודריש ר׳ אלעזר בן עזריה חדא שבתא. והיינו דאמר מר שבת של מי היתה של רבי אלעזר בן עזריה היתה ואותו תלמיד רבי שמעון בן יוחאי הוה:

(ע״ב) מתני׳ ר׳ נחוניא בן הקנה היה מתפלל בכניסתו לבית המדרש וביציאתו תפלה קצרה אמרו לו מה מקום לתפלה זו אמר להם בכניסתי אני מתפלל שלא יארע תקלה ע״י וביציאתי אני נותן הודאה על חלקי:

גמרא ת״ר בכניסתו מהו אומר יהי רצון מלפניך ה׳ אלהי שלא יארע דבר תקלה על ידי ולא אכשל בדבר הלכה וישמחו בי חברי ולא אומר על טמא טהור ולא על טהור טמא ולא יכשלו חברי בדבר הלכה ואשמח בהם. וביציאתו אומר מודה אני לפניך ה׳ אלהי ששמת חלקי מיושבי בית המדרש ולא שמת חלקי מיושבי קרנות שהם משכימים ואני משכים הם משכימים לדברים בטלים ואני משכים לדברי תורה אני עמל והם עמלים אני עמל ומקבל שכר והם עמלים ואינם מקבלים שכר אני רץ והם רצים אני רץ לחיי העולם הבא והם רצים לבאר שחת:

the Torah. I toil and they toil; I toil and hope to receive everlasting compensation, but they are working and will not receive everlasting compensation. I run and they run; I run to eternity in the world to come, while they run into the pit of a cave.' "

Our Rabbis taught: When R. Eliezer became ill his disciples came to visit him. "Rabbi," they said, "teach us the way of life so that we may deserve to inherit eternity in the world to come." He said unto them: "Be careful to honor your comrades; know to whom you pray; restrain your children from frivolous thoughts, and set them between the knees of learned men; by these means you will deserve eternity in the world to come." When R. Jochanan b. Zakai became ill his disciples visited him; as soon as he saw them he burst into tears. "Rabbi." they said to him, "light of Israel! the right pillar! Why weepest thou?" He replied thus: "Were I to be brought before a mortal king, who is here to-day, but in the grave to-morrow; who may become angry with me, but whose anger is not everlasting; who may imprison me, but whose imprisonment is not forever; who may kill me, but kill only for this world; and whom I may bribe, even then would I fear; but now when I am led to appear before the King of Kings, the Holy One, praised be He! who liveth through all eternity; if He is wroth, it is everlasting; if He imprison me, it is imprisonment forever; if He kill, one is killed forever; and I can neither appease with words nor bribe Him with money; moreover there are two paths before me, one leading to Gehenna and the other leading to Paradise, and I know not in which I am led. Should I not weep?"' They then said to him: "Rabbi, bless us." He said

תנו רבנן כשחלה רבי אליעזר נכנסו תלמידיו לבקרו אמרו לו רבי למדנו אורחות חיים ונזכה בהם לחיי העולם הבא. אמר להם הזהרו בכבוד חבריכם וכשאתם מתפללים דעו לפני מי אתם עומדים ומנעו בניכם מן ההגיון והושיבום בין ברכי תלמידי חכמים ובשביל כך תזכו לחיי העולם הבא. וכשחלה רבי יוחנן בן זכאי נכנסו תלמידיו לבקרו כיון שראה אותם התחיל לבכות. אמרו לו רבינו נר ישראל עמוד הימיני פטיש החזק מפני מה אתה בוכה. אמר להם אילו לפני מלך בשר ודם היו מוליכין אותי שהיום כאן ומחר בקבר שאם כעס עלי אין כעסו כעס עולם ואם אוסרני אין איסורו איסור עולם ואם ממיתני אין מיתתו מיתת עולם ואני יכול לפייסו בדברים ולשוחדו בממון ואעפ״כ הייתי בוכה. ועכשיו שמוליכין אותי לפני מלך מלכי המלכים הקב״ה שהוא חי וקים לעולם ולעולמי עולמים שאם כעס עלי כעסו כעס עולם ואם יאסרני איסורו איסור עולם ואם ממיתני מיתתו מיתת עולם ואין אני יכול לפייסו בדברים ולשוחדו בממון ולא עוד אלא שיש לפני שני דרכים אחד של גיהנם ואחד של גן עדן ואיני

to them: "May it be His will that your fear of God shall be as great as the fear of man." "Rabbi," they asked, "is that all?" Thereupon he answered: "Oh that! For when a man commits a crime [he does it in secrecy] saying 'no man should see me.' Although God seeth him everywhere." When at the point of dying he said to them: "Cleanse the house of all vessels on account of levitical impurity, and prepare a chair for Hezekiah, the King of Juda, who came [to take part in my procession]."

Our Rabbis taught that "Simon Happekuli has arranged the Eighteen Benedictions before Rabban Gamaliel at Jamnia, according to their present arrangement. Rabban Gamaliel said to the sages: 'Is there not anyone who knows how to compose a prayer concerning the Sadducees?' Thereupon Samuel the junior, came down and composed it. The following year he (Samuel the junior) forgot it (Fol. 29a) and for two or three hours he tried to recollect [but did not succeed]; still the congregation did not remove him [from the reader's place]." Why not? Has not R Juda in the name of Rab said: "If one errs in any part of the Eighteen Benedictions he should not be removed, but if he errs in the section referring to heretics he should be removed, in the apprehension that he is a heretic." Samuel the junior is different, since he himself composed it [therefore he shows no cause for suspicion]. But why should we not apprehend that perhaps he reconsidered it? Abaye said: "We have a tradition that a righteous person never becomes wicked." Is this so? Behold, it is written (Ez. 18, 24.) But when the righteous turneth away from his righteousness. This is said of a man who was

יודע באיזה מהן מוליכין אותי ולא אבכה. אמרו לו רבינו ברכנו. אמר להם יהי רצון שיהא מורא שמים עליכם כמורא בשר ודם. א״ל תלמידיו עד כאן אמר להם ולואי. תדעו כשאדם עובר עבירה אומר שלא יראני אדם. בשעת פטירתו אמר להם פנו כלים מפני הטומאה והכינו כסא לחזקיהו מלך יהודה שבא:

תנו רבנן שמעון הפקולי הסדיר י״ח ברכות לפני ר״ג על הסדר ביבנה. אמר להם ר״ג לחכמים כלום יש אדם שיודע לתקן ברכת המינים. ירד שמואל הקטן ותקנה. לשנה האחרת שכחה (דף כט) והשקיף בה ב׳ וג׳ שעות ולא העלוהו ואמאי לא העלוהו והא״ר יהודה אמר רב טעה בכל הברכות כולן אין מעלין אותו בברכת המינים מעלין אותו חיישינן שמא מין הוא. שאני שמואל הקטן דאיהו תקנה. וניחוש דילמא הדר בה. אמר אביי גמירי טבא לא הוי בישא. ולא והכתיב (יחזקאל יח כד) ובשוב צדיק מצדקתו ועשה עול. (דייק מדכתיב ובשוב צדיק ששב לרשעו דמעיקרא מהר״י ז״ל) ההוא רשע מעקרו אבל צדיק מעקרו לא. ולא והתנן אל תאמין בעצמך עד יום מותך שהרי יוחנן כ״ג שמש בכהונה גדולה פ׳ שנה ולבסוף נעשה צדוקי. אמר אביי הוא ינאי הוא יוחנן. רבא אמר ינאי לחוד יוחנן לחוד ינאי רשע מעקרו יוחנן צדיק

wicked in the beginning, but if one is righteous from the very beginning, it does not happen so. Is this so? Are we not taught: "Do not rely upon thyself [that thou art righteous] even until the last day of thy death; for R. Jochanan the High Priest served in the High Priesthood for eighty years and at last became a Sadducee." Abaye said: "Janai (the King) and Jochanan are the same person" [hence he was wicked in his early years]. Raba said: "Janai and Jochanan are two different persons; Janai was wicked from the very beginning, and Jochanan righteous from the very beginning." It is quite right according to the opinion of Abaye, but according to the opinion of Raba [who said that Jochanan was righteous from the very beginning], how should the question be answered? Raba may explain that a righteous person from the very beginning should also [not be relied upon] lest he become wicked. And if so., then why did not the Rabbis remove Samuel the junior? With Samuel the junior it is different; for he commenced to say it, and erred in the middle of it. For R. Juda in the name of Rab, and according to some in the name of R. Joshua b. Levi, said: "The above quotation [of Rab regarding the suspicion] refers only to him who has not even commenced to say it, but if he commenced the benediction and erred in the middle of it he may be allowed to finish it [without any suspicion]."

(Ib. b) Elijah, the brother of R. Sala Chasida, said to R. Juda "Do not get angry and thou wilt not sin. Do not get drunk and thou wilt not sin. And when thou art about to go on thy way, take counsel first with thy Possessor and then go out." What does it mean by, "Take counsel first with thy

מעקרו. לאביי ניחא אלא לרבא קשיא. אמר לך רבא צדיק מעקרו נמי דלמא הדר ביה. אי הכי אמאי לא אסקוהו. שאני שמואל הקטן דהא אתחיל בה דא״ר יהודה א״ר ואיתמא רבי יהושע בן לוי לא שנו אלא שלא התחיל בה אבל התחיל בה גומרה:

(ע״ב) א״ל אליהו לרב יהודה אחוה דרב סלא חסידא לא תרתח ולא תחטא. לא תרוי ולא תחטא. וכשאתה יוצא לדרך המלך בקונך וצא. מאי המלך בקונך וצא. אמר רבי יעקב אמר רב חסדא זו

Possessor and then go out." R. Jacob said in the name of R. Chisda: "This refers to the road-prayer which a man should say before he goes on his way." (Fol. 30a) And how shall he make this prayer? R. Chisda said standing, and R. Shesheth said, even while walking. R. Chisda and R. Shesheth were once walking along the road. [Suddenly] R. Chisda stopped and began to pray. "What is R. Chisda doing?" asked H. Shesheth of his attendant. "He stopped and said a prayer," was the reply of his attendant. Thereupon R. Shesheth ordered his attendant to stop also and to pray, remarking, "If thou canst be good do not be bad."

Our Rabbis taught: "A blind man or one who cannot determine the direction, let him direct his heart towards his Heavenly Father; for it is said (I Kings 8, 44.) They will pray unto the Lord. If he is outside of Palestine let him direct his heart toward Palestine, for it is said (Ib. 48.) They will pray unto Thee in the direction of their land. If he stand in Palestine let him direct his heart towards Jerusalem, for it is said (Ib. ib. 44.) They will pray unto the Lord in the direction of the city which thou hast chosen. If he stand in Jerusalem then let him direct his heart towards the Temple, for it is said (Ib. ib. 33.) And they will pray and praise unto this house. If he stand in the Temple then let him direct his heart towards the Holy of Holies; for it is said (Ib. ib. 30.) And they will pray towards this place. If he stand in the Holy of Holies let him direct his heart towards the Kaporeth. If he stand behind the cover of the ark, let him consider it as if he were standing in front of the Kaporeth. Hence, if one is in the east, he should face towards west; in the west, he should face towards east; in the

תפלת הדרך. (דף ל) והיכי מצלי לה. רב חסדא אמר מעומד. רב ששת אמר אפילו מהלך. רב חסדא ורב ששת הוו קא אזלי באורחא קם רב חסדא וקא מצלי אמר ליה רב ששת לשמעיה מאי קא עביד רב חסדא. אמר ליה קאי ומצלי. אמר ליה אוקמן נמי לדידי ואצלי מהיות טוב אל תקרי רע:

ת"ר סומא ומי שאינו יכול לכוין הרוחות יכוין לבו כנגד אביו שבשמים שנאמר (מ"א ח מד) והתפללו אל ה' אלהיהם. היה עומד בחוץ לארץ יכוין לבו כנגד א"י שנאמר (שם ח מח) והתפללו אליך דרך ארצם, היה עומד בארץ ישראל יכוין את לבו כנגד ירושלים שנאמר (שם ח מד) והתפללו אל ה' דרך העיר אשר בחרת, היה עומד בירושלים יכוין את לבו כנגד בית המקדש שנאמר (שם ח לג) והתפללו אל הבית הזה. היה עומד בבית המקדש יכוין את לבו כנגד בית קדשי הקדשים שנאמר (שם ח ל) והתפללו אל המקום הזה היה עומד בבית קדשי הקדשים יכוין את לבו כנגד בית הכפורת, היה עומד אחורי בית הכפורת יראה עצמו כאלו לפני הכפורת, נמצא עומד במזרח מחזיר פניו למערב, במערב מחזיר פניו למזרח, בדרום מחזיר

south, he should face towards the north; in the north, he should face towards the south. It is thus found that all Israel directs its heart towards one place [towards the Holy of Holies]." Where is the Biblical passage [to refer to this]? Thy neck is like the tower of David built on terraces (Songs 4, 4), i.e., a mound towards which all turn."

Chapter 5

Abaye was sitting before Rabba; the latter noticed that Abaye was very cheerful. Rabba said to him: "Does not the master agree with the passage (Ps. 2, 11.) Rejoice with treembling?" To which he answered: "I have the Tephilin on." R. Jeremiah was sitting before R. Zeira; the latter seeing that the former was very cheerful, remarked to him, "It is written (Ps. 14, 23.) In all painful labor there is profit." "I have Tephilin on," R. Jeremiah answered.

Mar, the son of Rabina, made a marriage banquet for his son; when he observed that the Rabbis were at the height of their merriment he brought in a very costly cup worth four hundred zouzim and broke it before them; and they grew sad. R. Ashi made a marriage feast for his son and when he noticed the Rabbis were at the height of their merriment (Fol. 31a) he brought in a costly cup made of white glass and broke it before them; and they grew sad. At the wedding of Mar the son of Rabina, the Rabbis said unto R. Hammma Zuti: "Sing to us master." He sang: "Woe, for we must die! Woe, for we must die!" "And what shall we respond to it?" asked they. "Sing ye,"

פניו לצפון, בצפון מחזיר פניו לדרום נמצאו כל ישראל מכוונים את לבם למקום אחד. א"ר אבין ואיתימא רבי אבינא מאי קרא (שיר ד ד) כמגדל דוד צוארך בנוי לתלפיות. תל שכל פיות פונים בו:

Chapter 5

(ע"ב) אביי הוה יתיב קמיה דרבה חזייה דהוה יתיב וקא בדח טובא א"ל לא סבר לה מר (תהלים ב יא) וגילו ברעדה. אמר ליה אנא תפלין מנחנא. רבי ירמיה הוה יתיב קמיה דר' זירא חזייה דהוה בדח טובא. א"ל (משלי יד כג) בכל עצב יהיה מותר כתיב. א"ל אנא תפלין מנחנא:

מר בריה דרבינא עבד הלולא לבריה חזנהו לרבנן דהוו קא בדחי טובא אייתי כסא דמוקרא בת ת' זוזי ותבר קמייהו ואעציבו. רב אשי עבד הלולא לבריה חזנהו לרבנן דהוו קא בדחי טובא (דף לא) אייתי כסא דזוגיתא חיוורתא ותבר קמייהו ואעציבו אמרו ליה רבנן לרב המנונא זוטי בהלולא דמר בריה דרבינא לישרי לן מר. אמר להו ווי לן דמיתנן ווי לן דמתנן. אמרו ליה אנן מה נעני בתרך. אמר להו הי תורה והי מצוה דמגנו עלן. א"ר יוחנן משום רשב"י אסור לאדם שימלא שחוק פיו

answered he, "Alas! where is the Torah [we have studied] and where are the meritorious deeds? [we have performed] to protect us?" R. Jochanan in the name of R. Simon b. Jochai said: "It is not permitted to a man to fill his mouth with laughter in this world, for it is said (Ps. 126, 2.) Then shall our mouths be filled with laughter, and our tongue with singing — when shall this be? At the time when — they shall say among the nations 'great things hath the Lord done for these.'" It is related of Resh Lakish that he never laughed from the time he heard this from R. Jochanan, his teacher.

Our Rabbis taught: "It is not proper to start to pray in a mood of sadness; nor in a mood of idleness, nor in a mood of laughter, nor in a mood of low talk, nor in a mood of jesting, nor in a mood of idle talk; but only in a mood of joy caused through the performance of a meritorious deed. Thus also shall one take leave of his friend neither in the mood of low talk, nor of laughter, nor of jesting, nor of idle talk; but immediately after the study of the Halacha (traditional law); for thus we find with our first prophets; they also finished their prophesies with matters of praise and consolation." And so has R. Mari, the grandson of R. Huna. the son of R. Jeremiah, recited [a tradition]: "A man shall not depart from his friend only immediately after reciting an Halacha; because by means of this his friend will always remember him." Just as it happened to R. Cahana, who accompanied R. Shimi b. Ashi, from Pum-Nahara to the place called "Between the Palm" in Babylonia. When they reached that place the latter said to the former: "Is it true, master, what people say that these palmtrees of Babylonia date from the days

בעוה״ז שנאמר (תהלים קכו ב) אז ימלא שחוק פינו ולשוננו רנה אימתי בזמן שיאמרו בגוים הגדיל ה׳ לעשות עם אלה. אמרו עליו על ר״ל שמימיו לא מלא שחוק פיו בעוה״ז מכי שמעה מר׳ יוחנן רביה:

תנו רבנן אין עומדין להתפלל לא מתוך עצבות ולא מתוך עצלות ולא מתוך שחוק ולא מתוך שיחה ולא מתוך קלות ראש ולא מתוך דברים בטלים אלא מתוך שמחה של מצוה ולא יפטר אדם מחבירו לא מתוך שיחה ולא מתוך שחוק ולא מתוך קלות ראש ולא מתוך דברים בטולים אלא מתוך דבר הלכה שכן מצינו בנביאים הראשונים שסיימו דבריהם בדברי שבח ותנחומים. וכן תני מרי בר בריה דרב הונא בריה דרבי ירמיה בר אבא אל יפטר אדם מחבירו אלא מתוך דבר הלכה שמתוך כך זוכרהו כי הא דרב כהנא אלוייה לרב שימי בר אשי מפום נהרא עד בי צניתא דבבל כי מטא להתם א״ל מר ודאי דאמרי אינשי הני צניתא דבבל איתנהו מאדם הראשון ועד השתא. אמר ליה אדכרתן מילתא דרבי יוסי בר׳ חנינא דאמר רבי יוסי בר׳ חנינא מ״ד (ירמיה ב ו) בארץ אשר

of Adam, the first man?" "Thou recallest to my mind," answered R. Cahaua, "what R. Jose, the son of R. Chanina said: 'What is meant by the passage (Jer. 2, 6.) Through a land through which no man had passed and where no man had dwelt. Since no man has passed through it, how is it possible for any man to have dwelt in it? It means to teach us that whatever land Adam, the first man, decreed should become inhabited did indeed become inhabited; but whatever land Adam, the first man, decreed shall not become inhabited, remained uninhabited.'"

Our Rabbis taught: He who prays shall direct his heart to Heaven. Abba Saul says: "We find a hint to this (Ps. 10, 17.) Thou wilt strengthen their hearts. Thou wilt cause thy ear to listen." We are taught that R. Juda says: "This was the custom of R. Akiba when he prayed with the community; he used to shorten his prayer in order to keep up with the assembly, so as not to trouble the assembly [to wait for him.]. But when he prayed privately, if one left him [praying] in one corner when he started, he would be found [at the completion of his prayer] in the next corner, because of his bowing and kneeling [during his prayer]." R. Hamnuna said: "How many important laws can we learn from the incident of Hannah? Now as for Hannah, she spoke in her heart (I Sam. 1, 13). We infer from this that one who prays must concentrate his attention. Only her lips moved (Ib.); we infer from this that he who prays must speak with his lips [thinking does not suffice]. But her voice could not be heard (Ib.); we infer from this that he who prays must not raise his voice loudly. Wherefore Eli regarded her as a. drunken woman (Ib.); we infer from this that it is

לא עבר כח איש ולא ישב אדם שם. וכי מאחר שלא עבר האיך ישב אלא לומר לך כל ארץ שגזר עליה אדם הראשון לישוב נתישבה וכל ארץ שלא גזר עליה אדם הראשון לישוב לא נתישבה:

תנו רבנן המתפלל צריך שיכוין את לבו לשמים. אבא שאול אומר סימן לדבר (תהלים י יז) תכין לבם תקשיב אזנך. תניא אמר רבי יהודה כך היה מנהגו של ר' עקיבא כשהיה מתפלל עם הצבור היה מקצר ועולה מפני טורח צבור וכשהיה מתפלל בינו לבין עצמו אדם מניחו בזוית זו ומוצאו בזוית אחרת. וכל כך למה מפני כריעות והשתחויות. אמר רב המנונא כמה הלכתא גברוותא איכא למשמע מהני קראי דחנה (ש"א א יג) והנה היא מדברת על לבה מכאן למתפלל צריך שיכוין לבו. רק שפתיה נעות מכאן למתפלל שיחתוך בשפתיו. וקולה לא ישמע מכאן שאסור להגביה קולו בתפלתו. ויחשבה עלי לשכורה מכאן שהשכור אסור להתפלל. (שם) ויאמר אליה עלי עד מתי תשתכרין אמר ר' אלעזר מכאן לרואה (ע"ב) בחברו דבר שאינו הגון צריך להוכיחו. (שם) ותען חנה ותאמר לא אדוני אמר עולא

unlawful for a drunkard to pray." And Eli said unto her, How long, wilt thou he drunk?' (Ib.) "We infer from this, said R. Elazar, "that if one notice (Ib. b.) an unbecoming thing in a friend it is one's duty to reprimand him." Hannah answered, and said: 'No, my Lord.' (Ib.) Ulla. and according to some R. Jose, the son of R. Chanina, said that Hannah remarked unto Eli, "Thou art not Judge in this matter nor does the Holy spirit rest upon thee, if thou suspect me of such a thing." Others say that Hannah spoke thus unto Eli: "Thou art not a Judge in this matter. Are there not then the Shechina and the Holy Spirit with thee, that thou judgeth me as guilty and not innocent?" Dost thou not know that I am a woman of a sorrowful spirit but neither wine nor strong drink have I drunk? (Ib.) "We infer from this," said R. Elazar, "that if a man is wrongly accused of anything he ought to inform his accuser of it." Esteem not thy handmaid as a worthless woman (Ib.) R. Elazar said, "We infer from this that a drunkard who prays, is as if he were worshipping idols; here is written Beliya'al (worthless) — as a worthless woman; and it is also written there (Deu. 13, 14.) There have gone forth men, children of worthless (Beliya'al), just as in the later instance it refers to idolatry, so also does it refer to idolatry here." Then Eli answered and said: 'Go in peace.' (Ib.) We infer from this," said R. Elazar, "that he who wrongly accuses his friend must appease him and moreover must bless him, as it is said (Ib. ib.) And may the God of Israel grant thy request."

(Fol. 32a) And the Lord spoke unto Moses, Go, get thee down! (Ex. 32, 7.) What is meant by get thee down? R. Elazar said:

"The Holy One, praised be He! said unto Moses, 'Come step down from your greatness, for would then greatness have been given to thee if not for Israel's sake? And now since Israel has sinned, there is no greatness for thee.' Hearing these words, Moses instantly became so weak that he lacked the strength to speak. But when Moses heard God's further utterance (Deu. 9, 14.) Leave me unto myself and I will destroy them, 'O' remarked he to himself, 'it looks as if this depends on me.' Whereupon, he immediately began to pray, asking mercy for Israel." It is similar to the parable of the king who was beating his son: the king's friend was sitting and observing it, being afraid to mediate and rescue the son: but as soon as he heard the king's remark. "Were it not for my friend who is sitting here I would kill you," he said to himself, "This depends on me": whereupon he immediately arose and rescued the son.

R. Simlai expounded: "A man should always arrange the praises of the Holy One, praised be He! and then pray for what he needs. Whence do we derive this? From Moses; for it is written (Deu. 3, 23.) And I besought the Lord at that time. And it is written also (Ib.) Thou hast begun to show Thy servant thy greatness, and Thy mighty hand; for what God is there in the heavens or on earth that can do aright like Thy works, and like Thy mighty deeds? And following this it is written Let me go over, I pray Thee, that I may see the good land, etc."

ב"ה למשה משה רד מגדולתך. כלום נתתי לך גדולה אלא בשביל ישראל עכשיו שישראל חטאו למה לי. מיד תשש כחו של משה ולא היה בו כח לדבר. כיון שא"ל (דברים ט יד) הרף ממני ואשמידם אמר משה דבר זה תלוי בי. מיד עמד ונתחזק בתפלה ובקש רחמים עליהם. משל למלך ב"ו שכעס על בנו והיה מכהו מכה גדולה והיה אוהבו יושב לפניו והיה מתירא להצילו. כיון שאמר אלמלא פלוני אוהבי היושב לפני הרגתיך. אמר דבר זה תלוי בי מיד עמד והצילו:

דרש רבי שמלאי לעולם יסדר אדם שבחו של הקב"ה ואח"כ יתפלל. מנא לן ממשה דכתיב (דברים ג כג) ואתחנן אל ה' בעת ההיא וכתיב ה' אלהים אתה החלות וגומר וכתיב בתריה אעברה נא ואראה את הארץ הטובה וגומר (ע"ב) א"ר אלעזר גדולה תפלה יותר ממעשים טובים שאין לך גדול במעשים טובים יותר ממשה רבינו אע"פ כן לא נענה אלא בתפלה שנאמר אל תוסף דבר אלי וסמיך ליה עלה ראש הפסגה. ואמר רבי אלעזר גדולה תפלה יותר מן הקרבנות שנאמר (ישעיה א יא) למה לי רוב זבחיכם

וכתיב ובפרשכם כפיכם. ואמר רבי אלעזר מיום שחרב בית המקדש נגעלו שערי תפלה שנאמר (איכה ג ח) גם כי אזעק ואשוע שתם תפלתי ואע"פ ששערי תפלה נגעלו שערי דמעה לא נגעלו שנאמר (תהלים לט יג) שמעה תפלתי ה' ושועתי האזינה אל דמעתי אל תחרש. ואמר רבי אלעזר מיום שחרב ביהמ"ק נפסקה חומת ברזל בין ישראל לאביהם שבשמים שנאמר (יחזקאל ד ג) ואתה בן אדם קח לך מחבת ברזל ונתת אותה קיר ברזל בינך ובין העיר. א"ר חנין אמר רבי חנינא כל המאריך בתפלתו אין תפלתו חוזרת ריקם מנא לן ממשה רבינו שנאמר (דברים ט יח) ואתפלל אל ה' וכתיב בתריה וישמע ה' אלי גם בפעם ההיא. איני והא אמר ר' חייא בר אבא אמר רבי יוחנן כל המאריך בתפלתו ומעיין בה סוף בא לידי כאב לב שנאמר (משלי יג יב) תוחלת ממושכה מחלה לב מאי תקנתיה יעסוק בתורה שנאמר (שם) ועץ חיים תאוה באה ואין עץ חיים אלא תורה שנאמר (שם ג יח) עץ חיים היא למחזיקים בה. לא קשיא הא דמאריך ומעיין בה הא דמאריך ולא מעיין בה. אמר רבי חמא בר חנינא אם ראה אדם שהתפלל ולא נענה יחזור ויתפלל שנא' (תהלים כז יד) קוה אל ה' חזק ויאמץ לבך וקוה אל ה'. תנו רבנן ד' צריכין חזוק אלו הן תורה ומעשים טובים

תפלה ודרך ארץ. תורה ומעשים טובים מנין שנאמר (יהושע א ז) רק חזק ואמץ מאד לשמור ולעשות ככל התורה חזק בתורה ואמץ במעשים טובים. תפלה מנין שנאמר קוה אל ה' חזק ויאמץ לבך וקוה אל ה'. דרך ארץ מנין שנאמר (ש"ב י יב) חזק ונתחזק בעד עמנו וגו':

(ע"ב) אמר ר"א גדולה תענית יותר מן הצדקה מה טעם זה בגופו וזה בממונו רבא לא גזר תעניתא ביומא דעיבא משום שנאמר (איכה ג מד) סכותה בענן לך מעבור תפלה:

(Ib. b) R. Elazar said: "Great is prayer, even more than good deeds; for there is none bigger in the performance of good deeds than our teacher Moses, still he was answered through prayers only; as it is said (Ib. ib. 26.) Let it suffice thee; do not continue to speak unto me any more of this matter; Immediately following it is said Get thee up unto the fop of Pisgah." R. Elazar also said: "Prayer is even more efficacious than sacrifice; "for it is said (Is. 1, 11.) For what serveth me the multitude of your sacrifice? Saith the Lord, and it is written further, And when you spread your hands, I shall withdraw my eyes from you." R. Elazar also said: "Since the day of the destruction of the Temple, the gates of prayer were locked up, as it is said (Lam. 3, 8.) Also when I cry aloud and make entreaty, He shutteth out my prayer; and even though the towers of prayer were locked up still the towers of tears are not locked, as it is said (Ps. 39, 13.) Hear my prayer, O Lord, and give ear unto my cry; at my tears Thou wilt surely not be silent." Further said R. Elazar: "Since the day of the destruction of the Temple, an iron wall separates Israel and the Heavenly Father, as it is said (Ezek. 4, 3.) Moreover take thou unto thyself an iron pan and set it up as a wall between thee and the city." R. Channin in the name of R. Chanina said: "He who prolongs in prayer will not return void (his prayers unfulfilled). Whence do we infer this? From our teacher Moses, for it is said (Deu. 9, 18.) And I threw myself down before the Lord; and it is further written And the Lord hearkened unto me also at that time." Is this so? Behold R. Chiya b. Abba in the name of R. Jochanan said: "Whoever prolongs in prayer and speculates on it (expecting its fulfillment as a reward for making it long) will, at the end, come to a heart sickness; for it is said (Pr. 13, 12.) Long deferred expectation maketh the heart sick. What is its remedy? Let him study the Torah, for close to it is said But a tree of life is a desire which is fulfilled; By a tree of life is meant nothing else but the Torah, for it is said (Ib. 3, 18.) A tree of life is she (the Torah) to those who lay hold on her." This is not difficult to explain; the latter deals with staying long in prayer and speculating on it, and the former deals with one who stays long in prayer but does not speculate on it. R. Chama b. Chanina said, "Although a man sees that his prayers are not answered, let him continue to pray; for it is said (Ps. 27, 14.) Wait on the Lord; be strong and let thy heart he of good courage; wait, I say, on the Lord." Our Rabbis taught: "Four things require fortitude in their observance: The Torah, good deeds, prayer, and social duties." The Torah and good deeds, whence do we know? It is said (Jos. 1, 7.) Be thou strong and firm that thou mayest observe to fulfill all the Torah; Be strong, refers to the Torah, And firm, refers to good deeds. Whence do we infer that prayer needs fortitude? It is said (Ps. 27, 14.) Wait on the Lord, be strong and He shall make thy heart firm; wait, I say, upon the Lord. 'Whence do we know that social duties require fortitude?

It is said (II. Sam 10, 12.) Be strong and let us strengthen ourselves for our people and for the cities of our God. R. Elazar said: "Fasting is even more meritorious than charity for the former is performed with the body and the latter is performed only with money." Raba never ordered a fast on a cloudy day; for it is said (Lam. 3, 44.) Thou hast covered thyself with a cloud that no prayer may pass through.

And Zion said, the Lord hath forsaken and forgotten me. (Is. 49, 14.) Is not forsaken and forgotten the same thing? Resh Lakish said: "The Congregation of Israel pleaded before the Holy One, praised be He! saying: 'Sovereign of the universe! Even a man who marries a second wife still bears in his mind the merits of the first, but Thou Lord has forgotten me!' 'My daughter,' replied The Holy One, blessed be He! I have created twelve stations in the heavens, and for each station I have created thirty legions [of stars], each legion contains thirty routes, each route thirty cohorts, each cohort has thirty camps and in each camp has been suspended three hundred and sixty-five thousand myriads of stars, equal to the number of days in the year; all these have I created for thy sake, and yet thou sayest thou art forsaken and forgotten.' Can a woman forget the suckling child so that she shall not have compassion on the son of her womb? (Ib. ib.) The Holy One, praised be He! said: 'Can I then forget the burnt offering of the rams and of the first-born which thou hast offered me, while you were in the desert?' Then again [the congregation of Israel] pleaded before the Holy One, praised be He! 'Sovereign of the universe! Since there is no forgetfulness before the throne

(ישעיה מט יד) ותאמר ציון עזבני ה' וה' שכחני היינו עזובה היינו שכוחה. אמר ר"ל אמרה כנסת ישראל לפני הקב"ה רבונו של עולם אדם נושא אשה על אשתו ראשונה וזוכר מעשה הראשונה אתה עזבתני ושכחני. התשכח אשה עולה אמר לה הקב"ה בתי שתים עשרה מזלות בראתי ברקיע ועל כל מזל ומזל בראתי לו שלשים חיל ועל כל חיל וחיל בראתי לו שלשים לגיון ועל כל לגיון ולגיון בראתי לו שלשים רהטון. ועל כל רהטון ורהטון בראתי לו שלשים קרטון. ועל כל קרטון וקרטון בראתי לו שלשים גסתרא. ועל כל גסתרא וגסתרא תליתי בו שלש מאות וששים וחמשא אלפי רבוא כוכבים כנגד ימות החמה וכולן לא בראתי אלא בשבילך ואת אמרת עזבתני ושכחתני. התשכח אשה עולה (ישעיה מט טו) אמר הקב"ה כלום אשכח עולות אילים ופטרי רחמים שהקרבת לפני במדבר. אמרה לפניו רבש"ע הואיל ואין שכחה לפני כסא כבודך שמא לא תשכח לי מעשי

of Thy Divine Majesty, then Thou mayest also not forget the incident of the golden calf?' The Lord said: 'This can also be forgotten.' (Ib.) Again she pleaded saying: 'Sovereign of the universe! Since there is forgetfulness before Thy exalted throne, then Thou mayest forget the Sinai affair, also?' 'Yet would I not forget thee,' (Ib.) replied the Lord." Thus we understand what R. Elazar, in the name of R. Oshia said: "This also can be forgotten (Ib.) refers to the golden calf; And yet would I not forget thee, refers to the Sinai event."

Our Rabbis taught: Once a pious man, while praying on the road, was met by a prince who saluted him, saying "Peace to you!" But the pious man did not respond. The prince waited till the end of his prayer. After he had finished his prayer, the prince said to him: "Good for nothing! behold! it is written in your Torah (Deu. 4, 9.) Only take heed to thyself, and guard thy soul diligently. It is also written (Ib. ib. 15.) Take ye therefore, good heed of your souls. When I saluted thee, why didst thou not answer me? If I had cut off thy head with a sword, who would be able to demand thy blood from my hand?" "Wait," the pious man said to him, "until I shall appease thee with a few words. If thou hadst been standing before a mortal king and one had saluted thee (Fol. 33a), wouldst thou have answered him?" "Nay," the prince replied. "And if thou hadst done so. what would [the king] have done unto thee?" "He would surely order my head to be cut off with a sword." replied the prince. The pious man then said unto him; "Behold now! If this is what you would have done if thou hadst stood before a mortal king, who is with us here today and may be in his grave to-

העגל, אמר לה (שם) גם אלה תשכחנה. אמרה לפניו רבש"ע הואיל ויש שכחה לפני כסא כבודך שמא תשכח לי מעשה סיני, אמר לה (שם) ואנכי לא אשכחך. והיינו דאמר רבי אלעזר א"ר אושעיא מאי דכתיב גם אלה תשכחנה זה מעשה עגל. ואנכי לא אשכחך זה מעשה סיני:

תנו רבנן מעשה בחסיד אחד שהיה מתפלל בדרך ובא הגמון אחד ונתן לו שלום ולא החזיר לו שלום המתין לו עד שסיים תפלתו. לאחר שסיים תפלתו אמר לו ריקא והלא כתיב בתורתכם (דברים ד ט) רק השמר לך ושמור נפשך מאד. וכתיב (שם ד טו) ונשמרתם מאד לנפשותיכם. כשנתתי לך שלום למה לא החזרת לי שלום אם הייתי חותך ראשך בסייף מי היה תובע את דמך מידי. אמר לו המתין לי עד שאפייסך בדברים, א"ל אילו לפני מלך ב"ו היית עומד ובא אחד ונתן לך שלום היית (דף לג) מחזיר לו שלים. אמר לו לאו. ואם היית מחזיר לו מה היו עושים לך. א"ל היו חותכין את ראשי בסייף. א"ל והלא דברים קל וחומר מה אתה שהיית עומד לפני מלך ב"ו שהיום כאן ומחר בקבר כך אני שהייתי עומד לפני מלך מלכי המלכים הקב"ה שהוא חי וקיים לעד ולעולמי עולמים על אחת כמה וכמה. מיד

morrow, how much more need I then to be careful when standing before the supreme King of kings, the Holy One, praised be He! who liveth and endureth forever to all eternity!" The prince became appeased and the pious man went peacefully home.

Our Rabbis taught: Once in a certain place, a wild ass used to injure the people; so they came and informed R. Chanina b. Dosa. "Show me the cave where the animal is hidden," said he to them. Whereupon they went and showed him. He then placed the sole of his foot on the hole, and when the animal came forth he hit it and the animal fell dead. R. Chanina then took it on his shoulder and brought it to the academy, saying to them: "My sons, see it is not the wild ass that kills, but sin kills." They then all exclaimed, "Woe unto the man who is met by a wild ass, but woe unto the wild ass when it meets R. Chanina b. Dosa," R. Ami said, "Great is knowledge, for it is the first benediction in the week day's prayer." Further said R. Ami, "Great is knowledge for it is placed between two Divine names, as it is said (I. Sam. 2, 3.) A God of knowledge is the Lord. Mercy is to be denied to him who has no knowledge; for it is said (Is. 27, 11.) They are a people of no understanding, therefore he that maketh them will not have

נתפייס אותו הגמון ונפטר אותו חסיד לביתו לשלום. (עקידת שע״ט) ת״ר מעשה במקום אחד שהיה בו ערוד והיה מזיק את הבריות. באו והודיעו לרבי חנינא בן דוסא. אמר להם הראוני את חורו. הלכו והראוהו חורו והניח עקבו על פתחו יצא ונשכו ומת אותו ערוד נטלו על כתיפו והוליכו לבית המדרש אמר להם בני ראו שאין ערוד ממית אלא חטא ממית. באותה שעה אמרו אוי לו לאדם שפגע בו ערוד ואוי לו לערוד שפגע בו רבי חנינא בן דוסא:

א״ר אמי גדולה דעה שנאמרה בתחלת ברכות של חול. וא״ר אמי גדולה דעה שנתנה בין שתי אותיות שנאמר (ש״א ב ג) כי אל דעות ה׳ וכל מי שאין בו דעה אסור לרחם עליו שנאמר (ישעיה כז יא) כי לא עם בינות הוא על כן לא ירחמנו עושהו. ואמר ר׳ אלעזר גדול מקדש שניתן בין שתי אותיות שנאמר (שמות טו יז) פעלת ה׳ מקדשי׳ה׳. ואמר ר׳ אלעזר כל אדם שיש בו דעה כאילו נבנה בהמ״ק בימיו. דעה ניתנה בין שתי אותיות. בית המקדש ניתן בין שתי אותיות. מתקיף לה רב אחא קרחינאה אלא מעתה גדולה נקמה שנתנה בין שתי אותיות דכתיב (תהלים צד א) אל נקמות ה׳. אמר ליה אין במילתה מיהא גדולה היא. והיינו דאמר עולא שתי נקמות הללו למה. אחד

mercy on them." R. Elazar said: "Great is the Temple for it is placed between two Divine names, as it is written (Ex. 15, 17.) Thou hast wrought for Thee to dwell in, O Lord, the sanctuary, O Lord!" R. Elazar also said: "Every man who possesses knowledge is considered worthy to cause the Temple to be built in his days, for knowledge is placed between two Divine names, and the Temple is placed between two Divine names." He was questioned by R. Acha of Karchina: "According to your opinion, retaliation must also be of great value, for it is written (Ps. 94, 1.) O God of vengeance, Lord!" "Yea," he replied, "when necessary it is of course of great value," and thus is meant by the saying of Ulla, "Why is the word vengeance repeated? O God of vengeance. Lord! O God of vengeance! One for a good purpose and one for a bad purpose; for good, as it is written (Deu. 33, 2.) He shone forth from Mt. Paran; for bad, as it is written (Ps. 94, 1.) O God of vengeance, Lord! O God of vengeance, shine forth!"

(Ib. b) A certain disciple prayed in the presence of R. Chanina, saying: "O God, who art Great, Mighty, Formidable, Magnificent, Strong, Terrible, Valiant, Powerful, Real and Honored." R. Chanina waited until he finished and then said to him: "Hast thou really finished all the praises of thy Master? Why do you enumerate so many? Behold! these three names (Great, Mighty and Formidable, which we use in the Eighteen Benedictions), we would not dare to utter, had not Moses, our teacher, pronounced them in the Torah (Deu. 10, 17.), and had not the men of the Great Synagogues ordained [the mention of these attributive names] in the prayer, and thou hast uttered

לטובה ואחד לרעה לטובה כדכתיב (דברים לג ב) הופיע מהר פארן לרעה דכתיב (תהלים צד א) אל נקמות ה׳ אל נקמות הופיע:

(ע״ב) ההוא דנחית קמיה דרבי חנינא אמר האל הגדול הגבור והנורא והאדיר והאמיץ והעזוז האמתי והיראוי החזק והודאי והנכבד. המתין לו עד דסיים. כי סיים אמר ליה סיימתינהו לכולהו שבחי דמרך למה לך כולי האי אנן הני תלת דאמרינן (הגדול הגבור והנורא) אי לאו דאמרינה משה רבינו באורייתא ואתו אנשי כנסת הגדולה ותקנינהו בתפלה אנן לא הוה אמרינן ואת שבחתיה כולי האי. משל (מגילה כד) למלך שהיו משבחין אותו באלף אלפין

so many words of praise and seemeth still inclined to go on; it is like one who complimenteth a king upon having a million silver denarim, when he really possesseth a million golden denarim. Would not such praise be a disgrace rather than an honor?"

R. Chanina said: "Everything is in the hnds of Heaven (under God's control) except fear of Heaven, as is written (Deu. 10., 12) And now, Israel, what doth the Lord, thy God, require of thee, but to fear the Lord, thy God." Is fear of God a small matter? Behold! R. Chanina in the name of R. Simon b. Jochai said: "Nothing is in God's storehouse except the treasure of fear of Heaven, as it is said (Ib.) And now, Israel, what doth the Lord, thy God, require of thee, but to fear the Lord, thy God." Aye, for one like Moses it was indeed a small matter, as R. Chanina said: "It is similar to a man who is asked for a large vessel. If he has it, it appears small to him, but if he has it not, even a small one would look large to him."

(Fol. 34a) Our Rabbis taught: "There are three things which are bad if used in great quantities; if used in small quantities however, they are very good. These are: leaven, salt and resistance." Our Rabbis taught: Once a disciple descended before the ark in the presence of R. Eliezer and prolonged his prayer. "See," said the other disciples to R. Eliezer, "how long he prays!" "Well," said the Rabbi to them, "is he praying longer than our teacher Moses, as written (Deu. 9, 25.) The forty days and the forty nights that I fell down." Again it happened that another disciple descended before the ark in the presence of R. Eliezer and made his prayer short; the other disciples said to R.

דיני כסף והיו לו אלף אלפין דיני זהב והלא גנאי הוא לו:

אמר רבי חנינא (מגילה כה) הכל בידי שמים חוץ מיראת שמים שנאמר (דברים י יב) ועתה ישראל מה ה' אלהיך שואל מעמך כי אם ליראה וגו'. אטו יראת שמים מלתא זוטרתי היא והאמר רבי חנינא משום ר' שמעון בן יוחאי אין להקב"ה בבית גנזיו אלא אוצר של יראת שמים שנאמר (ישעיה לג ו) יראת ה' היא אוצרו. אין לגבי משה מלתא זוטרתי היא דאמר רבי חנינא משל לאדם שמבקשים ממנו כלי גדול ויש לו דומה עליו ככלי קטן. קטן ואין לו דומה עליו ככלי גדול:

(דף לד) תנו רבנן שלשה רובן קשה ומיעוטן יפה ואלו הן שאור מלה וסרבנות. תנו רבנן מעשה בתלמיד אחד שירד לפני התיבה לפני ר' אליעזר והיה מאריך יותר מדאי. א"ל תלמידיו רבינו כמה ארכן הוא זה. א"ל כלום מאריך יותר ממשה רבינו דכתיב ביה (דברים ט כה) את ארבעים היום ואת ארבעים הלילה וגו'. שוב מעשה בתלמיד אחד שירד לפני התיבה לפני רבי אליעזר והיה מקצר יותר מדאי. א"ל תלמידיו כמה קצרן הוא זה. א"ל כלום מקצר יותר ממשה

Eliezer: "See how brief he is!" "Is he then briefer than Moses, our teacher," replied R. Eliezer, "as written (Num. 12. 13.) O God, do Thou heal her, I beseech Thee."

R. Jacob said in the name of R. Chisda: "Whoever prays for his friend need not mention the friend's name, as it is said (Ib.) O God! do Thou heal her, I beseech Thee, and he did not mention Miriam's name." ...

Our Rabbis taught: "These are the blessings [of the Eighteen Benedictions] during the recital of which a man should bow; the blessing of the Ancestors (the first one, or Aboth), at its beginning and its end; the blessing of Acknowledgment, (one before the last, or Modim), at its beginning and at its end; if one desire to bow at the end and the beginning of each and every blessing, he is to be taught not to do so."

(Ib. b) (Mishnah) It was related of R. Chanina b. Dosa that he was wont to pray for the sick and predict, "This one shall live, this one shall die." Whereupon the Rabbis once asked of him: "How do you know it?" "I notice," he answered, "when I pray; if the prayer flows readily from my tongue, I know that it is accepted; but if not I know that it is torn."'

(Gemara) Whence do we learn this? R. Joshua b. Levi said: "The text reads (Is. 57, 19.) Creating the fruit of the lips, peace, peace to him, that is afar off, and to him that is near, saith the Lord; and I will heal him.

R. Chiya b. Abba in the name of R. Jochanan said: "All that the prophets prophesied [concerning future glory] was only for a repentant sinner, but as for the perfectly

רבינו דכתיב ביה (במדבר יב יג) אל נא רפא נא לה:

אמר ר' יעקב אמר רב חסדא כל המבקש רחמים על חברו אינו צריך להזכיר שמו שנאמר (במדבר יב יג) אל נא רפא נא לה ולא קא מדכר שמה דמרים:

תנו רבנן אלו ברכות שאדם שוהה בהם. באבות תחלה וסוף, בהודאה תחלה וסוף, ואם בה לשוח בסוף כל ברכה וברכה ובתחלת כל ברכה וברכה מלמדין אותו שלא ישחה:

(ע״ב) משנה אמרו עליו על רבי חנינא בן דוסא שהיה מתפלל על החולים ואומר זה חי וזה מת. אמרו לו מנין אתה יודע. אמר להם אם שגורה תפלתי בפי יודע אני שהוא מקובל ואם לאו יודע אני שהוא מטורף:

גמרא מנא הני מילי. אמר רבי יהושע בן לוי אמר קרא (ישעיה נז יט) בורא ניב שפתים שלום שלום לרחוק ולקרוב אמר ה' ורפאתיו:

אמר רבי חייא בר אבא אמר רבי יוחנן כל הנביאים כולם לא נתנבאו אלא לבעלי תשובה אבל צדיקים גמורים

righteous the glory will be No eye has seen, O God, beside Thee! (Is. 6-1, 3)." And this is in contradiction of what R. Abuhu said: "Where the repentant sinners stand the perfectly righteous are not permitted to stand, for it is said (Ib. 57, 19.) Peace, peace unto him that is afar off, and to him that is near. First to him who is afar off (repentant) and then to him who is near (righteous from the very beginning)." But R. Jochanan said: "What is meant by Afar off? He who was far from the 'very beginning* of a transgression; and Near to him, means he who was 'close to a transgression' but turned away therefrom." Further said R. Chiya b. Abba in the name of R. Jochanan: "The prophecy of all the prophets referred only to the period of Messiah, but as for the future world, No eye has witnessed. O God, beside Thee!" And this disagrees with Samuel; for Samuel said: "There will be no difference between this world and the future one except in the subjugation of the Exile, as it is said (Deu. 15, 11.) For the needy will not cease out of thy land." Further said R. Chiya b. Abba in the name of R. Jochanan: "The glorious future of which all the prophets prophesied is only for him who marries his daughter to a Talmid Chacham (Scholar), and for him who does business with a Talmid Chacham, and for him who bestows of his wealth upon a Talmid Chacham; but as to the scholars themselves, No eye has witnessed, O God, beside Thee! happy is he who waits (patiently) for it." What is meant by No eye has witnessed? R. Joshuah b. Levi said: "This refers to the wine preserved in its grapes since the six days of creation." R. Samuel b. Nachmeini said: "This refers to Eden which no eye ever saw. And if thou wilt ask, 'Where did Adam, the first man live?' It was only in

(ישעיה סד ג) עין לא ראתה אלהים זולתך. ופליגא דר' אבהו דאמר ר' אבהו במקום שבעלי תשובה עומדים אין צדיקים גמורים עומדין שנאמר (שם נז יט) שלום שלום לרחוק ולקרוב לרחוק ברישא והדר לקרוב. ורבי יוחנן אמר לך מאי רחוק שהיה רחוק מעבירה מעיקרא. מאי קרוב שהיה קרוב לעבירה ונתרחק ממנה השתא. וא"ר חייא בר אבא א"ר יוחנן כל הנביאים לא נתנבאו אלא לימות המשיח אבל לעולם הבא עין לא ראתה אלהים זולתך. ופליגא דשמואל דאמר שמואל אין בין העולם הזה לימות המשיח אלא שעבוד גליות בלבד שנא' (דברים טו יא) כי לא יחדל אביון מקרב הארץ. ואמר רבי חייא בר אבא אמר רבי יוחנן כל הנביאים כלן לא נתנבאו אלא למשיא בתו לתלמיד חכם ולעושה פרקמטיא לתלמיד חכם ולמהנה לתלמיד חכם מנכסיו אבל תלמידי חכמים עצמן עין לא ראתה אלהים זולתך יעשה למחכי לו. מאי עין לא ראתה אמר רבי יהושע בן לוי זה יין המשומר בענביו מששת ימי בראשית. רבי שמואל בר נחמני אמר זו עדן שלא ראתה עין מעולם. וא"ת אדם הראשון היכן היה בגן ושמא תאמר גן זה עדן ת"ל (בראשית ג י) ונהר יוצא מעדן להשקות את הגן. (תענית פ"ק ע"ש מהרש"א) גן לחוד ועדן לחוד:

the garden [of Eden]. And if thou wilt say that 'Garden' and 'Eden' are the same, it is therefore said (Gen. 2, 10.) And a river went out of Eden to water the garden [which shows that] 'Garden' and 'Eden' are two distinct places."

Our Rabbis taught: It happened once, that the son of Rabban Gamaliel took sick. The latter sent two learned men to R. Chanina b. Dosa asking him to beseech [the Lord] to have mercy on him. As soon as R. Chanina saw them coming he went up to the upper chamber and besought [the Lord] to have mercy on the sick. Coming down he said to the two learned men: "You may go home, for the fever has already left him." "Art thou a prophet?" they asked him". "Neither a prophet, nor the son of a prophet," he answered them, "but I have this tradition. If my prayer flow readily from my tongue, I know that it has been accepted, but if not, I know that it has been rejected." So they wrote down the exact hour when he told them [that the sick man was delivered], and when they came to Rabban Gamaliel, he said to them: "I swear that it happened neither before nor after the hour, but exactly at the time you were told that my son was relieved; at that moment [the sick] asked us for a drink of water." On another occasion it happened that when R. Chanina b. Dosa went to R. Jochanan b. Zackai to study the Torah the son of R. Jochanan b. Zackai took sick. The latter then said: "Chanina, my son, beseech [the Lord] to have mercy on my son that he may live." He placed his head between his knees and besought [God] to have mercy on his son. Whereupon he got well. Then R. Jochanan b. Zackai said: "If b. Zackai had kept his head between his knees

ת"ר מעשה וחלו בנו של ר"ג ושגר ב' ת"ח אצל ר"ח בן דוסא לבקש רחמים עליו כיון שראה אותם עלה לעליה וביקש רחמים עליו בירידתו אמר להם לכו שכבר חלצתו חמה. אמרו לו וכי נביא אתה. אמר להם לא נביא אני ולא בן נביא אני אלא כך מקובלני (מבית אבי אבא) אם שגורה תפלתי בפי יודע אני שהוא מקובל ואם לאו יודע אני שהוא מטורף. ישבו וכתבו וכוונו אותה שעה וכשבאו אצל ר"נ א"ל העבודה לא חסרתם ולא התרתם אלא כך היה מעשה באותה שעה חלצתו חמה ושאל לנו מים לשתות. ושוב מעשה ברבי חנינא בן דוסא שהלך ללמוד תורה אצל רבן יוחנן בן זכאי וחלה בנו של ריב"ז א"ל חנינא בני בקש עליו רחמים ויחיה. הניח ראשו בין ברכיו ובקש עליו רחמים וחיה. אמר רבן יוחנן ב"ז אלמלי הטיח ב"ז את ראשו בין ברכיו כל היום כלו לא השגיחו עליו. א"ל אשתו וכי חנינא גדול ממך. א"ל לאו אלא הוא דומה כעבד לפני המלך ואני דומה כשר לפני המלך:

for the whole day, it would have been of no effect." "Why," asked his wife, "is he greater than you?" "Nay," replied R. Jochanan, "but he is likened unto a servant before a king [who can enter the king's chamber whenever he wishes]; while I am as a prince before the king [who can enter only at certain times or by invitation] ."

R. Chiya b. Abba said in the name of R. Jochanan: "A man shall not pray in a house where there are no windows, for it is said (Dan. 6, 10-11.) Where he had open windows in his upper chamber, he kneeled upon his knees in the direction of Jerusalem and prayed three times every day." R. Cabana said: "I consider him insolent who prays in a valley [where people pass by]." Further said R. Cahana: "I consider him insolent who mentions his iniquities [while repenting], for it is said (Ps. 32, 1.) Happy is he whose transgression is forgiven, whose sin is covered."

ואמר ר' חייא בר אבא אמר רבי יוחנן אל יתפלל אדם אלא בבית שיש שם חלונות. שנא' (דניאל ו י-יא) וכוין פתיחן ליה בעליתה נגד ירושלם. אמר רב כהנא חציף עלי מאן דמצלי בבקתא, ואמר רב כהנא חציף עלי מאן דמפרש חטאיה שנא' (תהלים לב א) אשרי נשוי פשע כסוי חטאה:

Chapter 6

(Fol. 35a) How shall the Benediction on fruit be said, etc? Whence do we derive [that benedictions are to be said before eating]? Our Rabbis taught: All its fruit be holy for praises giving unto the Lord (Lev. 19, 24). "We infer that a benediction is to be said before and a benediction after [eating]." "From this, said R. Akiba, "we derive that it is prohibited to a man to taste anything before saying a benediction."

Our Rabbis taught: "It is prohibited to enjoy anything of this world without saving a

(דף לח) כיצד מברכין על הפירות וכו' מנא הני מילי דת"ר (ויקרא יט כד) קדש הלולים לה' מלמד שטעונין ברכה לפניהם ולאחריהם מכאן אמר רבי עקיבא אסור לאדם שיטעום כלום קודם שיברך:

תנו רבנן אסור לאדם שיהנה מן העולם הזה בלא ברכה

benediction, and he who enjoys [the least thing] in this world without saving a benediction defrauds [the Lord]. What shall his remedy be? Let him go to a learned man." What can a learned man do for him when he already has transgressed the prohibition? "But," said Raba, "let him go unto a learned man first; study the laws of benedictions that he may avoid sacrilege." R. Juda said in the name of Samuel: "He who enjoys [the least thing] in this world without having said a benediction is considered as if he had enjoyed something of the things dedicated to Heaven, for it is said (Ps. 24, 1.) Unto the Lord belongeth the earth and all that filleth it." R. Levi pointed out the following contradiction: "It is written (Ib. ib.) Unto the Lord belongeth the earth and all that filleth it, and it is also written (Ib. 115, I6.) The Heavens are the Heavens of the Lord; but the earth hath He given to the children of man. It is not difficult to reconcile [these two verses]. The former refers to the time before he pronounced the benediction [it still belongs to Heaven], (Ib. b.) and the latter refers to the time after he pronounced the benediction [then it belongs to man]." R. Chanina b. Papa said: "He who enjoys [anything] in this world without saying a benediction is considered as if he has robbed the Holy One, praised be He! and the Congregation of Israel, for it is said (Pr. 28, 24.) Whoso robbeth his father or his mother and saith it is no transgression, he is the companion of a destroyer. His father, refers to the Holy One, praised be He! as it is said (Deu. 32, 6.) Is He not thy father who hath bought thee; Or his mother, refers to nothing else but the Congregation of Israel., as it is said (Pr. 1, 8.) Hear, my son, the instructions of your father and cast not aside

וכל הנהנה מן העולם הזה בלא ברכה מעל. מאי תקנתיה ילך אצל ת״ח. ילך אצל תלמיד חכם מאי עביד ליה הא עבד לאיסוריה. אלא אמר רבא ילך אצל חכם מעיקרא וילמדנו ברכות כדי שלא יבא לידי מעילה. אמר רב יהודה אמר שמואל כל הנהנה מן העולם הזה בלא ברכה כאלו נהנה מקדשי שמים שנאמר (תהלים כד א) לה׳ הארץ ומלואה. רבי לוי רמי כתיב לה׳ הארץ ומלואה וכתיב (שם קטו טז) השמים שמים לה׳ והארץ נתן לבני אדם. לא קשיא כאן קודם ברכה (ע״ב) כאן לאחר ברכה. אמר רבי חנינא בר פפא כל הנהנה מן העולם הזה בלא ברכה כאלו גוזל להקב״ה וכנסת ישראל שנאמר (משלי כח כד) גוזל אביו ואמו ואומר אין פשע חבר הוא לאיש משחית. אביו זה הקב״ה שנאמר (דברים לב ו) הלא הוא אביך קנך ואין אמו אלא כנסת ישראל שנאמר (משלי א ח) שמע בני מוסר אביך ואל תטוש תורת אמך. מאי חבר הוא לאיש משחית. אמר רבי חנינא בר פפא חבר הוא לירבעם בן נבט שהשחית את ישראל לאביהם שבשמים:

the teaching of your mother." What is meant by He is a companion of a destroyer? R. Chanina b. Papa said: "He is a companion of Jeroboam, the son of Nebat, who has corrupted Israel in their relation to their Heavenly Father."

(Ib. b) R. Chanina b. Papa pointed out the following contradiction: "It is written (Hos. 2, 11.) And I shall take away my corn in its time. It is also written (Deu. 11, 14.) That thou mayest gather in thy corn and thy wine and thy oil. It is not difficult to reconcile [these two verses]. The latter refers to the time when Israel is doing the will of God, and the former refers to the time when Israel is not doing the will of God." Our Rabbis taught: That thou mayest gather in thine corn. (Ib.) Why is this commandment necessary? [Would not the people do it as a matter of course?] Because, it is written (Joshua, 1, 8.) This book of Torah shall not depart out of thy mouth. One may perhaps say that those words are meant literally [that a man must never cease studying], therefore it is written Thou shalt gather in the season, thy corn, thy wine and thy oil, conduct yourselves in regard to them as is the custom of the world." This is according to R. Ishmael; but R. Simon b. Jochai says: "How is it possible, if a man plows in the plowing season, sows in the sowing season, reaps in the harvest season, threshes in the threshing season, and winnows when there is a wind? What will become of the Torah? [For there will not remain any time to study]. "But said R. Simon b. Jochai, "when Israel is doing the will of God then their work is done through others, as is said (Is. 61, 5.) And strangers shall stand and feed your flocks. But when Israel is not performing the will of God, then

(ע״ב) רבי חנינא ב״פ רמי כתיב (הושע ב יא) ולקחתי דגני בעתו וכתיב (דברים יא יד) ואספת דגנך. לא קשיא כאן בזמן שישראל עושין רצונו של מקום כאן בזמן שאין ישראל עושין רצונו של מקום. ת״ר ואספת דגנך וגו' מה תלמוד לומר לפי שנאמר (יהושע א ח) לא ימוש ספר התורה הזה מפיך יכול דברים ככתבן ת״ל ואספת דגנך הנהג בהם מנהג דרך ארץ דברי רבי ישמעאל. רבי שמעון ב״י אומר אפשר אדם חורש בשעת חרישה וזורע בשעת זריעה וקוצר בשעת קצירה ודש בשעת דישה וזורה בשעת הרוח תורה מה תהא עליה. אלא בזמן שישראל עושין רצונו של מקום מלאכתן נעשית ע״י אחרים שנאמר (ישעיה סא ה) ועמדו זרים ורעו צאנכם ובזמן שאין ישראל עושין רצונו של מקום מלאכתן נעשית ע״י עצמן שנאמר ואספת דגנך ולא עוד אלא שמלאכת אחרים נעשית על ידם שנאמר (דברים כח מח) ועבדת את אויביך. אמר אביי הרבה עשו כרבי ישמעאל ועלתה בידם והרבה עשו כרשב״י ולא עלתה בידם. אמר להו רבא לרבנן במטותא מינייכו דלא תיתו

their work is to be done by themselves, as it is said (Deu. 11, 14.) And thou shalt gather in thy corn in season; moreover the work of other people is done by Israel, as is said (Deu. 28, 48.) Thou shall serve thine enemies." Abaye said: "Many who conducted themselves according to the opinion of R. Ishmael succeeded, but many who conducted themselves according to the opinion of R. Simon b. Jochai were not successful." Raba [being the head of an academy] was in the habit of saying to the disciples: "I beg of you, do not come before me [to the academy] during the days of Nisan (in Spring) nor during the days of Tishrei (in Fall), in order that you may not have any trouble in supporting yourselves during the entire year." Rabba b. b. Chana in the name of R. Jochanan quotes R. Juda b. Elai: "Come and see the great difference between the former generations and the later ones; the former generations made the study of the Torah their regular engagement and their vocation a temporary profession, and both endured with them. But the later generations made the study of the Torah their temporary engagement and their vocation a regular profession and neither endured with them."

(Fol. 40a) R. Juda said in the name of Rab: "A person must not eat before he feeds his cattle, as it is written (Ib. 11, 15.) And I will give grass in thy field for thy cattle, and it continues And thou shalt eat and be satisfied."

Raba the son of Samuel said in the name of R. Chiya: "After every meal eat salt, and after every drink, drink water, and then willst thou not be hurt." We are also taught that "After every meal eat salt, and after every drink, drink water, and then willst thou not be hurt." Another [Baraitha] teaches: "If he ate every kind of food but salt, if he drank every kind of drink but water, in the day he would worry because of an ill odor from his month and at night he would worry because of croup." Our Rabbis taught: "He who [drinks so much water as to] cause his food to swim, will never be disposed to stomach disease." How much shall one drink? R. Chisda said: "A kiton for each loaf of bread". R. Mari in the name of R. Jochanan said: "He who is accustomed to eat lentils once in thirty days will keep away sickness, but they are not to be eaten every day, because they cause a bad odor." Further said R. Mari in the name of R. Jochanan: "Mustard eaten once in thirty days drives out sickness but if eaten every day it is apt to affect the heart." R. Chiya, the son of R. Ashi. said in the name of Rab: "He who is used to small fish will never be disposed to stomach sickness; moreover small fish cause the strengthening of the whole body of a man." R. Chamba b. Chanina said: "He who is used to black cumin will not be disposed to heart trouble." The following objection was raised; Rabban Simon b. Gamaliel said; "Black cumin is one sixtieth of a deadly drug, and he who sleeps at the easterly side of his threshing floor, his blood is upon his head." This is not difficult to explain. Rabban Simon b. Gamaliel refers to smelling it, but eating it is indeed healthful.

(Fol. 43b) One more thing said R. Zutra b. Tubia in the name of Rab; others say R. Chanan b. Bizna said it in the name of R. Simon; still others say R. Jochanan said it in the name of R. Simon b. Jochai: "It is better for a man to be thrown into a fiery furnace than be the means of bringing another to shame in public. We infer this from Tamar, as is written (Gen. 38, 25.) She sent to her father-in-law saying, 'By the man who owns these, am I with child.' and she said. 'Acknowledge, I pray thee, the ownership of these, the signet, the scarf, and the staff. And Juda acknowledged it and said, 'She has been more righteous than I.'" [Tamar thus preferred to be burnt rather than to disclose Juda's name for fear of bringing public shame upon him.] Our Rabbis taught: "Six things are a disgrace to a learned man: He shall not go out perfumed; he shall not wear patched shoes; he shall not walk alone at night; he shall not talk with a woman on the street; he shall not sit at the table with ignorant men; he shall not enter the synagogue late." Some add to this, "He shall not take long steps when walking, and he shall not walk with a proud unbending gait." He shall not go out perfumed. R. Abba, the son of R. Chiya b. Abba, in the name of R. Jochanan said: "This refers to places where immorality prevails." R. Shesheth said it refers only to his clothes, but not to his body, as it is healthful. Regarding the hair [as to perfume], R. Papa says it is in the same class as clothes; others contend it is part of the body. He shall not wear patched shoes. This will support the opinion of R. Chiya b. Abba who said that it is a disgrace for a scholar to go out with patched shoes. Is it really so? Behold! R. Chiya b. Abba himself used to go out with patched shoes. Mar Zutra the son of R. Nachman said: "This is prohibited only when there is a patch upon a patch, then only on the leather, not on the sole, and only during the summer and in the street; but, during the winter or in the house it does not matter. He shall not walk alone at

לאדם שיפיל עצמי לתוך כבשן האש ואל ילבין פני חברו ברבים מנ"ל מתמר שנא' (בראשית לח כה) היא מוצאת והיא שלחה אל חמיה לאמר לאיש אשר אלה לו אנכי הרה, ותאמר הכר נא למי החתמת והפתילים והמטה האלה. ויכר יהודה ויאמר צדקה ממני. תנו רבנן ששה דברים גנאי לו לת"ח. אל יצא כשהוא מבושם לשוק ואל יצא במנעלים הממולאים ואל יצא יחידי בלילה ואל יספר אם אשה בשוק ואל יכנס באחרונה לבית המדרש ואל יסב בחבורה של עמי הארץ, וי"א אף אל יפסיע פסיעה גסה ואל יהלך בקומה זקופה. אל יצא כשהוא מבושם לשוק א"ר אבא בריה דרבי חייא בר אבא אמר רבי יוחנן במקום שחשודים על משכב זכור. א"ר ששת לא אמרן אלא בבגדו אבל בגופו זיעה מעברא ליה. א"ר פפא ושערו כבגדו דמי ואמרי ליה כגופו דמי. אל יצא במנעלים הממולאים מסייע ליה לר' חייא בר אבא דאמר ר' חייא בר אבא גנאי הוא לת"ח שיצא במנעלים המטולאים, איני והא רבי חייא בר אבא נפיק. אמר מר זוטרא בריה דרב נחמן בטלאי על גבי טלאי. ולא אמרן אלא בפנתא אבל בגילדא לית לן בה, ובפנתא לא אמרן אלא באורחא אבל בביתא לית לן בה, ולא אמרן אלא בימות החמה אבל בימות הגשמים לית לן בה. ואל יצא יחידי בלילה משום חשדא. ולא

night. Because of suspicion. He shall not talk with a woman on the street. R. Chisda said: "This refers even to his own wife." We have also a Baraitha to the same effect: "Even to his own wife, to his own daughter or to his own sister; for not every one is acquainted with his family." He shall not enter the synagogue late; for he may be called lazy; He shall not sit at the table with ignorant men, for he may adopt their bad manners. He shall not walk fast, because the master said: "Big steps take away one five hundredth of the light of a man's eye," [and if his eyes suffer] what shall be the remedy? Let him drink the cup of Habdala, and he will become well. He shall not walk with proud, unbending gait., because the master said, "He who walks even four cubits with a proua, unbending gait is considered to have spurned [with his haughty head] the feet of the Shechinah, for it is written (Is. 6, 3.) The whole earth is full of His glory."

(Fol. 44a) When R. Dimi came he told a story of a town belonging to King Janai, situated upon the royal mound. From that city there went forth every week six hundred thousand cans filled with fish, for the laborers who were busy collecting the trees there. When Rabin came he said: "King Janai has one single tree on the royal mound whence once a month they collected forty seahs of young pigeons of three different breeds." When R. Isaac came he told of a town named Gufnith in Palestine where there were eighty couples of brother priests who married eighty couples of sister priestesses and when the Rabbis searched in that neighborhood between Sura and Nehardea, they were not able to find husbands for the daughters of R. Chisda. These daughters were finally compelled to marry Rami and Ukba the sons of Chama although they were not priests.

(Ib. h) R. Janai in the name of Rab said: "The egg is better than anything that equals the size of an egg." When Rabin came he said: "A soft-boiled egg is better than six ounces of fine flour." When R. Dimi came, be said: "A soft-fried egg is better than six ounces of flour, a hard fried one [is better] than four ounces [of flour], a soft, or hard boiled one, if it is as big as an egg, the latter is better, but not so with meat." Our Rabbis taught: "A milt is good for the teeth but not for the stomach; vetch is bad for the teeth but is good for the stomach: all raw vegetables make the face green, and all unripe things affect men; every living thing, if eaten alive, strengthens life: every part which is near the [source of] life (as near the throat) also strengthens life; cabbage is a nourishing food, beetroot is good for medicinal use. Woe unto the house where turnip enters!"

Chapter 7

(Fol. 45a) When three men [over thirteen years of age] dine together [on food which requires previous thereto the washing of the hands], they are bound to say the after-meal grace in Mezuman (in company), etc. (Gemara) whence do we infer this? R. Assi said: "Scripture says (Ps. 34, 4.) Oh, you magnify the Lord with me, and let us exalt His name together." R. Abuhu said: "We infer from this. (Deu. 32, 3.) When I will proclaim the name of the Lord; ascribe ye greatness to our God." R. Chanan b. Abba said: "Whence do we infer that a man shall not answer Amen louder than the one that says the benedictions? It is said (Ps. 34, 4.) Oh, magnify the Lord with me, and let us exalt His name together." R. Simon b. Pazi said: "Whence do we infer that the Methurgeman (Interpreter) shall not raise his voice louder than the reader? It is said (Ex. 19, 19.) Moses spoke and God answered him with a loud voice; it was not necessary to say with a loud voice, and what is intimated by saying a loud voice? Just as loud as the voice of Moses." We have also a Baraitha to the same effect: "The Methurgeman shall not raise his voice louder than the reader. If the Methurgeman cannot raise his voice equal to that of the reader, then the reader should lower his voice [in order that the Methurgeman should be heard]."

(Fol. 47b) We are taught: Who is [to be considered] an Am-Ha'aretz? "He who does not observe the law of levitical cleanliness in his food," so says R. Meier. Acheirim say: "He who does not tithe his fruit in accordance with the law"; The Samaritans practice the latter correctly; for it is a Biblical law; and the master said, "Whatever command the Samaritans have undertaken to observe, they fulfill it more accurately than the Israelites."

Our Rabbis taught: "Who is [to be considered] a common man? He who does not read the Sh'm'a, (Hear O Israel, etc.), both morning and evening," so says R. Eliezer. R. Joshua says: "He who does not put on Tephilin (phylacteries)." Ben Azai says: "He who does not wear Tzitzis (fringes).'" R. Nathan says: "He who has no Mezuzah on his door post." R. Jonathan b. Joseph says:

"He who has children and does not bring them up in the study of the Torah." Acheirim say: "Even if one has studied the Bible and the Mishnah, but has failed to be in attendance upon scholars (as a disciple), he also is considered an Am Ha'aretz." Further said R. Joshua b. Levi: "A man shall always come to the synagogue early so that he may have an opportunity to be counted among the first ten. Thous a hundred men come after the first ten, the first ten will be rewarded for all of the others." How can you imagine that the first ten obtain the reward of all? But say rather that the reward of every one of the first ten will equal the reward of all the others together.

(Fol. 48a) R. Nachman said: "A child who understands to whom the benediction is offered is persona grata, to be counted among the three who appeal to the partakers of a meal to say grace after the meal (Mezuman)." Abaye and Rabba, when small, were sitting before Rabba. "To whom do you pray?" Rabba asked them. "To God," both answered." "But where is God?" he asked them. Raba lifted up his hand and pointed towards the ceiling, and Abaye went outside and pointed towards Heaven. "Both of you," remarked Rabba, "will become Rabbis. It is as the people say: 'When the pumpkin is still small, you can tell from its blossoms how it will turn out.'" King Janai and his queen were eating together, and since Janai had killed all the Rabbis, they had no learned person to recite for them the after-meal grace when they had finished their meal. "Who can give us a man, to recite for us the after-meal grace?" the king asked of his wife. Whereupon she replied, "Swear to me, that if I bring thee a man, thou wilt

אומרים אפילו קרא ושנה ולא שמש תלמידי חכמים הרי זה עם הארץ. ואמר ריב"ל לעולם ישכים אדם לבהכ"נ כדי שיזכה וימנה עם עשרה הראשונים שאפילו מאה באים אחריו קבל שכר כולם. שכר כולם ס"ד. אלא אימא נותנים לו שכר כנגד כולם:

(דף מח) אמר רבי נחמן קטן היודע למי מברכין מזמנין עליו. אביי ורבא הוו יתבי קמיה דרבה אמר להו רבה למי מברכין, אמרו ליה לרחמנא. ורחמנא היכא יתיב, רבא אחוי לשמי טללא אביי נפק לברא אחוי כלפי שמיא. אמר להו רבה תרוויכו רבנן הויתו, היינו דאמרי אינשי בוצין בוצין מקטפיה ידיע. ינאי מלכא ומלכתתא כריכו ריפתא בהדי הדדי ומדקטל להו לרבנן לא הוה ליה איניש לברוכי להו. אמר לה לדביתהו מאן יהב לן גברא דמברך לן אמרה ליה אישתבע לי דאי מייתינא לך גברא דלא מצערת ליה אשתבע לה. אייתיתיה לשמעון בן שטח אחוה אותביה בין דידיה לדידה אמר ליה חזי במה יקרא עבידנא לך אמר ליה לאו את קא מוקרית לי אלא אורייתא

not harm him." He swore to her, and she brought him Simon b. Shetach, her brother. The king gave him a seat between himself and his queen, saying: "Behold, how much I honor you." Whereupon R. Simon b. Shetach replied: "Not thou, but the Torah honors me; as it is written (Pr. 4, 8.) Exalt her and she shall promote thee; she will bring thee to honor, when thou embraceth her." King Janai then said unto the queen: "See how they (the Pharisees) do not recognize (royal) authority." Finally he gave R. Simon a cup [of wine] with which to recite the grace. So R. Simon b. Shetach said: "How can I say the grace? Shall I say, Blessed is He, because Janai and his associates have eaten of His (food)?'" Thereupon he drank the contents of the cup; whereupon they gave him another one, with which he said the grace. R. Abba, the son of R. Chiya, said in the name of R. Jochanan, that Simon b. Shetach [who said the after-meal grace on a cup of wine] did so according to his own opinion only; for thus has R. Chiya b. Abba said in the name of R. Jochanan: "Never can a man recite the after-meal grace for others unless he eats a piece of cornbread at least as large as an olive."

(Ib. b) R. Nachman said: "Moses ordained Birchath Hazan (the grace of the food), at the time when the Manna had descended for Israel. Joshua ordained Birchath Ha'aretz (the grace of the land), upon entering Palestine. David and Solomon both ordained the grace of Bonei Jerusalem (Build O Jerusalem): Have mercy upon Israel, Thy people; on Jerusalem, Thy city; on Zion, the residence of Thy glory, and of the great and holy house of David, Thy anointed, was ordained by David; and On the great and holy house which is called by Thy name, was ordained by Solomon, The grace of Hatob Vehameitib (who hath done good and caused goodness), was ordained by the people of Jabne, in memory of those killed in Bether, for R. Mathna said: "The very day on which those killed in Bether were permitted to be buried, the grace of Hatob Vehameitib was ordained in Jabne; Hatob (who hath done good), for those who were killed caused no stench; Vehameitib (who caused goodness), that they were permitted to be buried."

Our Rabbis taught: "Whence do we learn that the after-meal grace is a Biblical law? Is is written (Deu. 8, 10.) When thou hast eaten and art satisfied, then shalt thou bless the Lord, thy God. Whence do we learn that we must say a grace before we eat? It is written (Ib. ib.) Which he has given thee, i.e., as soon as he gives you, must you say the grace."

R. Meier said: "Whence do we derive that as a man blesses God for good tidings, so shall he bless God for evil tidings? It is written (Deu. 8, 11.) Which he hath given thee, the Lord, thay God, i.e., He is your judge whatever the sentence He decrees upon thee, whther it be a good or an evil dispensation."

(Fol. 51a) R. Jochanan said: "He who is careful to recite a grace on a full cup of wine, will be given boundless inheritance; as it is said (Deu. 33, 23.) And full with the blessing of the Lord take thou possession of the West and the South." R. Jose, the son of R. Chanina, said: "His reward will be to inherit both worlds, this world and the world to come."

הטוב והמטיב הטוב שלא הסריחו והמטיב שניתנו לקבורה:

ת"ר מנין לברכת המזון מן התורה שנאמר (דברים ח י) ואכלת ושבעת וברכת. אין לי אלא לאחריו לפניו מנין ת"ל אשר נתן לך, משנתן לך:

ר"מ אומר מנין שכשם שמברך על הטובה כך מברך על הרעה ת"ל (דברים ח יא) אשר נתן לך ה' אלהיך דיינך בכל דין שדנך בין מדה טובה ובין מדת פורעניות:

(דף נא) אמר רבי יוחנן כל המברך על כוס מלא נותנין לו נחלה בלא מצרים שנאמר (דברים לג כג) ומלא ברכת ה' ים ודרום ירשה. ר' יוסי ברבי חנינא אמר זוכה ונוחל שני עולמים העולם הזה והעולם הבא :

Chapter 8

Chapter 9

(Fol. 54a) Our Rabbis taught: "He who sees the passages where Israel crossed the sea, the Jordan, the passage of the brook of Arnon, the stones of the declivity of Beth Charan, the stone which Og attempted to throw upon Israel, the stone upon which Moses was sitting when Joshua fought Amalek, Lot's wife who became a pillar of salt, and the walls of Jericho which sank in their foundations, should give praise and thanksgiving to God." (Ib. b) The stone which Og, King of Bashan, tried to throw upon Israel is delivered by tradition as follows: "The camp of Israel [I see]," said he, "extends three miles. I shall therefore go and uproot a mountain three miles in extent and throw it upon them and kill them." He went and uprooted a mountain three miles in extent, and raised it above his head. But the Holy One, praised be He! sent a host of ants to the mountain and they bored a hole in it causing it to fall over his head and rest on his shoulderers. He tried to throw it oft, but his teeth protruding one into the other, had riveted it upon him and he was not able to throw it off. Thus is understood the passage (Ps. 3, 8.) Thou hast broken the teeth of the wicked; and as R. Simon ben Lakish explained it, for R. Simon b. Lakish said: "Do not read it Shibarta (Thou hast broken) but

Chapter 9

(דף נד) ת"ר הרואה מעברות הים ומעברות הירדן, מעברות נחלי ארנון, אבני אלגביש במורד בית חורן, ואבן שבקש לזרוק עוג מלך הבשן על ישראל, ואבן שישב עליה משה בשעה שעשה יהושע מלחמה בעמלק ואשתו של לוט, וחומת יריחו שנבלעה במקומה על כולן צריך שיתן הודאה ושבח לפני המקום. (ע"ב) אבן שביקש עוג מלך הבשן לזרוק על ישראל גמרא גמירי לה. אמר מחנה ישראל כמה הוי תלתא פרסי איזיל ואיעקר טורא בר תלתא פרסי ואשדי עלייהו ואיקטלינהו אזל עקר טורא בר ג' פרסי ואותביה ארישיה אייתי הקב"ה עליה קומצי ונקבוה ונחית ליה אצואריה בעא למשלפיה משכוה שיניה להאי גיסא ולהאי גיסא ולא מצי למישלפה והיינו דכתיב (תהלים ג ח) שני רשעים שברת וכדרשב"ל דאמר רב שמעון בן לקיש אל תקרי שברת אלא שרבבת. משה כמה הוי עשר אמין, שקל נרגא בת עשר אמין ושוור עשר אמין ומחייה בקרסוליה וקטליה. אמר רב יהודה אמר

read it Shirbabta (that became ramified), i.e., Thou hast caused to branch out." What was Moses' height? Ten cubits; he seized an axe ten cubits long, sprang up ten cubits, and struck Og's ankle a mighty blow which killed him. R. Juda in the name of Rab said: "Four classes of people are in duty bound to return thanks to God. Those who have returned from a voyage at sea; those who have traveled in the desert; those who have recovered from a serious illness, and those who are liberated from prison." Whence do we learn this concerning those that have returned from a voyage at sea? It is written (Ps. 107, 23-31.) They who go down to the sea in ships, etc. These have seen the wonders of the Lord. For he spoke, and he raised the stormy wind. They would mount up to heaven, they would go down to the depths. They would reel to and fro, etc. And they were rejoiced because they were silent. They shall therefore give thanks unto the Lord. Whence do we infer this concerning those who have traveled in the deserts? It is written (Ib. ib. 4-8.) They wandered about in the wilderness, hungry and thirsty. Then they cried unto the Lord, and he led them forth upon the right road. Therefore they shall give thanks unto the Lord. Whence do we infer this concerning those who have recovered from a serious illness? It is written (Ib. ib. 17-2.) Fools, because of their transgression. All manner of food their soul abhorreth. But when they cry unto the Lord. He sendeth his word and healeth them. They therefore shall give thanks unto the Lord. Whence do we know this concerning those who have been liberated from prison? it is written (Ib. ib. 10-20.) Such as sit in darkness and in the shadow of death. Because they have rebelled against the words of God. And

רב ארבעה צריכין להודות ואלו הן. יורדי הים והולכי מדברות ומי שהיה חולה ונתרפא ומי שהיה חבוש בבית האסורים ויצא. יורדי הים מנלן דכתיב (תהלים קז כג -לא) יורדי הים באניות וגו' המה ראו מעשי ה' וגו' ויאמר ויעמד רוח סערה וגו' יעלו שמים ירדו תהומות וגו' יחוגו וינועו וגו' ויצעקו אל ה' בצר להם וממצוקותיהם יוציאם. וישמחו כי ישתקו וגו' יודו לה' חסדו וגו'. הולכי מדברות מנלן דכתיב (שם) תעו במדבר וגו' רעבים גם צמעים וגו' ויצעקו אל ה' וגו' וידריכם בדרך ישרה וגו' יודו לה' חסדו וגו'. מי שהיה חולה ונתרפא מנלן דכתיב אוילים מדרך פשעם וגו' כל אכל תתעב נפשם וגו' ויצעקו אל ה' וגו' ישלח דברו וירפאם וגו' יודו לה' חסדו וגו'. ומי שהיה חבוש בבית האסורים ויצא מנלן דכתיב יושבי חשך וצלמות וגו' כי המרו אמרי אל וגו' ויכנע בעמל לכם וגו' ויצעקו אל ה' וגו' יוציאם מחשך וצלמות וכו' יודו לה' חסדו וכו'. מאי מברך אמר רב יהודה ברוך גומל חסדים טובים. ואמר אביי צריך לאודויי קמי עשרה דכתיב (שם) וירוממוהו בקהל עם וגו'. מר זוטרא אמר ותרין מינייהו רבנן דכתיב ובמושב זקנים יהללוהו. ר"י ור"א דאמרי תרוויהו בזמן שבית המקדש קיים מזבח מכפר על ישראל, ועכשיו שלחנו של אדם מכפר:

he humbled their hearts with trouble But when they cry unto the Lord He bringeth them out of the darkness. They, therefore, shall give thanks unto the Lord. How shall they say the grace? R. Juda said: "Blessed art thou who bestoweth kindness." Abaye said: "It should be said in the presence of ten persons, as it is written (Ib. ib. 32) And they must exalt him in the congregation of people." Mar Zutra said: "And two of the ten shall be learned men, as it is written (Ib. ib.) And in the assembly of the elders must they praise Him." (Fol 55a) R. Jochanan and R. Elazar both said: "As long as the Temple was in existence, the altar was [the means of] atonement for Israel, but now [since there is no Temple], each man's table is [the means of] atonement."

R. Juda said further: "Three things may cause to shorten a man's days and years: Refusing to read the Torah when offered to him; refusing to recite the [customary] grace over a cup [of wine], and leading a dominating life. Refusing to read the Torah, as it is written (Deu. 30, 20.) For he (the Torah) is thy life and the length of thy days. Refusing to recite the benediction over a cup of wine, as it is written (Gen. 12, 3.) And I will bless them that will bless thee. And he who leads a dominating life, as R. Chama b. Chanina said: "Joseph died before his brethren because he dominated them."

(Fol. 55a) R. Jochanan said: "Three things God Himself proclaimeth: Famine, plenty and a good chief of the community. Famine, as it is written (II Kings 8. 7.)' The Lord hath called for a famine; Plenty, as it is written (Ezek. 36, 29.) And I will call for corn and

ואמר רב יהודה שלשה דברים מקצרין ימיו ושנותיו של אדם, מי שנותנין לו ס"ת לקרוא ואינו קורא וכוס של ברכה לברך ואינו מברך והמנהיג עצמו ברבנות. מי שנותנין לו ספר תורה לקרוא ואינו קורא דכתיב (דברים ל כ) כי הוא חייך ואורך ימיך. וכוס של ברכה לברך ואינו מברך דכתיב (בראשית יב ג) ואברכה מברכיך ומקללך אאור. והמנהיג עצמו ברבנות דאמר רב חמא בר חנינא מפני מה מת יוסף קודם אחיו מפני שהנהיג עצמו ברבנות:

(דף נה א) אמר רבי יוחנן שלשה דברים הקב"ה מכריז עליהם בעצמו ואלו הן רעב ושבע ופרנס טוב. רעב דכתיב (מ"ב ח ז) כי קרא ה' לרעב. שבע דכתיב (יחזקאל לו כט) וקראתי אל הדגן

increase it; A good chief of the community, as it is written (Ex. 31, 2.) Behold, I have called by name, Bezalel." R. Isaac said: "A chief of a community is not to be appointed unless the community be consulted first; as it is written (Ex. 35, 30.) And Moses said to the children of Israel, behold God hath called by name Bezalel. i.e., The Holy One, praised be He! said thus to Moses, 'Moses! is Bezalel worthy enough for you?' 'Sovereign of the universe,' replied Moses, 'if he is worthy in thine eyes, then he certainly is worthy enough for me.' Then said God to him: 'Consult then, the children of Israel.' Moses thereupon went and said thus to the children of Israel: 'Is Bezalel worthy of you?' They said, 'If he is worthy for the Holy One, praised be He! and for thee, then he is surely worthy enough for us.' " R. Samuel b. Nachmeini in the name of R. Jonathan said: "The name Bezalel was given to him because of his wisdom; for when the Holy One, praised be He! said unto Moses, ' Go, tell Bezalel to erect for me a Mishkan, ark and vessels.' Moses went and told it to him in the reverse order — make ark, vessels and a Mishkan. [Upon hearing the order] Bezalel said: 'Moses, our teacher, the custom of the world is that a man first builds a house and then brings into it vessels, and thou sayest to me I should first make the ark, and then the Mishkan; where shall I put the vessels if I make them first? Perhaps the Holy One, praised be He! said first Mishkan and then the ark and the vessels?' Thereupon Moses said to him: 'Perhaps in the shadow of God hast thou been that thou knowest.'" [Thus Bezalel means — Bezal (in the shadow), El (of God)]. R. Juda said in the name of Rab: "Bezalel knew how to arrange the letters with which heaven and earth were created,

והרביתי אותו. פרנס טוב דכתיב (שמות לא ב) ראה קראתי בשם בצלאל. אמר ר׳ יצחק אין מעמידין פרנס על הצבור אלא אם כן נמלכין בצבור שנאמר (שם לה ל) ויאמר משה אל בני ישראל ראו קרא ה׳ בשם בצלאל. אמר ליה הקב״ה למשה משה הגון עליך בצלאל. אמר ליה רבונו של עולם אם לפניך הגון לפני לא כ״ש אמר לו אף על פי כן לך אמור להם לישראל הלך ואמר להם לישראל הגון עליכם בצלאל. אמרו לו אם לפני הקדוש ברוך הוא ולפניך הגון לפנינו לא כל שכן. אמר רבי שמואל בר נחמני א״ר יונתן בצלאל על שם חכמתו נקרא שבשעה שאמר לו הקב״ה למשה לך אמור לבצלאל עשה לי משכן ארון וכלים הלך משה והפך ואמר לו עשה ארון וכלים ומשכן אמר לו משה רבינו מנהגו של עולם אדם בונה בית ואחר כך מכניס לתוכו כלים ואתה אומר עשה כלים ארון ומשכן כלים שאני עושה, להיכן אכניסם שמא כך אמר לך הקב״ה עשה משכן ארון וכלים. אמר ליה שמא בצל אל היית וידעת. אמר רב יהודה אמר רב יודע היה בצלאל לצרף אותיות שנבראו בהן שמים וארץ כתיב הכא (שמות לה לא) וימלא אותו רוח אלהים בחכמה ובתבונה ובדעת וכתיב התם (משלי ג יט) ה׳ בחכמה יסד ארץ כונן שמים בתבונה וכתיב (שם ד) בדעתו תהומות נבקעה אמר

for it is written here (Ex. 35, 31.) And He hath filled him with the spirit of God, in wisdom (Chachma) in uderstanding (Bithbuna), and in knowledge, and it is written (Pr. 3, 19.) The Lord hath founded the earth through wisdom (Chachma); He hath established the heavens through understanding (Tebuna). And it is further written By His knowledge were the depths split open." R. Jochanan said: "The Holy One, praised be He! doth not give wisdom to a man unless he possesses some; as it is said (Dan. 2, 21.) Who giveth wisdom unto the wise, and knowledge to those who possess understanding." When R. Tachalifa of the west (Palesine) heard this he went and related it to R. Abuhu, whereupon the latter replied: "What you infer from that passage, we derive from another; it is written (Ex. 31, 6.) And in the heart of all that are wise-hearted have I put wisdom."

רבי יוחנן אין הקב״ה נותן חכמה אלא למי שיש בו חכמה שנאמר (דניאל ב כא) יהב חכמתא לחכימין ומנדעא לידעי בינה. שמע רב תחליפא בר מערבא אזל אמרה קמיה דרבי אבהו אמר ליה אתון מהתם מתניתו להו אנן מהכא מתנינן לה דכתיב (שמות לא ו) ובלב כל חכם לב נתתי חכמה:

R. Chisda said: "Every dream is good except that of fasting." Further said R. Chisda: "Of a bad dream the worry is sufficient [to dissipate it], and of a good one the joy is sufficient [to dissipate it]." R. Joseph said: "Even to me [though blind] the humor of a good dream causes it to dissipate." Further said R. Chisda: "A bad dream is much better than a good one [because it may result in repentance]." Further said R. Chisda: "Neither a good dream nor a bad one is fully fulfilled." Again said R. Chisda: "A dream not interrupted is like a letter not read." Further said R. Chisda: "A bad dream is more severe than being lashed, for it is said (Ecc. 3, 14.) And God hath so made it that men should be afraid of Him, and Rabba b. b. Chana said in the name of R. Jochanan: 'This refers to a bad dream.' " The prophet that hath had a

אמר ר״ח כל חלום ולא טוות, ואמר רב חסדא חלמא בישא עציבותיה מסתייה חלמא טבא חדויה מסתייה. אמר רב יוסף חלמא טבא אפילו לדידי בדיחותיה מפכחא ליה. ואמר רב חסדא חלמא בישא עדיף מחלמא טבא ואמר רב חסדא לא חלמא טבא מתקיים כוליה ולא חלמא בישא מתקיים כוליה. ואמר רב חסדא חלמא דלא מפשר כאגרתא דלא מיקריא. ואמר רב חסדא חלמא בישא קשה מנגדא שנאמר (קהלת ג יד) והאלהים עשה שייראו מלפניו ואמר רבה בר בר חנה א״ר יוחנן זה חלום רע. (ירמיה כג כח) הנביא אשר אתו חלום יספר חלום ואשר דברי אתו

dream, let him relate his dream; and he that hath received my word, let him speak my word of truth. What hath the straw to do with the corn? Saith the Lord (Jer. 23, 28). What relation has corn and straw to a dream? R. Jochanan in the name of R. Simon b. Jochai said: "Just as it is impossible for corn to be without straw, so it is impossible for a dream to be without absurdities."

R. Berachia said: "There may be a dream which thought in part fulfilled, yet is impossible of being entirely fulfilled. We can derive it from Joseph, for it is written (Gen. 37, 9.) The sun and the moon and the eleven start. — Shall we indeed come, I and thy mother, and thy brothers (Ib. b). And at that time his mother was dead." R. Levi said: "A man should look forward to the realization of a good dream even for as long as twenty-two years; as it is written (Gen. 37, 2.) These are the generations of Jacob, Joseph was seventeen years old [when he had the dreams], and it is written also (Ib. 41, 46.) And Joseph was thirty years old when he stood before Pharaoh. From seventeen to thirty are thirteen years, to which add the seven years of plenty and the two years of famine, will make the total of twenty-two years." R. Huna said: "To a good man bad dreams are shown, and to a bad man good dreams." We have also a Baraitha to the same effect: "During all the years of David he never dreamed a good dream, and during all the years of Achitophel he never dreamed a bad dream." R. Bizna b. Zabda, in the name of R. Akiba, who spoke in the name of R. Panda, who, in turn, spoke in the name of R. Nachum, who quoted R. Birim, said: "A venerable man by the name of R. Bana'ah had told him there were twenty-four places

ידבר דברי אמת מה לתבן את הבר נאום ה', וכי מה ענין בר ותבן אצל חלום א"ר יוחנן משום רשב"י כשם שא"א לבר בלא תבן כך א"א לחלום בלי דברים בטלים:

אמר ר' ברכיה חלום אף על פי שמקצתו מתקיים כולו אינו מתקיים מנלן מיוסף דכתיב (בראשית ל"ז ט) והנה השמש והירח וגו' הבוא נבוא אני ואמך ואחיך להשתחוות לך ארצה (שם ע"ב) וההיא שעתא אמיה לא הויא. א"ר לוי לעולם יצפה אדם לחלום טוב עד כ"ב שנה מנ"ל מיוסף שנא' (שם ב) אלה תולדות יעקב יוסף בן שבע עשרה שנה וכתיב (שם מא מו) ויוסף בן שלשים שנה בעמדו לפני פרעה, משבע עשרה עד שלשים כמה הואי תליסר, שבע דשבעא ותרתין דכפנא הוי עשרין ותרין. אמר רב הונא לאדם טוב אין מראין לו חלום טוב ולאדם רע אין מראין לו חלום רע. תניא נמי הכי כל שנותיו של דוד לא ראה חלום טוב וכל שנותיו של אחיתופל לא ראה חלום רע. אמר רב ביזנא בר זבדא א"ר עוקבא א"ר פנדא אמר רבי נחום א"ר בירים משום זקן אחד ומנו רבי בנאה עשרים וארבעה פותרי חלומות היו בירושלים. פעם אחת חלמתי חלום והלכתי אצל כולם מה שפתר לי זה לא פתר לי זה וכולם נתקיימו

in Jerusalem for the interpretation of dreams; that once he had a dream and went to each one of these places; each one gave a different interpretation and each was fulfilled." This establishes what is written: "Every dream is in accord with its interpretation." Is this a passage? Yes, as R. Elazar said, for R. Elazar said: "Whence do we learn that every dream is realized according to its interpretation? It is written (Gen. 41, 13.) And just as he interpreted it, so it was."

R. Jochanan said: "Three dreams are bound to be realized: that which is dreamed in the morning; that which is dreamed by one's neighbor: and a dream which is interpreted within a dream." Some add to this "A dream that is dreamed by the same person twice": as it is written (Gen. 41, 32.) And for that the dream was doubled unto Pharaoh.

(Fol. 57b) Three things restore the mind of a man: melody, scenery and sweet odor. Three things develop the mind of a man: a fine house, a handsome wife and elegant furniture. Five things have in them a sixtieth part of the five other things: fire, honey, the Sabbath, sleep and dreams. Fire [has] a sixtieth of Gehenna; honey [has] a sixtieth of Manna; the Sabbath [has] a sixtieth of the world to come; sleep [has] a sixtieth of death, and dreams [have] a sixtieth of prophecy.

(Fol. 58a) Our Rabbis taught: "He who sees Jewish troops or bands shall say the fol-following grace: 'Praised be He who understandeth their secrets (the minds of men);' for their knowledge is not equal to one another's, just as their features are not like one another's.'" Ben Zoma saw troops

בי לקיים מה שנא' כל החלומות הולכין אחר הפה אטו כל החלומות הולכין אחר הפה קרא הוא, אין וכדברי אלעזר דאמר רבי אלעזר מנין שכל החלומות הולכין אחר הפה שנאמר (בראשית מא יג) ויהי כאשר פתר לנו כן היה:

אמר רבי יוחנן שלשה חלומות מתקיימין, חלום של שחרית וחלום שחלם לו חברו וחלום שנפתר בתוך חלומו ויש אומרים אף חלום שנשנה שנאמר (שם מא לב) ועל השנות החלום:

(נז ע״ב) ג' משיבין דעתו של אדם, אלו הן: קול ומראה וריח. ג' מרחיבין דעתו של אדם ואלו הן דירה נאה ואשה נאה וכלים נאים. חמשה אחד מששים ואלו הן אש דבש שבת ושינה וחלום, אש אחד מששים לגיהנם, דבש אחד מששים למן, שבת אחד מששים לעולם הבא, שינה אחד מששים למיתה, חלום אחד מששים לנבואה:

(דף נח ע״א) תנו רבנן הרואה אוכלוסי ישראל אומר ברוך חכם הרזים, שאין דעתן דומות זו לזו ואין פרצופיהן דומות זו לזו. בן זומא ראה אוכלוסא על גב מעלה בהר הבית אמר ברוך חכם הרזים

on the elevation of the Temple mound. He said: "Blessed is He who understandeth their secrets, and blessed is He who created them all to serve me." He (b. Zoma) said: "Behold, how much labor did Adam, the first man, have until he got bread to eat; plowed, sowed, reaped, heaped together in sheaves, threshed winnowed, cleansed, ground, sieved, kneaded and baked; only after all these was he able to eat; but I rise in the morning and find all this done and prepared for me. And how much labor did Adam, the first man, have before he found a garment with which to clothe himself; he sheared the sheep, whitened the wool, dispersed it, spinned it, weaved, dyed, and sewed; only after [doing] all these did he find garments to clothe himself; but I rise in the morning and find everything done for me. All nations are anxious to come to the door of my house, and I rise and find everything [prepared] for me." Ben Zoma was accustomed also to say: "What says a good guest? 'The master of the house troubled himself so much for me; he brought so much wine for me; he brought so much meat for me, and he brought so many rolls for me; and all this trouble was on my account only.' But what says a bad guest? 'What trouble was the master of the house put to. How little wine he brought, how little meat he brought, how little rolls he brought, and all this trouble was for the sake of his own wife and children only [not for me] .' Concerning the good guest, the passage says (Job 36, 24.) Reflect that thou shouldst magnify his work, but regarding the bad guest it says (Ib. 37, 24.) Therefore do men fear him." And the man mas old in the days of Saul (I Sam. 17, 12.) Raba, and according to some R. Zebid, and according to others, R. Oshiya,

וברוך שברא כל אלו לשמשני, הוא היה אומר כמה יגיעות יגע אדה"ר עד שמצא פת לאכול חרש וזרע וקצר ועמר ודש וזרה ובירר וטחן והרקיד ולש ואפה ואח"כ אכל, ואני משכים ומוצא כל אלו כשהוא מתוקן לפני, וכמה יגיעות יגע אדה"ר עד שמצא בגד ללבוש גזז ולבן ונפץ וטוה וארג וצבע ותפר ואחר כך מצא בגד ללבוש, ואני משכים ומוצא כל אלו כשהוא מתוקן לפני. כל אומניות שוקדות ובאות לפתח ביתי ואני משכים ומוצא כל אלו לפני. הוא היה אומר אורח טוב אומר כמה טרחות טרח בעל הבית לפני כמה יין הביא לפני וכמה בשר הביא לפני וכמה גלוסקאות הביא לפני, כל הטורח שטרח לא טרח אלא בשבילי. אבל אורח רע אומר מה טרחות טרח בעל הבית זה מה יין הביא מה בשר הביא מה גלוסקאות הביא, כל מה שטרח לא טרח אלא בשביל אשתו ובניה על אורח טוב מהו אומר (איוב לו כב) זכור כי תשגיא פעלו וגו'. על אורח רע כתיב (שם לז כד) לכן יראוהו אנשים. (ש"א יז יב) והאיש בימי שאול זקן בא באנשים וגו' אמר רבא ואי תימא רב זביד ואיתימא רב אושעיא זה ישי אבי דוד שיצא באוכלוסא ונכנס באוכלוסא ודרש באוכלוסא. אמר עולא נקטינן אין אוכלוסא בבבל, תנא אין אוכלוסא פחותה מס' רבוא. ת"ר הרואה מלכי ישראל

said: "This is Jesse, David's father, who used to go out with troops and enter with troops, and lectured before a crowd." Ulla said: "We have a tradition that Babylon has no troops." In a Baraitha we are taught: They are not called "troops" if loss than sixty myriads. Our Rabbis taught: "He who sees Kings of Israel shall say, 'Blessed be He who shared his honor with those who fear Him'; and if he see kings of other nations he shall say, 'Blessed be He who shared His honor with [one who is] flesh and blood.' Seeing wise men of Israel, he shall say, 'Blessed be He who shared his wisdom with those who fear Him'; and if he see the wise men of other nations he shall say, 'Blessed be He who gave from his wisdom to [one who is] flesh and blood.'" R. Jochanan said: "A man should always try his utmost to go out to meet the Kings of Israel, and not only to meet the Kings of Israel [did the Rabbis urge], but also to meet kings of other nations, because if he will have merit [to see the King Messiah] he will then note the distinction between the Kings of Israel and the kings of other nations." R. Shesheth was blind, yet, when the whole community once went out to meet the king, he went out with them and was met by a certain heretic who laughed at him saying: "All the earthen pitchers are indeed going to the stream [to draw water]; whither do the broken vessels go?" "Come!" R. Shesheth said unto him, "I will show thee that I know more than you do." When the first company of troops passed by making a great noise, the heretic asked, "Has the king passed?" "No." replied R. Shesheth. When a second group of troops passed, the heretic again asked whether the king had passed. Again R. Shesheth answered "No." A third company passed in a very quiet manner. The

אומר ברוך שחלק מכבודו ליראיו, מלכי עובדי כוכבים אומר ברוך שנתן מכבודו לבשר ודם, חכמי ישראל אומר ברוך שחלק מחכמתו ליראיו. חכמי עובדי כוכבים אומר ברוך שנתן מחכמתו לבשר ודם. א"ר יוחנן לעולם ישתדל אדם לצאת לקראת מלכי ישראל ולא לקראת מלכי ישראל בלבד אלא אפי' לקראת מלכי עובדי כוכבים שאם יזכה יבחין בין מלכי ישראל למלכי עובדי כוכבים. רב ששת סגי נהור הוה הוו קאזלי כולי עלמא לקבולי אפי מלכא וקם אזל בהדייהו רב ששת, אשכחיה ההוא מינאה א"ל חצבי לנהרא כגני לייא, אמר ליה תא חזי דידענא טפי מינך, חליף גונדא קמייתא כי קא אוושא א"ל חליף מלכא א"ל לאו חליף אחריתי א"ל חליף מלכא, א"ל לאו. אתאי תליתאה דהוה שתקא, א"ל אתא מלכא א"ל אין א"ל מנא ידעת, א"ל מלכותא דארעא כעין מלכותא דרקיעא דכתיב (מ"א יט יב) ואחר הרעש אש לא באש ה' ואחר האש קול דממה דקה, כי אתא מלכא פתח רב ששת וקאמר ברוך, א"ל ההוא צדוקי למאן דלא חזית לידה קא מברכת. ומאי הוי עליה דההוא מינאה, איכא דאמרי חברוהי כחלינהו לעיניה ואיכא דאמרי רב ששת נתן עיניו בו ונעשה גל של עצמות:

heretic asked: "Is the king coming now?" Whereupon R. Shesheth answered: "Yes." The heretic asked him how he knew this. R. Shesheth replied: "The kingdom on the earth is like the kingdom in Heaven, for it is written (I Kings 19, 12.) After the earthquake there was a fire, but the Lord was not in the fire; after the fire there, was heard the sound of a soft whisper." When the king approached. R. Shesheth began to say, "Praised be He, etc.; whereupon the heretic interrupted him saying: "Since you do not see, how can you bless?" What happened to that heretic? Some say his associates pierced his eyes; according to others, R. Shesheth himself looked at him and he thereupon became a heap of bones.

R. Shila lashed a certain man for having committed adultery. The man went over to the Government [of the Roman Empire], and informed them that there was a man among Israel who executed judgment without the permission of the king. The king sent a representative who, when he arrived, asked R. Shila: "Why did you lash that man?" "Because," answered R. Shila, "he committed adultery." "Have you any witness who saw it?" the representative asked. "Yes," he replied. Thereupon Elijah came in the image of a man and testified. "If so," said the representative, "he should be killed." "Well," replied R. Shila, "since the day we were exiled from our land, we have had no authority to exercise capital punishment; you may do as you please with him." While they were deciding what to do with that man, R. Shila began to praise God, saying Thine, O Lord, are the greatness and the might and glory, and the victory and the majesty, yea, all that is in the heavens and

רבי שילא נגדיה לההוא גברא דבעל זונה אזל אכל קורצא בי מלכא אמר איכה גברא חד ביהודאי דדאין דינא כלא הורמנא דמלכא. שדר עליה פריסתקא בי אתא א״ל מ״ט נגדתיה לההוא גברא אמר להו משום דבעל חמרא, אמרו ליה אית לך סהדי אמר להו אין, אתא אליהו ז״ל אתדמי להו כאיניש ואסהיד אמרו ליה אי הכי בר קטלא הוא. אמר אנן מיומא דגלינן מארעין לית לן רשותא למקטל אתון מאי דבעיתון עבידו ביה. עד דמעייני ביה בדינא פתח רב שילא ואמר (דה״א כט יא) לך ה׳ הגדולה והגבורה והתפארת והנצח וההוד כי כל בשמים ובארץ, אמרו ליה מאי קאמרת אמר להו הכי קאמינא בריך רחמנא דיהב מלכותא דארעא כעין מלכותא דרקיעא

on the earth; Thine, O Lord are the kingdom, and thou art exalted as the head above all (I Chr. 29, 11). "What art thou saying?" he was asked. "Thus I said," he answered," "Praised be the all merciful who giveth the kingdom on earth just as the kingdom in the heaven, and who bestowed the rulership upon you who love justice." "Since you esteem the honor of the kingdom so highly let this man, therefore be the Judge who shall preside over all judicial affairs." He thereupon gave R. Shila a cane [as a token of a judge] saying: "Execute judgment." When he was through he said: "Since that passage was the cause of such a miracle I would explain it." Thereupon he went to the academy and expounded: Thine, O Lord, are the greatness, refers to the act of creation, as it is written (Job 9, 10,) Who doth great things which are quite unsearchable; And the might, refers to the redemption of Egypt, and so says the passage (Ex. 14, 31) And Israel saw that great power which the Lord hath shown; And the glory, refers to the incident of the sun and the moon which Joshua stopped in their course; as is said (Josh. 10, 13.) And the sun stood still and the moon stopped; And the victory, refers to the downfall of Babylon, and so says the passage (Is. 63, 3.) And their blood was sprinkled on my garments; And the majesty, this refers to the battle of Arnon, as it is said (Num. 21, 14.) Therefore mention is made in the books of wars of the Lord of Voheb in Suph, etc.; Yea, all that is in the heaven and on the earth, this refers to the war of Sisra and so says the passage (Judge 5, 20.) From heaven they fought; and Thine, O Lord, is the kingdom, refers to the war of Amalek, as is said (Ex. 17. 16.) And he said. Because the Lord hath sworn on his throne; And thou art exalted, this refers to

ויהיב לכו שולטנא ורחמי דינא, אמרו חביבא עליה יקרא דמלכותא כולי האי. יהבי ליה קולפא א"ל דון דינא. כי הוה נפק וכו' אמר הואיל ואיתעביד לי ניסא בהאי קרא דרשינן ליה נפק לבי מדרשא ודרש לך ה' הגדולה זה מעשה בראשית וכה"א (איוב ט י) עושה גדולות עד אין הקר, והגבורה זו יציאת מצרים וכה"א (שמות יד לא) וירא ישראל את היד הגדולה, והתפארת זו חמה ולבנה שעמדו לו ליהושע שנא' (יהושע י יג) וידום השמש וירח עמד, והנצח זו מפלתה של רומי וכה"א (ישעיה סג ג) ויז נצחם על בגדי, וההוד זו מלחמת נחלי ארנון שנא' (במדבר כא יד) על כן יאמר בספר מלחמות ה' את והב בסופה וגו', כי כל בשמים ובארץ זו מלחמת סיסרא שנאמר (שופטים ה כ) מן שמים נלחמו הכוכבים ממסלותם וגו', לך ה' הממלכה זו מלחמת עמלק וכן הוא אומר (שמות יז טז) כי יד על כס יה, והמתנשא זו מלחמת גוג ומגוג וכה"א (יחזקאל לח ג) הנני אליך גוג נשיא ראש משך ותובל, לכל לראש אמר רב חנן בר אבא אפילו ריש גרגותא מן שמיא מוקמי. במתניתא תנא משמיה דר"ע לך ה' הגדולה זו קריעת ים סוף, והגבורה זו מכת בכורות, והתפארת זו מתן תורה, והנצח זו ירושלים, וההוד זו בנין בית המקדש (יהי רצון שיבנה במהרה

בימינו):

the war of Gog and Magog, and so says the passage (Ezck. 38, 3.) Behold, I will be against thee, O God, the prince of Besh, Meshech and Thubal; As the head above all, R. Chana b. Abba said: "This means that even a superintendent over the well [which is made to water the fields] is also appointed in Heaven." In a Baraitha we are taught in the name of R. Akiba: Thine, O Lord, are the greatness, refers to the miracle of dividing the Red Sea; The might, refers to the plague of the first-born (in Egypt); The glory, refers to the giving of the Torah; And the victory, refers to Jerusalem; The majesty, refers to the rebuilding of the Temple may it he His will that it be built within our days.

(Ib. b) Ulla and R. Chisda were once traveling together, when they came up to the gate of the house of R. Chana b. Chanilai; R. Chisda looked at it, became faint and sighed, "Why sighest thou?"' asked Ulla; "since as Rab said, sighing breaks half of a body, for it is written (Ezek. 21, 11.) Sigh, therefore, O son of man, with the breaking of thy loins, etc.; and R. Jochanan said: 'A sigh breaks up the entire body, for it is said (Ib. ib. 12.) And it shall be when they say unto thee, "Wherefore sighest thou? that thou shalt answer, for the tidings, because it cometh, and the whole heart shall melt,'" etc. To this R. Chisda replied: "How can I help sighing over this house, where sixty bakers used to he employed during the day, and sixty during the night, to bake bread for the poor and the needy; and R. Chana always had his hand in his purse, for he thought a respectable poor man might come along, and while he would put his hand in his purse [to take out a coin] it might cause the poor man shame [for being compelled to apply for charity];

(ע״ב) עולא ורב חסדא הוו קאזלי באורחא כי מטו אפתחא דבי רב חנא בר חנילאי נגד רב חסדא ואתנח אמר ליה עולא אמאי קא מתאנחת והאמר רב אנחה שוברת חצי גופו של אדם שנאמר (יחזקאל כא יא) ואתה בן אדם האנח בשברון מתנים וגו׳. ורבי יוחנן אמר כל גופו של אדם שנאמר (שם) והיה כי יאמרו אליך על מה אתה נאנח וכהתה כל רוח וגו׳. אמר ליה היכי לא אתנח ביתא דהוו בה שיתין אפייתא ביממא ושיתין אפייתא בליליא ואפיין לכל מאן דצריך ולא שקיל ידא מן כיסא דסבר דילמא אתא עניא בר טובים ואדמטו ליה לכיסא קא מכסיף. ותו הוו פתיחין ליה ד׳ בבי לארבע רוחתא דעלמא וכל דהוה עייל כפין נפיק כי שבע והוה שדי ליה חטי ושערי בשני בצורת

besides, he kept four doors open, one facing each direction, and whoever entered hungry went out satisfied. Moreover in time of famine he scattered wheat and barley outside, so that those who were ashamed to take help openly by day might come and take it by night; and now his house has fallen into ruin. Should I not sigh?" So Ulla said to him, "Thus R. Jochanan said: 'Since the destruction of the Temple it was decreed that the houses of the righteous shall become ruins, for it is written (Is. 5, 9.) Truly many houses shall become desolate. Yea, great and beautiful ones without an inhabitant!' 'Still,' added Rabbi Jochanan, 'the Holy One, praised be He! will again people it, for it is written (Ps. 125, 1.) Those who trust in the Lord are like Mt. Zion. Just as the Holy One, praised be He! is ready to rebuild Mt. Zion so will the Holy One, praised be He! rebuild the houses of the righteous.'" Ulla noticed that R. Chisda was still not comforted. He said to him therefore: "It is sufficient for the slave to have as much as his master [but not more]."

Rab said: "The memory of a dead one is not erased from the heart [of his relatives] before twelve months have elapsed, for it is written (Ps. 31, 13.) I am forgotten as a dead man out of the heart, I am become like a lost vessel."

(Fol. 60a) Our Rabbis taaught: "It once happened that when Hillel the Old was coming along the road and heard a sorrowful cry he said, 'I am sure it is not in my house.' And concerning such men, says the passage (Ps. 112, 7.) Of an evil report shall he not be afraid; his heart is firm, trusting in the Lord." Raba said: "We can infer this passage in whatever way we desire, either from the beginning to the end, or from the end to the beginning; from the beginning to the end: Of an evil report shall he not be afraid, [because] his heart is firm trusting in the Lord, or from the end to the beginning: [Having] his heart firm trusting in the Lord, he shall not be afraid of an evil report." A certain disciple followed R. Ishmael, the son of R. Jose, in the market of Zion, whereupon the latter noticed that the disciple was frightened; he said to him: "Hast thou sinned? for it is written (Is. 33, 14.) In Zion sinners are in fear." The disciple asked him, "Is it not written (Pr. 28, 13.) Happy is the man that always feareth." 'This refers to the Torah'" [was R. Ishmael's answer]. Juda b. Nathan was following R. Hamnuna and noticed that he groaned; Juda b. Nathan said: "That man is inviting afflictions upon himself, for it is written (Job 3, 25.) For the thing which I greatly feared, is come upon me, and that which I was afraid of is come unto me." Has it not been written also (Pr. 28, 14.) Happy is the man that always feareth? The last refers to the Torah.

(Fol. 60b) R. Huna said in the name of Rab, who spoke in the name of R. Meier, and it is so taught also in a Baraitha in the name of R. Akiba: A man shall always be accustomed to say, "All that God doth is done well"; as it once happened to R. Akiba who was traveling over the country and had with him an ass, a rooster and a lamp. At nightfall he reached a village where he sought lodging for the night, and it was refused. "All that God doth is done well," said he. He proceeded toward the forest where he resolved to spend the night. A lion came and ate up his ass; a cat came and devoured the rooster, and the wind extinguished the lamp. "All that God doth is done well," he said. That same night a ravaging army came and captured the village, and then R. Akiba said joyfully: "Is not what I said true? All that is done by Heaven is done well'" [for the enemy passed through the forest where R. Akiba slept that night, and if the ass had brayed, if the rooster had crowed or if the soldiers had seen the light, he would surely have met his death]." (Fol. 61b) And thou shalt love thy Lord thy God with all thy heart, and with all thy soul and with all thy might (Deu. 6, 4). We are taught that R. Eliezer the great says: "Since it is said With all thy soul, why then is it necessary to say With all thy might, and since it is said With all thy might, why then is it necessary to say With all thy soul. To teach that if there is a man to whom the soul is considered dearer than money, to him is said With all thy soul; while for him who values money more than his life, to him is said And with all thy might." But R. Akiba said. With all thy soul means. "Even when thy life is taken away from thee." Our Rabbis taught that the [Roman] Government once issued a decree forbidding Israel to study the Torah. What did R. Akiba do? He installed many congregations in public places and sat and lectured to them. Whereupon Papus b. Juda found him and said to him: "Akiba! art thou not afraid of this nation?" R. Akiba replied: "Art thou Papus, called the wise? Listen, and I will relate a parable to thee. A fox, walking by the river side, noticed the fishes therein swimming to and fro., so he said to them, 'Why are ye running?' 'Because we fear the nets that are placed for us,' they replied. 'Come to shore then,' said the fox to them, 'and live with us just as my ancestors lived with your ancestors.' The fishes

לטב. ביה בלילה אתא גייסא שבויה למתא אמר להו לאו אמרי לכו כל מה שעשה הקב״ה הכל לטובה. (דף סא ע״ב) ואהבת את ה׳ אלהיך וגו׳ תניא ר״א הגדול אומר אם נאמר בכל נפשך למה נאמר בכל מאדך ואם נאמר בכל מאדך למה נאמר בכל נפשך, לומר לך אם יש לך אדם שגופו חביב עליו מממונו לכך נאמר בכל נפשך, ואם יש לך אדם שממונו חביב עליו מגופו לכך נאמר ובכל מאדך. ר״ע אומר בכל נפשך אפי׳ נוטל את נפשך. ת״ר מעשה שגזרה מלכות גזירה על ישראל שלא יעסקו בתורה מה עשה ר״ע הלך והקהיל קהלות ברבים וישב ודרש. מצאו פפום בן יהודה א״ל עקיבא אי אתה מתיירא מפני אומה זו א״ל אמשול לך משל למה הדבר דומה לשועל שהיה מהלך על הנהר ראה דגים שהיו רצים לכאן ולכאן אמר להם מפני מה אתם רצים אמרו לו מפני הרשתות והמכמורות הבאות עלינו, אמר להם רצונכם שתעלו ליבשה ונדור אני ואתם כדרך שדרו אבותי ואבותיכם, אמרו לו אתה הוא שאומרים עליך פקח שבחיות, לא פקח אתה אלא טפש אתה, ומה במקום חיותנו אנו מתיראים, במקום מיתתנו לא כל שכן, ואף אנו כך בזמן שאנו עוסקים בתורה דכתיב בה (דברים ל כ) כי הוא חייך ואורך ימיך אנו מתיראים, כשאנו פוסקין מדברי תורה עאכ״ו. אמרו לא

exclaimed, 'Art thou called the wisest of the beasts? Thou art not wise but very foolish. If we are in danger in the element in which we live (in the water), how much greater would we be in danger in the element in which we die (on shore).' So is it with us; if at the time we study the Torah, of which it is written (Deu. 30, 20.) It is thy life and the prolongation of thy days, we are in such fear of danger, how much greater would be the danger if we cease studying the Torah?" It is related that not many days elapsed when R. Akiba was arrested and imprisoned; Papus also was arrested and placed in the same prison. "Papus, what brought thee here?" asked R. Akiba; Papus replied: "Happy art thou R. Akiba, that thou art arrested for studying the Torah! Woe to me, Papus, that I was arrested because of vanity!" When R. Akiba was led forth to execution, it was just at the time of the morning Sh'm'a. As they tore his flesh with iron curry-combs, he was devotedly taking upon himself the yoke of the Heavenly Kingdom with love. His disciples asked of him:' "Rabbi, how long [wilt thou continue your prayers]?" "O," answered he, "all my life I worried as to how I could fulfill the ordinance. [Love thy God] with all thy soul, which means 'even if thy soul be taken from you'; I asked myself when would such an opportunity come to hand that I might fulfill it? And now when it finally came to hand shall I not fulfill it?" With a long-drawn out voice he was saying the word Echad (One) [from Hear O Israel, the Lord our God is One]. when his soul departed. A Heavenly voice went forth and said "Happy ought thou be, R. Akiba, that thy soul departed with the word Echad." The ministering angels then pleaded before the Holy One, praised be He! saying: "Sovereign

היו ימים מועטים עד שתפסוהו לר״ע וחבשוהו בבית האסורים ותפסו לפפום בן יהודה וחבשוהו אצלו, אמר לו פפום מי הביאך לכאן אמר לו אשריך ר״ע שנתפסת על ד״ת אוי לי שנתפסתי על דברים בטלים. בשעה שהוציאוהו לר״ע להריגה זמן ק״ש היה והיו סורקין את בשרו במסרקאות של ברזל והיה מתכוין לקבל עליו עול מלכות שמים באהבה, אמרו לו תלמידיו רבינו עד כאן אמר להם כל ימי הייתי מצטער על הפסוק הזה בכל נפשך ואפי' הוא נוטל את נפשך אמרתי מתי יבא לידי ואקיימנו ועכשיו שבא לידי לא אקיימנה היה מאריך באחד עד שיצתה נשמתו באחד, יצתה בת קול ואמרה אשריך ר״ע שיצתה נשמתך באחד, אמרו מלאכי השרת לפני הקב״ה רבש״ע זו תורה וזו שכרה, אמרו (תהלים יז יד) ממתים ידך ה' ממתים מחלד. אמר להם חלקם בחיים, יצתה בת קול ואמרה לו אשריך ר״ע שאתה מזומן לחיי העוה״ב:

of the universe, is this the Torah's reward? Is it not said (Ps. 17, 14.) Let me die through Thine own hand (a natural death) O Lord, of those who die of age." "Their share shall be in life," was God's answer. Thereupon a Heavenly voice went forth and said, "Happy art thou, Akiba, that thou art chosen for the bliss of futurity."

(Fol. 6'2b) If the Lord hath instigated thee against me (I Sam. 26, 19). R. Elazar said: "Thus spoke the Holy One, praised, be He! unto David, 'Art thou calling me instigator? I will cause thee to stumble even with that which school children know'; for it is written (Ex. 30, 12.) When thou takest the sum of the children of Israel of those who are to he numbered, then shall each man pay a ransom for his soul [which means that Israel should not be counted unless a ransom is given for that act]. Immediately after this it happened (I Chr. 21, 1.) And Satan moved against Israel and enticed David. It is also written (II Sam. 24, 1.) He instigated David against them to say ' Go number Israel and Judah,' and since he counted them without taking a ransom from them, it is written immediately thereafter And the Lord sent a pestilence into Israel from morning even to the time appointed. What is meant by From morning even to the time appointed? Samuel, the senior, and son-in-law of R. Chanina. said in R. Chanina's name: "From the time of the slaughter of the perpetual-daily-morning-offering until the sprinkling of its blood." And R. Jochanan said: "Until noon," And He said to the angel, that destroyed among, the people great (Ib. ib. 16). What is meant by great? R. Elazar said: "Thus said the Holy One, praised be He! 'Take me the greatest of them in whom

(דף סב ע״ב) (ש״א כו יט) אם ה׳ הסיתך בי. אמר ר״א אמר ליה הקב״ה לדוד מסית קרית לי הרי אני מכשילך בדבר שאפי׳ תינוקות של בית רבן מכירין בו שנאמר (שמות ל יב) כי תשא את ראש בני ישראל לפקדיהם ונתנו איש כופר נפשו, מיד (דה״א כא א) ויעמוד שטן על ישראל וכתיב (ש״ב כד א) ויסת את דוד בהם לאמר לך מנה את ישראל וכיון דמנינהו לא שקל מינייהו כופר דכתיב (שם) ויתן ה׳ דבר בישראל מהבקר ועד עת מועד, מאי ועד עת מועד. א״ר שמואל סבא חתניה דרבי חנינא משמיה דרבי חנינא משעת שחיטת תמיד ועד זריקתו. ורבי יוחנן אמר עד חצות ממש. (שם) ויאמר למלאך המשחית בעם רב, מאי רב אמר רבי אלעזר א״ל הקב״ה למלאך טול הרב שבהן שיש בו ליפרע מהן כמה חובות. באותה שעה מת אבישי בן צרויה ששקול כרובה של סנהדרין. (דה״א כא טו) ובהשחית ראה ח׳ וינחם על הרעה. מאי ראה אמר רב יעקב אבינו ראה שנאמר (בראשית לו ב) ויאמר יעקב כאשר ראם ושמואל אמר

there is [merit enough] with which to pay their debts (sins). At that moment Abishai b. Zeruyah. who was the equal of the majority of the Sanhedrin, died. But as he was destroying, the Lord looked on and bethought Himself (I Chr. 21, 15). What did He see? Rab said: "He saw our father Jacob," for it is written (Gen. 32, 3.) And when Jacob saw them (Ra'ah) he said, etc. Samuel said: "He saw the ashes of Isaac, for it is said (Ib. 22. 8.) God will show us the lamb for them." R. Isaac Napbcha said: "He saw the atonement money [which was donated for the construction of the Tabernacle], for it is said (Ex. 31, 16.) And thou shall take the atonement money"; and R. Jochanan said: "He saw the Temple, for it is written (Gen. 22, 14.) On the mount of the Lord it shall he seen." Upon the same point R. Jacob b. Ide and R. Samuel b. Nachmeini differ. One said, "He saw the atonement money,"' and the other said "He saw the Temple." The following statements will prove the correctness of the opinion of the one who said that "He saw the Temple"; for it is said (Ib. ib.) As it is said to this very day. On the mount of the Lord it shall he seen.

(Fol. 63a) It was taught that Hillel the Elder said: "When people imbibe (learning), diffuse it; when they reject (learning), gather it in. If thou see that the Torah is beloved by the generation, then, diffuse it [teach it even though there are others that teach them]; for it is said (Pr. 11, 24.) There is a man that scattereth gifts and yet his wealth is increased, but if thou see that the Torah is not beloved by the generation, then gather it in (do not teach it); for it is said (Ps. 119, 126.) It is time to act for the Lord; they have broken thy law." R. Kapara once preached:

אפרו של יצחק ראה שנא׳ (שם כב ח) אלהים יראה לו השה, ר' יצחק נפחא אמר כסף כפורים ראה שנא׳ (שמות ל טז) ולקחת את כסף הכפורים, ורבי יוחנן אמר בית המקדש ראה דכתיב (בראשית כב יד) בהר ה' יראה, פליגי בה רבי יעקב בר אידי ורבי שמואל בר נחמני, חד אומר כסף כפורים ראה וחד אומר בית המקדש ראה, ומסתברא כמאן דאמר בית המקדש ראה שנאמר (שם) אשר יאמר היום בהר ה' יראה:

(דף סג) אמר רבא האי קרא מרישיה לסיפיה מדריש מסיפיה לרישיה מדריש, מרישיה לסיפיה מדריש עת לעשות לה' מה טעם משום הפרו תורתך. מסיפיה לרישי׳ מדריש הפרו תורתך מה טעם משום עת לעשות לה', תניא הלל הזקן אומר בשעת המכנסים פזר בשעת המפזרים כנס אם ראית דור שהתורה חביבה עליו פזר שנא׳ (משלי יא כד) יש מפזר ונוסף עוד ואם ראית דור

"If a thing is cheap, be quick and buy it [for it will surely rise]. Where there is no man (leader) try to be a man yourself." Abaye said: "We infer from these words that in any gathering where there are enough men one should not try to make himself prominent." Surely! This is more than plain! He needs it in the case of the stranger who comes and finds a man only his equal [the stranger should not try to do anything without the consent of the native]. R. Kapara expounded: "Which small section contains the essential parts of the Torah? In all thy ways acknowledge Him and He shall direct thy path (Pr. 3, 6)." Raba said: "Even in matters of iniquity." R. Kapara preached: "A man should always teach his son an occupation which is clean and easy." What is that? R. Chisda said, "Needle work."

We are taught that Rabbi says: "Never shall a man try to acquire too many friends within his house, for it is said (Pr. 18, 24.) A man's many companions are hurtful to him." We are taught that Rabbi says: "A man should avoid appointing a supervisor over his household for had not Potiphar appointed Joseph the supervisor over his household, the trouble [he had] would not have occurred." We are taught that Rabbi says: "Why has the section referring to the Nazarite been arranged close to the section of Sota? To tell us that if one sec a Sota in her corrupted state he shall obstain from wine." Hezekiah, the son of R. Parnach, said in the name of R. Jochanan: "Why has the section referring to the Sota been arranged close to the section of Terumah and tithes? To tell us that whoever has Terumah and tithes and does not give them to the priest will finally be obliged [to go] to the Priest on

שאין התורה חביבה עליו כנס שנא׳ עת לעשות לה׳ הפרו תורתך. דרש בר קפרא זלת קפוץ קנה מינה באתר דלית גבר תמן הוי גבר. אמר אביי ש"מ באתרא דאית גבר תמן לא תהוי גבר, פשיטא לא נצרכה אלא כששניהם שוים, דרש בר קפרא איזו היא פרשה קטנה שכל גופי תורה תלויין כה (שם ג ו) בכל דרכיך דעהו והוא יישר אורחותיך. אמר רבא אפילו לדבר עבירה, דרש בר קפרא לעולם ילמד אדם את בנו אומנות נקייה וקלה, מאי היא אמר רב יהודה מחטא דתלמיותא:

תניא רבי אומר לעולם אל ירבה אדם ריעים בתוך ביתו שנאמר (משלי יח כד) איש רעים להתרועע. תניא רבי אומר אל ימנה אדם אפוטרופוס בתוך ביתו שאלמלא מינה פוטיפר את יוסף אפוטרופוס בתוך ביתו לא בא לאותו דבר, תניא רבי אומר למה נסמכה פרשת נזיר לפרשת סוטה לומר לך שכל הרואה סוטה בקלקולה יזיר עצמו מן היין. אמר חזקיה בריה דרבי פרנך אמר רבי יוחנן למה נסמכה פרשת סוטה לפרשת תרומות ומעשרות לומר לך שכל שיש לו תרומות ומעשרות ואינו נותנן לכהן סוף נצרך לכהן על ידי אשתו, שנאמר (במדבר ה י) ואיש את קדשיו לו יהיו וסמיך ליה איש איש כי

account of his wife, as it is said (Num. 5, 10.) And every man's hallowed things shall be his, and immediately succeeding this is written If the wife of any man go saide; and after this is written: Then shall the man bring his wife, etc. And moreover poverty will at last overtake him and he will become a recipient of that same thing which he refused to give, as it is said And every man's hallowed things shall be his [i.e.. And every man's hallowed things, — if he gives it not to the priest, — shall he his own, — for his own necessities]." R. Nachman b. Isaac said: "If, on the other hand, he give [deliberately the tithes to the priest], he will become rich, as it is said (Ib.) Whatever any man giveth to the priest shall belong to him, i.e., he shall have much wealth." R. Huna b. Brachia in the name of R. Elazar Hakapar said: "To him who associates the Heavenly name in his troubles (praising the Lord even for misfortune), his means of support will be doubled, as it is said (Job 22, 25.) Yea, the Almighty shall be thy defence, and thou shall have plenty of silver." R. Samuel b. Nachmeini said: "His maintenance will come as quickly as a bird flies; for it is said (Ib.) And thou shalt have plenty of silver." R. Tubia said in the name of R. Joshiya: "He who is careless about the study of the Torah, will have no strength to withstand a day of adversity; as it is said (Pr. 24, 10.) If thou faint in the day of adversity, thy strength i small." R. Ami b. Mathun in the name of Samuel said: "Even [if he weaken himself] from one meritorious deed; for it is said If thou faint, i.e., from whatever the weakening; may be."

R. Saffra said that R. Abuhu related When Chanania the son of R. Joshua's brother went into exile, he made leapyears and fixed days for the new moon outside of Palestine. The Rabbis sent two disciples after him, R. Jose b. Kippar and the grandson of R. Zechariah b. Kebutal [to warn him against such an act]. As soon as R. Chanania saw them he said: "For what have ye come here?" "To learn the Torah from you have we come," they replied. He then introduced them [before the public]: "They are the prominent men of this generation whose fathers served in the Temple as we have been taught (in a Mishnah). Zechariah b. Kebutal says, 'Many a time have I read before him in the book of Daniel.'" He began to teach them and of everything he said levitically unclean they said clean; prohibited, they said permitted; so that he began denouncing them, saying, "These men are false and of a wicked nature." "It is too late," said they to him. "What thou hast already built thou canst not destroy; what thou hast already repaired thou canst not break." Thereupon he asked them: "Why have ye said clean of things which I declared unclean, and allowed things which I declared prohibited?" Whereupon they answered him: "Because thou hast made leap years and hast fixed days for the new moon outside of Palestine." He said to them, "Had not R. Akiba b. Joseph made leap years and fixed days for the new moon outside of Palestine?" "R. Akiba was different," they answered him, "because none greater than he was left in Palestine." "Have I left any one bigger than I am in Palestine?" "The kids (young scholars) have grown to be wethers (great scholars) of horns [who are able to measure their intellectual strength with thee], and they sent us unto thee saying thus. 'Go tell him in our names: If he will listen it is well but if not let him be under ban, (Fol. 63b) and warn

שנים וקובע חדשים בחוצה לארץ, שגרו אחריו שני ת״ח רבי יוסי בן כיפר ובן בנו של זכריה בן קבוטל כיון שראה אותם אמר להם למה באתם אמרו לו ללמוד תורה באנו הכריז עליהם אנשים הללו גדולי הדור הם ואבותיהם שמשו בבית המקדש כאותה ששנינו זכריה בן קבוטל אומר הרבה פעמים קריתי לפניו בספר דניאל התחיל הוא מטמא והם מטהרים הוא אוסר והם מתירין הכריז עליהם אנשים הללו של שוא הם של תוהו הם. אמרו לו כבר בנית ואי אתה יכול לסתור כבר גדרת ואי אתה יכול לפרוץ, אמר להם מפני מה אני מטמא ואתם מטהרים אני אוסר ואתם מתירים. אמרו לו מפני שאתה מעבר שנים וקובע חדשים בחוצה לארץ. אמר להם והלא עקיבא בן יוסף היה מעבר שנים וקובע חדשים בחוץ לארץ. אמרו לו הנה רבי עקיבא שלא הניח כמותו בארץ ישראל, אמר להם אף אני לא הנחתי כמותי בארץ ישראל אמרו לו גדיים שהנחת נעשו תישים בעלי קרנים והם שגרוני אצלך וכך אמרו לנו לכו ואמרו לו בשמנו אם שומע מוטב ואם לאו יהא בנדוי ואמרו לאחינו שבגולה אם שומעים מוטב ואם לאו יעלו להר, אחיה יבנה מזבח חנניה ינגן בכנור ויכפרו כלם ויאמרו אין להם חלק באלהי ישראל. מיד געו כל העם בבכיה ואמרו חס ושלום יש לנו חלק באלהי

our exiled brethren that if they will listen it is well, but if not let them ascend the mountain (to make a heathen altar), Achiya will be the builder [of such an altar] and Chanania (of above) shall play violin and let them all deny Eternity and say we have no more a share in the God of Israel.'" Immediately after they finished this message, the people commenced to weep loudly and said, "God forbid such a thing. [Our sincere desire is] to keep on having a share in the God of Israel." And why were the Rabbis so severe in their warning? Because it is said (Is. 2, 3.) Out of Zion shall come forth the Torah and the words of the Lord out of Jerusalem. It could quite be understood had the two disciples declared unclean whatever Chanania declared clean, as this would have been permissible, but how was it that what he declared unclean they declared clean? Have we not taught: "If one sage declared a thing [levitically] unclean another one has no right to declare it clean; if one prohibited a thing, the other one is not permitted to declare it allowed." They did it because the people should not be guided by him.

Our Rabbis taught: When our Rabbis entered the academy of Jabne, they found R. Juda, R. Jose, R. Nechemia. and R. Elazar, the son of R. Jose the Galilean, there. They all began to expound in honor of hospitality to the stranger. R. Juda, the chief speaker in every place, began in honor of the Torah and preached. "It is written (Ex. 33, 7.) And Moses took his tent, and pitched it outside the camp. Can we not conclude this from the rule of a fortiori: that if the Lord's ark which was at a distance of only twelve miles, the Torah says (Ib. ib.) And it came to pass that

ישראל. וכל כך למה. משום שנאמר כי מציון תצא תורה ודבר ה' מירושלים, בשלמא הוא מטהר והן מטמאין לחומרא אלא הוא מטמא והן מטהרים היכי הוה והתניא חכם שטמא אין חבירו רשאי לטהר אסר אין חבירו רשאי להתיר. קא סברי כי היכי דלא נגררו בתריה:

ת"ר כשנכנסו רבותינו לכרם ביבנה היו שם רבי יהודה ורבי יוסי ורבי נחמיה ור"א בנו של ר"י הגלילי פתחו כולם בכבוד אכסניא ודרשה פתח רבי יהודה ראש המדברים בכל מקום בכבוד תורה ודרש (שמות לג ז) ומשה יקח את האהל ונטה לו מחוץ למחנה והלא דברים ק"ו ומה אדון ה' שלא היה מרוחק אלא י"ב מיל אמרה תורה (שם) והיה כל מבקש ה' יצא אל אהל מועד ת"ח

every one who sought [instruction of] the Lord went out unto the Tabernacle of the congregation, surely, then scholars who travel from one town to another and from one land to another, should be called those who sought the Lord." And the Lord spoke unto Moses face to face. (Ib.) R. Isaac said: "Thus saith the Holy One. praised be He! unto Moses 'Moses, let us cheer each other up in the Halacha by discussion.'" And some say: "Thus said the Holy One. praised be He! unto Moses: 'Moses, just as I have been kind enough to thee, so be thou kind (forbearing) to Israel and return the tent unto its former place.' " And then he returned unto the camp, etc. (Ib.) R. Abuhu said: "Thus said the Holy One. praised be He! unto Moses: 'Now the people will say. The teacher (God) be angry and the scholar (Moses) be angry, what will become of Israel? If thou wilt return the tent unto its place, it will be well, if not Joshua b. Nun, thy disciple, will serve instead of thee;' and thus is understood what is written [immediately after this]. And he (Moses) returned unto the camp." Raba said: "Nevertheless, the words were not uttered for no purpose; for it is said And his servant, Joshua b. Nun, a young man, departed not out of the tent. (Ib.)" [Showing that he remained there since] .

R. Juda again opened in honor of the Torah and expounded Be attentive, and hearken, O Israel, this day art thou become a people. (Deu. 27, 9). "Was the Torah then given unto Israel on that day? Behold! forty years had already elapsed. But this is stated for the purpose of inferring from it that the Torah shall always be as dear and beloved by its students, as if that very day it had been given on Mt. Sinai." R. Tanchum, son of R.

שהולכים מעיר לעיר וממדינה למדינה ללמוד תורה אעכ"ו. (שם) ודבר ה' אל משה פנים אל פנים א"ר יצחק א"ל הקב"ה למשה משה אני ואתה נסביר פנים בהלכה. איכא דאמרי כך א"ל הקב"ה למשה כשם שאני הסברתי לך פנים כך אתה הסבר פנים לישראל והחזר האהל למקומו, ושב אל המחנה וגו' אמר רבי אבהו א"ל הקב"ה למשה עכשיו יאמרו הרב בכעס ותלמיד בכעס ישראל מה תהא עליהם אם אתה מחזיר האהל למקומו מוטב ואם לאו יהושע בן נון תלמידך משרת תחתיך והיינו דכתיב ושב אל המחנה, אמר רבא אע"פ כן לא יצא הדבר לבטלה שנא' ומשרתו יהושע בן נון נער לא ימיש מתוך האהל:

ועוד פתח רבי יהודה בכבוד תורה ודרש (דברים כז ט) הסכת ושמע ישראל היום הזה נהיית לעם וכי אותו היום נתנה תורה לישראל והלא אותו יום סוף ארבעים שנה היה אלא ללמדך שחביבה תורה על לומדיה בכל יום ויום כיום שנתנה מהר סיני. אמר רבי תנחום בריה דרבי חייא איש כפר

Chiya, the man from the village of Achu, said: "You may infer it from the following. A man who is accustomed to read the Sh'm'a, reads it every day, morning and evening; and if he miss but one evening it seems to him as if he had never read the Sh'm'a." Be attentive, i.e., organize yourself into a company for the purpose of studying the Torah, because the Torah can be acquired only if studied in company; for R. Jose, the son of R. Chanina, said: "What is meant by the passage (Jer. 50, 36.) The sword is against the lying soothsayers and they shall become foolish, i.e., the sword is against the learned who sit alone and study the Torah in privacy. Moreover, they become foolish; for it is written here Veno'alu (and they shall become foolish), and it is written there (Num. 12, 11.) No'alnu (wherein we have acted foolishly). Moreover, they will commit sins; for it is said (Ib.) And wherein we have sinned (No'alnu), and if you wish [I conclude] from this (Is. 19, 13.) The prince of Tzo-an are become fools (No'alu)." We can explain in another way: Be attentive and listen, Expose yourselves to being smitten over the study of the Torah, as Resh Lakish said: "Whence do we infer that the Torah will be preserved with him only who is ready to die for her? It is said (Num. 19, 14.) This is the Torah, when a man dieth in a tent." We may explain in another way: Be attentive and listen, O Israel; Be quiet, listen, and then explain it, as Raba said "A man shall first study and then think how to explain it." It was said in the academy of R. Janai, "What is meant by the passage (Pr. 30, 33). For the pressure of milk bringeth forth butter, and the pressure of the nose bringeth forth blood, so the pressure of wrath bringeth forth strife? That is, In whom can you find

עכו תדע שהרי אדם קורא ק״ש שחרית וערבית וערב אחד אינו קורא דומה כמי שלא קרא ק״ש מעולם. הסכת עשו כתות כתות ועסקו בתורה לפי שאין התורה נקנית אלא בחבורה כדרבי יוסי בר חנינא דאמר רבי יוסי בר חנינא מאי דכתיב (ירמיה נ לו) הרב אל הבדים ונואלו חרב על שונאיהם של ת״ח שיושבין בד בבד ועוסקין בתורה ולא עוד אלא שמטפשין כתיב הכא וגואלו וכתיב התם (במדבר יב יא) אשר נואלנו ולא עוד אלא שחוטאין שנא' ואשר חטאנו, ואי בעית אימא מהכא (ישעיה יט יג) נואלו שרי צוען, דבר אחר הסכת ושמע ישראל כתתו עצמכם על דברי תורה כדריש לקיש דאמר ריש לקיש מנין שאין דברי תורה מתקיימים אלא במי שממית עצמו עליה שנא' (במדבר יט יד) זאת התורה אדם כי ימות באהל, ד״א הסכת ושמע ישראל הם ואחר כך כתת כדרבא דאמר רבא לעולם ילמוד אדם ואחר כך יהגה, אמרי דבי רבי ינאי מאי דכתיב (משלי ל לג) כי מיץ חלב יוציא חמאה ומיץ אף יוציא דם ומיץ אפים יוציא ריב. במי אתה מוצא חמאה של תורה במי שמקיא חלב שינק משדי אמו עליה. ומיץ אף יוציא דם כל תלמיד שכועס עליו רבו פעם ראשונה ושותק זוכה להבחין בין דם טמא לדם טהור ומיץ אפים יוציא ריב כל תלמיד שכועס עליו רבו פעם

the butter (the prime) of Torah? who has vomited the milk of his mother's breast on account of her (the Torah). And the pressure of the nose bringeth forth blood, i.e., every disciple who is silent when the provocation of his teacher is upon him the first time, will be rewarded with the knowledge of being able to distinguish between ritually purified blood and unpurified blood. So the pressure of wrath bringeth forth strife, i.e., every disciple who remains silent at the provocation of his teacher once and a second time will be rewarded with the knowledge of being able to distinguish between civil and criminal laws; for we are taught (in a Mishnah) that R. Ishmael says: "He who wants to become wise shall study the civil laws for there is no store (of wisdom) in the entire Torah richer than this (civil law), which is like a flowing well." R. Samuel b. Nachmeini said: "What is meant by the passage (Pr. 30, 32.) If thou hast become degraded by lifting thyself up or, if thou hast devised evil, put thy hand to thy mouth, i.e., He who lowers himself (exposes his ignorance) for the sake of learning the Torah. shall finally be raised; if he muzzle his mouth (is ashamed to ask his teacher) he will have to put his hand to the mouth [when he in turn is questioned]."

R. Nechemiah opened in honor of the one who exercised hospitality [toward strangers] and preached: And Saul said unto the Kenite, 'Go. depart, get you down from the midst of Amalekites lest I destroy thee with them, whereas ye acted kindly with the children of Israel at their coming up out of Egypt (I Sam. 15, 6). "Behold, can this not be concluded through the rule of a fortiori? If Jethro who did not come near Moses for anything else

ראשונה ושניה ושותק זוכה להבחין בין דיני ממונות לדיני נפשות דתנן רבי ישמעאל אומר הרוצה שיתחכם יעסוק בדיני ממונות שאין לך מקצוע בתורה יותר מהן שהן כמעין נובע. אמר רבי שמואל בר נחמני מ״ד (משלי ל לב) אם נבלת בהתנשא ואם זמות יד לפה. כל המנבל עצמו על דברי תורה סופו להתנשא ואם זמם יד לפה:

פתח רבי נחמיה בכבוד אכסניא ודרש מ״ד (ש״א טו ו, ע׳ בחדושי הלכות) ויאמר שאול אל הקיני לכו סורו רדו מתוך עמלקי פן איסיפך עמו ואתה עשית חסד עם כל בני ישראל, והלא דברים ק״ו ומה יתרו שלא קרב את משה אלא לכבוד עצמו כך, המארח ת״ח בתוך ביתו ומאכילו ומשקהו ומהנהו מנכסיו על

but his own honor was so rewarded, how much more then should a man he rewarded, who takes learned men in his house, feeds them, gives them drink and lets them enjoy of his wealth?' R. Jose opened in honor of the one who is hospitable and preached: Thou shalt not abhor an Edomite, for he is thy brother; thou shalt not abhor an Egyptian, because thou wert a stranger in his land (Deu. 23, 8). "Can this not be concluded through the rule of a fortiori? If the Egyptians who came nigh unto Israel for their own benefit only, as is said (Gen. 47, 6.) And if thou knowest that there are among them men of activity, then appoint them rulers over my cattle, were so protected; how much more then, should he be protected who takes in a learned man and gives him food and drink and lets him enjoy of their wealth?" R. Elazar, the son of R. Jose, the Galilean opened in honor of him who is hospitable to the stranger: And the Lord blessed ObedEdom. and all his household, (II Sam. 6, 11). "Behold, we can infer this through the rule of a fortiori; if keeping the house clean, in honor of the Holy Ark with the Tablet, which neither eats nor drinks, was blessed, how much more will he be blessed who keeps a learned man and gives him food and drink and permits him to enjoy of his wealth?" Of what did the blessing (of Obed-Edom) consist? R. Juda b. Zabida said: "It was that Chamoth and her eight daughters-in-law each gave birth to six at a time, as it is said (I Chr. 26, 5.) Pe'ulthai the eighth because God blessed him, etc., sixty-two were all that Obed-Edom had."

(Fol. 64a) R. Abin the Levite said: "He who forces time will in return be pressed by time; but to him who gives way to time (yielding patiently to circumstances), time will give way. [We know it] from the incident of Rabba and R. Joseph, for R. Joseph was called Sinai (Erudite scholar) and Rabba was called Okar Harim (Dialectician). One of them was wanted [to become the head of an academy] so they sent into Palestine [to inquire to which one the office should be offered]: "Sinai or Okar Harim, which one is the better?" Whereupon they were answered that Sinai should be preferred, because all need the possessor of wheat (versed in the Mishnah and the Baraitha). And yet R. Joseph did not accept, for the Chaldeans (soothsayers) foretold unto him, "Thou wilt reign only twelve years." So Rabba became the head and after reigning twenty-two years, R. Joseph became head for twelve and a half years. During all the years in which Rabba was the head, R. Joseph [never conducted himself in any manner of domination]. Not even a barber did he call into his house. Again said R. Abin the Levite: "What is meant by that which is written (Ps. 20, 2) May the Lord answer thee in the day of distress. He should strengthen thee, the God of Jacob; The God of Jacob and not the God of Abraham and Isaac? We infer from this that the owner of the beam must take hold at the thickest part of it [if he desire to remove it successfully]." Further said R. Abin the Levite: "He who enjoys a meal at which a learned man is present is considered as if he were enjoying of Divine Glory, for it is said (Ex. 18, 12.) And Aaron came, with all the elders of Israel, to eat bread with the father-in-law of Moses, before God. Were they then eating before God? Behold it was before Moses that they ate? But we learn from this that whoever partakes of a meal at which a learned man is

עומדת לו מדרבה ורב יוסף. דרב יוסף סיני ורבה עוקר הרים אצטריכא להו שעתא שלחו להתם סיני ועוקר הרים איזה מהם קודם. שלחו להו סיני קודם שהכל צריכין למרי חטיא. אף על פי כן לא קבל עליו רב יוסף דאמרי ליה כלדאי מלכת תרתין שנין. מלך רבה עשרין ותרתין שנין מלך רב יוסף תרתין שנין ופלגא כל הנך שני דמלך רבה אפי׳ אומנא לביתיה לא קרא. וא״ר אבין הלוי מ״ד (תהלים כ ב) יענך ה׳ ביום צרה ישגבך שם אלהי יעקב, אלהי יעקב ולא אלהי אברהם ויצחק מכאן לבעל הקורה שיכנס בעוביה של קורה. וא״ר אבין הלוי כל הנהנה מסעודה שתלמיד חכם שרוי בתוכה כאלו נהנה מזיו השכינה שנאמר (שמות יח יב) ויבא אהרן וכל זקני ישראל לאכל לחם עם חותן משה לפני האלהים וכי לפני האלהים אכלו והלא לפני משה אכלו אלא לומר לך כל הנהנה מסעודה שתלמיד חכם שרוי בתוכה כאלו נהנה מזיו השכינה:

present, is considered to be enjoying the Divine Glory."

And further said R. Abin the Levite: "He who leaves his friend [after escorting him a distance] must not say 'Go in peace' but Go with peace.' for Jethro said unto Moses (Ex. 4, 18.) Go with peace. He went and succeeded, but David said to Abshalom (II Sam. 15, 9.) Go in peace. He went and hanged himself." Further said R. Abin the Levite: "He who takes leave of the dead body [after burial] must not say 'Go with peace' but 'Go in peace,' for it is said (Gen. 15, 15.) But thou shalt come to thy fathers in peace." R. Levi b. Chiya said: "He who goes out from the synagogue [after prayer] and enters the house of learning and studies the Torah will be permitted to wait on the Divine Presence, for it is said (Ps. 84, 8.) They go from strength to strength; each of them will appear before God in Zion." R. Elazar in the name of R. Chanina said: "Scholars advance peace in the world, as it is said (Is. 54, 13.) And all thy children shall be taught by the Lord and great shall be the peace of thy children. Read not Banaich (Thy Children), but read it Bonaich (thy builders)"; Great peace have they who love thy Torah and there is no stumbling for them (Ps. 119, 115). Peace be within thy rampart, prosperity within thy palaces (Ib. 122, 7). For my brethren and associates' sake I would fain speak peace concerning Thee (Ib.). For the sake of the house of the Lord our God. I would seek thy good. The Lord will give strength unto his people; The Lord will bless his people with peace.

THE END OF BERACHOTH.

ואמר רבי אבין הלוי הנפטר מחברו אל יאמר לו לך בשלום אלא לך לשלום שהרי יתרו שאמר לו למשה (שמות ד יח) לך לשלום עלה והצליח דוד שאמר לו לאבשלום (ש״ב טו ט) לך בשלום הלך ונתלה. וא״ר אבין הלוי הנפטר מן המת אל יאמר לו לך לשלום אלא לך בשלום שנא׳ (בראשית טז טז) ואתא תבא אל אבותיך בשלום. א״ר לוי בר חייא היוצא מבהכ״נ ונכנס לבהמ״ד ועוסק בתורה זוכה להקביל פני השכינה שנאמר (תהלים סד ח) ילכו מחיל אל חיל יראה אל אלהים בציון אמר רב חייא בר אשי אמר רב ת״ח אין להם מנוחה לא בעולם הזה ולא בעולם הבא שנא׳ (תהלים סד ח) ילכו מחיל אל חיל יראה אל אלהים בציון. אמר רבי אלעזר א״ר חנינא ת״ח מרבים שלום בעולם שנאמר (ישעיה נד יג) וכל בניך למודי ה׳ ורב שלום בניך, אל תקרי בניך אלא בוניך (תהלים קיט קטו) שלום רב לאוהבי תורתיך ואין למו מכשול (שם קכב ז) יהי שלום בחילך שלוה בארמנותיך (שם) למען אחי ורעי אדברה נא שלום בך (שם) למען בית ה׳ אלהינו אבקשה טוב לך (שם) ה׳ עוז לעמו יתן ה׳ יברך את עמו בשלום:

סליק מסכת ברכות.

Made in the USA
Las Vegas, NV
07 March 2025